Trans

Transgression means to 'cross over': borders, disciplines, practices, professions, and legislation. This book explores how the transgression of boundaries produces new forms of architecture, education, built environments and praxis.

Based on material from the 10th International Conference of the AHRA, this volume presents contributions from academics, practising architects and artists/activists from around the world to provide perspectives on emerging and transgressive architecture. Divided into four key themes – boundaries, violations, place and art practice – it explores global processes, transformative praxis and emerging trends in architectural production, examining alternative and radical ways of practising architecture and reimagining the profession.

The wide range of international contributors are drawn from subject areas such as architecture, cultural geography, urban studies, sociology, fine art, film-making, photography and environmentalism, and feature examples from regions such as the United States, Europe and Asia.

At the forefront of exploring inter-disciplinary and trans-disciplinary research and practice, *Transgression* will be key reading for students, researchers and professionals with an interest in the changing nature of architectural and spatial disciplines.

Louis Rice is a Senior Lecturer at the Department of Architecture and the Built Environment, University of the West of England, Bristol, UK.

David Littlefield is a Senior Lecturer at the Department of Architecture and the Built Environment, University of the West of England, Bristol, UK.

CRITIQUES: Critical Studies in Architectural Humanities
A project of the Architectural Humanities Research Association

Series Editor: Jonathan Hale (University of Nottingham)
Editorial Board:
Sarah Chaplin
Mark Dorrian (Newcastle University)
Murray Fraser (University College London)
Hilde Heynen (Catholic University of Leuven)
Andrew Leach (Griffith School of Environment)
Thomas Mical (Carleton University)
Jane Rendell (University College London)
Adam Sharr (Newcastle University)
Igea Troiani (Oxford Brookes University)

This original series of edited books contains selected papers from the AHRA Annual International Conferences. Each year the event has its own thematic focus while sharing an interest in new and emerging critical research in the areas of architectural history, theory, culture, design and urbanism.

Volume 1: Critical Architecture
Edited by: Jane Rendell, Jonathan Hill, Murray Fraser and Mark Dorrian

Volume 2: From Models to Drawings: Imagination and Representation in Architecture
Edited by: Marco Frascari, Jonathan Hale and Bradley Starkey

Volume 3: The Politics of Making
Edited by: Mark Swenarton, Igea Troiani and Helena Webster

Volume 4: Curating Architecture and the City
Edited by: Sarah Chaplin and Alexandra Stara

Volume 5: Agency: Working With Uncertain Architectures
Edited by: Florrian Kossak, Doina Petrescu, Tatjana Schneider, Renata Tyszczuk and Stephen Walker

Volume 6: Architecture and Field/Work
Edited by: Suzanne Ewing, Jérémie Michael McGowan, Chris Speed and Victoria Clare Bernie

Volume 7: Scale
Edited by: Gerald Adler, Timothy Brittain-Catlin and Gordana Fontana-Giusti

Volume 8: Peripheries
Edited by: Ruth Morrow and Mohamed Gamal Abdelmonem

Volume 9: Architecture and the Paradox of Dissidence
Edited by: Ines Weizman

Volume 10: Transgression: Towards an expanded field of architecture
Edited by: Louis Rice and David Littlefield

AHRA provides an inclusive and comprehensive support network for humanities researchers in architecture across the UK and beyond. It promotes, supports, develops and disseminates high-quality research in all areas of architectural humanities.

www.ahra-architecture.org

Transgression

Towards an expanded field of architecture

**Edited by Louis Rice and
David Littlefield**

Routledge
Taylor & Francis Group

LONDON AND NEW YORK

First published 2015
by Routledge
2 Park Square, Milton Park, Abingdon, Oxon OX14 4RN

and by Routledge
711 Third Avenue, New York, NY 10017

Routledge is an imprint of the Taylor & Francis Group, an informa business

British Library Cataloguing-in-Publication Data
A catalogue record for this book is available from the British Library

Library of Congress Cataloging-in-Publication Data
Transgression : towards an expanded field of architecture / [edited by]
Louis Rice and David Littlefield.
  pages cm. – (Critiques: critical studies in architectural humanities)
  Includes bibliographical references and index.
  1. Architecture – Philosophy. 2. Architectural practice. 3. Architecture
  and society. I. Rice, Louis, editor. II. Littlefield, David, editor.
  NA2500.T73 2014
  720.1–dc23   2014022951

ISBN: 978-1-138-81891-0 (hbk)
ISBN: 978-1-138-81892-7 (pbk)
ISBN: 978-1-315-74491-9 (ebk)

Typeset in Univers
by HWA Text and Data Management, London

MIX
Paper from
responsible sources
FSC
www.fsc.org   FSC® C013056

Printed and bound in Great Britain by
TJ International Ltd, Padstow, Cornwall

Contents

Contents

Illustration credits

Advertisements for architecture

1   Image: Bernard Tschumi
2   Image: Bernard Tschumi
3   Image: Bernard Tschumi
4   Image: Bernard Tschumi
5   Image: Bernard Tschumi
6   Image: Bernard Tschumi
7   Image: Bernard Tschumi

The fly and the satellite

1   NASA image AS08-14-2383, NASA. Image courtesy of the Earth Science and Remote Sensing Unit, NASA Johnson Space Center. http://eol.jsc.nasa.gov
2   NASA image AS17-148-22727, NASA. Image courtesy of the Earth Science and Remote Sensing Unit, NASA Johnson Space Center. http://eol.jsc.nasa.gov
3   NASA Earth Observatory image by Robert Simmon, using Suomi NPP VIIRS data provided courtesy of Chris Elvidge (NOAA National Geophysical Data Center). http://earthobservatory.nasa
4   Astronaut photograph ISS026-E-33647 taken on 14 March 2011. Image courtesy of the Earth Science and Remote Sensing Unit, NASA Johnson Space Center; http://eol.jsc.nasa.gov
5   NASA Earth Observatory image by Jesse Allen and Robert Simmon, using data from the NASA/GSFC/METI/ERSDAC/JAROS, and U.S./Japan ASTER Science Team. http://earthobservatory.nasa
6   NASA Earth Observatory images by Jesse Allen and Robert Simmon, using data from the NASA/GSFC/METI/ERSDAC/JAROS, and U.S./Japan ASTER Science Team. http://earthobservatory.nasa.gov

Space and its assembled subjects

1   Reproduced by permission of Abaris Books
2   Diagrams by author
3   Untitled diagram, from page 106 in Jacques Lacan, *The Four Fundamental Concepts of Psychoanalysis* (1981) Copyright © 1973 Editions du Seuil. English translation

copyright © 1977 Alan Sheridan. Used by permission of W.W. Norton & Company, Inc. and Editions du Seuil

4   Montage by the author including anonymous photograph of climbers in Mousetrap Zawn, Gogarth, Anglesey. Reproduced by permission of Jack Geldard

5   Montage by author including LeQueu's 'Le Rendezvous de Bellevue' ... (plate 146 from *Architecture Civile*) and two self-portraits (from *Figures Lascives*) Copyright © 1986 by Thames and Hudson, Ltd. Reproduced by permission of Thames and Hudson, Ltd

6   Montage by the author including plan of the Wexner Center for the Arts at The Ohio State University by Peter Eisenman. Image courtesy of Eisenman Architects

7   Montage by the author including photograph © Fondation Le Corbusier. Reproduced by permission of DACS on behalf of La Fondation Le Corbusier. © FLC/ADAGP, Paris and DACS, London 2014

Transgression and ekphrasis in Le Corbusier's *Journey to the East*

1   © FLC-ADAGP
2   © FLC-ADAGP
3   © FLC-ADAGP
4   © FLC-ADAGP
5   © FLC-ADAGP
6   © FLC-ADAGP
7   © FLC-ADAGP
8   © FLC-ADAGP
9   Courtesy National Museum Belgrade
10   © FLC-ADAGP
11   © FLC-ADAGP
12   © FLC-ADAGP

R-Urban

1   Source: aaa
2   Source: aaa
3   Source: aaa
4   Source: aaa
5   Source: aaa

Informal architecture/s

1   Photo: Louis Rice
2   Photo: courtesy S. de Maat
3   Photo: Louis Rice
4   Photo: Louis Rice

Diffuse transgression

1   Copyright: Dana Vais
2   Copyright: Dana Vais

Transgression and temperance

1 Provenance: postcards and photographs (reproduced from negatives) from the John Gale Collection and Miscellaneous Collection (donor unknown). Rights holder (digital file) University of Sheffield, Rights holder (work) University of Sheffield
2 Drawings held by the NFA: accession numbers 178M9-1–178M9-14. Rights holder (digital file) University of Sheffield, Rights holder (work) University of Sheffield
3 Drawings held by the NFA: accession numbers 178M9-1–178M9-14. Rights holder (digital file) University of Sheffield, Rights holder (work) University of Sheffield

Art/architecture practice

1 Rights reserved © Didier Faustino
2 Rights reserved © Didier Faustino. Courtesy of the artist and Galerie Michel Rein, Paris/Brussels
3 Rights reserved © Didier Faustino
4 Rights reserved © Didier Faustino. Courtesy of the artist and Galerie Michel Rein, Paris/Brussels

Rupturing the surface of the known

1 Photo: Michael Petrus
2 Photo: Michael Petrus
3 University of Virginia School of Architecture
4 University of Virginia School of Architecture
5 University of Virginia School of Architecture
6 University of Virginia School of Architecture
7 Photo: Michael Petrus
8 Photo: Michael Petrus

Architecture in the material space of possible transgression

All images courtesy and copyright of Nathaniel Coleman

Rogue Game

1 Photo by Warren and Mosley. The *Rogue Game* series (2007–ongoing by Sophie Warren and Jonathan Mosley with Can Altay)
2 Photo by Max McClure
3 Photo by Sophie Warren and Jonathan Mosley
4 Photo by Sophie Warren and Jonathan Mosley
5 Photo by Max McClure

We-Minotaur-Labyrinth-Root

1 Image courtesy and copyright of Rebecca Krinke
2 Image courtesy and copyright of Rebecca Krinke
3 Image courtesy and copyright of Victoria Walters
4 Image courtesy and copyright of Victoria Walters

Contributors

Editors

Louis Rice is an architect, academic and educator who spent over a decade as a practising architect in France and the UK. For the last five years he has worked as a Senior Research Fellow and Senior Lecturer at the University of the West of England in Bristol; as course leader for urban design and the MA in Architecture.

David Littlefield is a Senior Lecturer at the Department of Architecture and the Built Environment, University of the West of England.

Contributors

Can Altay is an artist and Assistant Professor in the Faculty of Architecture at Istanbul Bilgi University. He investigates the functions, meaning, organisation and reconfigurations of public space. His 'settings' provide critical reflection on urban phenomena and artistic activity. His work is staged and manifested through the spaces, exhibitions and publications he produces. Recent public projects include: 'Inner Space Station' (New York, 2013); 'Distributed' (London, 2012); 'The Church Street Partners' Gazette' (London, 2010–13) and 'PARK: bir ihtimal' (Istanbul, 2010). Altay is the editor of *Ahali: an anthology for setting a setting*, 2013 published by Bedford Press, AA Publications, London.

Ella Bridgland has worked in the cultural and education group at John McAslan + Partners in London, and currently works for Tom Dixon Design Research Studio. She graduated from Sheffield School of Architecture (SSoA) in 2013 with a first class degree, where her final third year project was nominated for the RIBA Yorkshire prize. She was a University of Sheffield SURE researcher, with Stephen Walker, in Summer 2012 where she developed a particular interest in the temporary role of architecture within a wider social context.

Sara Brolund de Carvalho is an architect and artist based in Stockholm. Her ongoing independent research revolves around the relation between accessibility to public meeting spaces and the growth of urban grass root movements. She is currently working with the art/architecture research project 'Action Archive' together with architects and researchers Helena Mattsson and Meike Schalk. The project is currently part of an exhibition at Tensta Konsthall in Stockholm and is affiliated with KTH School of Architecture, Stockholm. She is also collaborating with architect Anja Linna in the project 'Our common spaces'. In 2014 Brolund de Carvalho will contribute to a Swedish anthology on civic participation in the planning process, with a text reflecting on the historical role of the architect in situations of urban conflicts.

Robert Brown is Professor and Head of Architecture at Plymouth University. His research interests include the relation of socio-cultural identity to place; recent publications include chapters in *The Territories of Identity* (2013), *Nu-topia – a critical view of future cities* (2012), *The SAGE Handbook of Architectural Theory* (2012), and an award-winning article (Jeffrey Cooke Prize for outstanding research) in *Traditional Dwellings and Settlements Review*. He is a steering group member of the AHRA, European Architectural History Association referee panel member, and a member of ARENA.

Nathaniel Coleman is Reader in History and Theory of Architecture at Newcastle University. He first studied architecture at the IAUS, received his BFA and BARCH degrees from RISD, his MUP degree in Urban Design from CCNY, and his PhD from UPenn. Author of *Utopias and Architecture* (2005), and editor of *Imagining and Making the World: Reconsidering Architecture and Utopia* (2011), his most recent book, *Lefebvre for Architects* will be published later in 2014. He has also recently guest edited a special issue of *Utopian Studies* on Architecture and Utopia. Nathaniel has also published numerous journal articles and book chapters, and presented his research on the problematic of architecture and Utopia, the city, and architecture education nationally and internationally. He is particularly interested in Utopia's generative potential.

Phoebe Crisman is Associate Professor of Architecture at the University of Virginia, where she teaches design studios and lectures on architecture theory and urbanism. Crisman also directs the Global Studies – Environments + Sustainability interdisciplinary major. Her essays are published in *Peripheries*, *Agency: Working with Uncertain Architectures, The Hand and the Soul: Essays on Ethics and Aesthetics, Journal of Architecture, Places,* and the *Journal of Architectural Education*. Crisman has received numerous awards for the' Learning Barge', 'Money Point', and 'Paradise Creek' design research projects. Educated at Harvard University and Carnegie Mellon, she is a licensed architect, urbanist, and principal of Crisman+Petrus Architects.

Colm Donnelly is a Senior Research Fellow and Director of the Centre of Archaeological Fieldwork at Queen's University Belfast. Colm is an historical archaeologist who specialises in Medieval and seventeenth-century buildings, with a particular interest in tower houses, the subject of his doctoral research. A founding member of the Irish Post-Medieval Archaeology Group in 1999, he is also an experienced field archaeologist and teaches field archaeology modules at Queen's. Colm has directed excavations at sites across Northern Ireland over the past 20 years and, since 2010, he has led a transatlantic excavation and education programme between the University of Massachusetts in Lowell, USA and Queen's University Belfast.

Didier Faustino is an artist and architect, who works on the intimate relationship between body and space. His approach is multifaceted, from installation to experimentation, from the creation of subversive visual art to spaces exacerbating the senses. Didier Faustino created the Bureau des Mésarchitectures in 2002. He received the Académie d'Architecture's Dejean prize for lifetime achievement in 2010 and was nominated several times for the Chernikhov Prize (Moscow). He is currently working on prestigious architectural projects in France and among the world, for example, to create a library and a cultural centre in Mexico, or for the creation of an experimental house in Spain for the Solo House projects.

Gordana Korolija Fontana-Giusti is an architect, urban designer, architectural historian and theorist, and the Professor at University of Kent, School of Architecture, where she is the Director of CREAte – Centre for Research in European Architecture. Fontana-Giusti has published scholarly papers in *The Journal of Architecture, ARQ* and the *AA-Files*; and is the author of *Foucault for Architects* (2013), co-editor and author of *Scale: Imagination, Perception and Practice in Architecture* (2012) and the co-editor and author of the *Complete Works of Zaha Hadid* (with Patrik Schumacher, 2004).

Lorens Holm is Reader in Architecture and Director of the Geddes Institute for Urban Research at the University of Dundee. He has taught at the Architectural Association, the Bartlett, the Mackintosh, and Washington University in St. Louis. His teaching/research focuses on the thought threads that link architecture to philosophy, history, psychoanalysis, and machines. Publications include *Brunelleschi Lacan Le Corbusier: architecture space and the construction of subjectivity* (2010). His papers have appeared in *The Journal of Architecture*, *Perspecta*, *Critical Quarterly*, *Architecture Theory Review*, and *Assemblage*.

Anja Linna is an architect and musician based in Malmö and Stockholm, Sweden. Situated within feminist and critical spatial practice, her independent research focus on participatory methods for architecture and urban planning. In her M.Arch. diploma (KTH School of Architecture 2013) Linna developed tools for architects to work carefully and socially engaged with urban regeneration projects. In a current research project, 'Våra gemensamma rum' ('Our common spaces'), she and architect Sara Brolund de Carvalho explore how common and collective spaces in the city are important for social community building, using methods from art practice and feminism. The project has been awarded with grants from the housing company Einar Mattson and the Swedish Arts Grants Committee.

Keith McAllister is a Lecturer and the Stage 03 Co-ordinator in Architecture at Queen's University of Belfast. A practising Chartered Architect, his ongoing academic research is focused primarily on the relationship between architecture and fear, especially for those populations without a voice. He has practised architecture in Russia, Italy and the UK.

Constantin Petcou is a Paris-based architect whose work stresses the intersection between architecture, urbanism, and semiotics. He has co-edited *Urban Act: A Handbook for Alternative Practice* (2007) and *Trans-Local-Act: Cultural Practices Within and Across* (2010). He is a co-founder of atelier d'architecture autogérée (aaa), a collective that conducts explorations, actions, and research concerning socio-political practices in the contemporary city. aaa acts through 'urban tactics', encouraging inhabitants to self-manage disused urban spaces, engage in nomadic and reversible projects, and initiating interstitial practices. aaa has been laureate of Zumtobel Prize for Sustainability and Humanity 2012, Curry Stone Design Prize 2011, the European Prize for Urban Public Space 2010 and the Prix Grand Public des Architectures contemporaines en Métropole Parisienne 2010.

Doina Petrescu is a Professor of Architecture and Design Activism at the University of Sheffield. She is the other co-founder of atelier d'architecture autogérée (aaa). Her research focuses on gender and space in contemporary society as well as participation in architecture. Her approach broadens the scope of architectural discourse by bringing cultural, social, and political issues to inform the design and thinking processes in architecture. Her research methodology combines approaches from architectural theory and design, contemporary arts, social sciences, political philosophy, and feminist theory. She is the editor of *Altering Practices: Feminist Politics and Poetics of Space* (2007) and co-editor of *Architecture and Participation* (2005), *Urban Act* (2007), *Agency: Working with Uncertain Architectures* (2009), and *Trans-Local-Act: Cultural Practices Within and Across* (2010).

Gunnar Sandin is Associate Professor in Architecture at Lund University, Sweden, where he is also Director of Research Studies. He is Chair of the Program Committee of the Swedish Research School in Architecture (ResArc). He has published his research in the fields of architecture theory, semiotics, art theory and aesthetics, such as the recent article 'Democracy on the margin', in *Architectural Theory Review*. His doctoral thesis 'Modalities of Place' (2004) discusses theories on site specificity in an interdisciplinary perspective. He currently leads the land use oriented research project 'The Evolutionary Periphery'.

Bernard Tschumi is an architect based in New York and Paris. First known as a theorist, he exhibited and published *The Manhattan Transcripts* (1976–1981) and wrote *Architecture and Disjunction* (1994), a series of theoretical essays. Major built works include the Parc de la Villette, the New Acropolis Museum, Le Fresnoy Center for the Contemporary Arts, Muséo Parc Alésia and the Paris Zoo. His most recent book is *Architecture Concepts: Red is Not a Color* (2012), a comprehensive collection of his conceptual and built projects. His drawings and models are in the collections of several major museums, including MoMA in New York and the Centre Pompidou in Paris.

Renata Tyszczuk is Senior Lecturer in Architecture at the University of Sheffield and a founding member of the Agency Research Centre. Her research explores questions concerning global environmental change and provisionality in architectural thinking and practice. She is the co-editor of *Atlas: Geography, Architecture and Change in an Interdependent World* (2012); *Agency: Working with Uncertain Architectures* (2009); and the co-founding editor of *field:* the online journal of architecture. In 2013 she was awarded a British Academy Mid-Career Fellowship.

Dana Vais is associate professor at the Faculty of Architecture and Urbanism, Technical University of Cluj, Romania, where she teaches theory, modern and contemporary history, and architecture studio. She earned both her architecture degree (1989) and her PhD (2000) at the University of Architecture and Urbanism 'Ion Mincu' in Bucharest. Her visiting appointments include University of Cincinnati OH/USA (Fulbright fellow), École d'architecture Paris Belleville, Inst.Sup. d'Architecture Saint-Luc de Wallonie Liège, Technical University of Budapest, University of Novi Sad. She publishes in the fields of theory, criticism and recent history in architecture and urbanism.

Stephen Walker is a Reader in Architecture at Sheffield School of Architecture (SSoA), where he is Director of the Graduate School. His research broadly encompasses art, architectural and critical theory, and examines the questions that such theoretical approaches can raise about particular moments of architectural and artistic practice. He received an RIBA Trust Award in 2012 to support research into the architecture of travelling fairs.

Victoria Walters is a Research Fellow in Visual Culture at Winchester School of Art, University of Southampton. She holds a doctorate from the University of Ulster on the art practice of German twentieth-century artist Joseph Beuys. She is a member of the Mapping Spectral Traces network and SIEF (the International Society for Ethnology and Folklore) and contributes to one of the society's working groups, Place Wisdom. Victoria's publications include *Joseph Beuys and the Celtic Wor(l)d: a language of healing* (2012) and *Beuysian Legacies in Ireland and Beyond: Art, Culture and Politics* co-edited with Professor Christa-Maria Lerm Hayes (2011). Her research interests include the work of Joseph Beuys, theories of language, the relationship between art and anthropology and art and ecology. She is currently exploring research through practice as well as theory.

Introduction

Louis Rice and David Littlefield

The potency of the word *"transgress"* is hardly reflected in its Latin etymology – to go or walk across. The language is benign, but symbolically loaded: to violate, to infringe, to go beyond the boundaries. To transgress is to break, violate, infringe, or exceed the bounds of: laws, commands, moral principles or other established standard of behaviour. Writers as far back as Horace Walpole and Edgar Allan Poe established links between (aberrant) architectural space and psychological conditions, and twentieth-century thinkers from Georges Bataille to Michel Foucault and Henri Lefebvre have lent theoretical weight to the idea of architecture as the expression of social norms, codes and hierarchies. As Lefebvre states 'space is a social product'[1]; so to challenge, or go beyond, architectural codes, expectations and values is to challenge society itself.

Transgression, the tenth international conference of the Architectural Humanities Research Association (UWE Bristol, 22–23 November 2013) was set up to ask how those working within spatial practice (architects, planners, urban designers, artists etc) can think and work transgressively; we asked what transgression means and where society places the limits within which these professions work. The aim of the conference was to explore ideas of spatial, social and conceptual transgression – its history, notions of (and the need for) limits, its use as a spatial metaphor and as a conceptual and practical tool. Importantly, many of those involved within this research theme are conscious of positioning 'transgression' within notions of inter/trans/multi-disciplinary working. Transgression is an attitude within which one operates and crosses boundaries, challenging norms, risking censure, exploring hybridity and pushing beyond the periphery of established practice.

Foucault (2003), in his lectures concerning the abnormal at the Collège de France in the mid-1970s, described the advent of the 'discipline of normalisation',[2] that is, the process within which the eighteenth- and nineteenth-century state established a framework of power. Foucault describes how the ab/normal, including aberrations such as the 'human monster', came to be formulated in terms of the law and medical judgement.

> The monster is the transgression of natural limits, the transgression of classifications, of the table, and of the law as table.[3]

Those who infringed the societal norms described by Foucault – biological and behavioural freaks – have since become normalised by society. Mary Shelley, of course, described how the hybrid, the transgressive new, can become unsettling or problematic; the crossing of established borders, confusing the purity of categories and even exceeding what is considered to be finite limits can result in creations for which civilised society can find no accommodation. 'Remember that I am thy creature: I ought to be thy Adam, but I am rather the fallen angel'[4] says Frankenstein's unnamed monster to the eponymous inventor, in despair. Foucault describes how definitions of madness and criminality have been adjusted; what was once deemed transgressive is no longer considered so. The avant-garde, similarly, has become normalised (or society has adjusted its framework for what is acceptable) allowing once outrageous movements such as Dadaism and Surrealism to become part of the canon of authorised history. Therefore, rather than working within the frameworks of society to produce spaces which reflect and reinforce that society, architecture can adopt a critical practice – to become active and, suggests Bernard Tschumi, to adopt a new language and attitude towards practice and society. Indeed, as Tschumi writes on page 12 (this volume):

> Architecture is filled with constraints. These constraints, these rules, these regulations (whether they are city regulations, budgets or other limits) are things we learn to deal with, to play with even. We must learn to make these constraints, dare I say, part of the project. Unless we make these limits pleasurable our lives as architects would be miserable. Much of architecture is a game where one simply takes advantage of the disadvantage; redefining the invisible opponent (the rule; the limit; the constraint) as a positive factor.

Both Bataille and Bakhtin have described how transgression negotiates a relationship with limits, but crucially neither proposes that this relationship be destructive. Rather, it is one of applying pressure, nudging or manipulating the limits (of experience, for example, or cultural expectation) with the aim of throwing them into stark relief – or even reinforcing those limits once they have been made explicit. *'Transgression pushes the limits of experience'*, wrote Bakhtin. Bataille suggested a further definition:

> Transgression opens the door into what lies beyond the limits usually observed, but it maintains those limits just the same. Transgression is complementary to the profane world, exceeding its limits but not destroying it.[5]

In other words, challenges to the norm can have the effect of reinforcing, repositioning or clarifying the norm – perhaps shifting it, perhaps shifting the centre ground from which the periphery is determined, or perhaps allowing those peripheries to expand or become more porous. In order to transgress, one needs to know where the boundaries are; in order to have boundaries, one needs to acknowledge the possibility they may be exceeded.

Bataille explored this notion of cultural boundary in his 1928 novel *The Story of the Eye*, a description of ever more daring and outrageous sexual exploits framed within a play of surreal symbolic references/connections (eye, egg, testicles). The descriptions of the narrator press on a wide range of social, religious and cultural boundaries, both challenging and making absolutely explicit the presence of those boundaries and their frailty. At one point, relatively early in the narrative, a teenage orgy collapses into noisy chaos and terror, causing the parents to enter the room:

> Indeed, by bursting in, the parents managed to wipe out the last shreds of reason, and in the end the police had to be called, with all the neighbours witnessing the outrageous scandal.[6]

Here, then, order reasserts itself; limits had been identified, tested and reasserted, but nothing was quite the same again.

Consider dirt. Anthropologist Mary Douglas (1966) famously described dirt as 'matter out of place'.[7] Dirt is constructed culturally in relation to a specific context and specifically in contradistinction to that space. Dirt, suggested Douglas, transgresses the boundary which separates where it ought to be from where it actually is. Douglas' definition of dirt suggests a transgression in relation to (or 'out of') a place. However, one could go further: dirt does not belong to *a* place, nor by implication or corollary, does it belong anywhere else: dirt belongs nowhere. Dirt is where it should not be, moreover, dirt should not *'be'*. Dirt is often hidden from view (or consolidated at or beyond an edge), removed, ignored or eradicated: 'in the most radical and effective way: we make them invisible by not looking and unthinkable by not thinking'.[8] Dirt is often related to non-material issues of religion, purity, ideology and imperfection. There are religious overtones to dirt; and many other culturally specific interpretations of that which is theoretically and/or spiritually clean or dirty. In a reverse trajectory; dirt (*qua* soil) has been transvalued with positive significations. The term has been re-appropriated as part of the ecological movement and climate-change strategy as a beneficent entity. Dirt involves many important biological and atmospheric qualities that could ameliorate global climate-change. This recuperation of the term 'dirt' involves a re-examination of the function of dirt, soil, earth, excreta as nature and natural, rather than a culturally constructed 'transgression'. Dirt, then, can be considered in entirely oppositional ways, as both good and bad, as physical and conceptual, as both a transgression in itself and a transgression between modes.

This theoretical background becomes compelling when brought into an architectural focus: where do architectural boundaries lie? How might those working within spatial practice (architects, planners, urban designers, artists) think and work transgressively? Where does society place the limits within which these professions work and how might those limits shift? What happens when a planning authority is presented with a utopia? Might a structure of social value be ever permitted to fall into ruination? How can transgressive behaviour and processes alter the nature of constructed space, the mode of habitation, or the ways in which space is perceived? Does, indeed, architecture have the capacity to be subversive? The 'Transgression' project aimed to determine how the term 'transgression' can stimulate invention and generate insight into architectural understanding, design practice and concepts of space. Transgression is a lens through which one can recast these accepted narratives.

Such questions pose a question: why transgress at all? The term 'transgression' implies more than breaking the rules; there is within the term a certain distaste, the anxiety of breaking of a taboo. Mikhail Bakhtin's work on the notion of the carnival suggests why it might actually be *good* to transgress. The carnival, he argued, celebrates a temporary relaxing of the normal rules – a transgression that firstly acknowledges the society's limits and boundaries and then, through exceeding those boundaries, in a sense completes them: 'It asserts and denies, it buries and revives. Such is the laughter of the carnival'.[9] We might ask ourselves what might be the architectural equivalent to the carnival; what spatial practice or regenerative activity might exploit the self-conscious transgression, and affirmation, of rarely contested rules? If architecture can be considered a social art then practitioners and theorists must move *beyond* what Lefebvre describes as the reproduction of the social relations of production. That is, rather than working within the frameworks of society to produce spaces which reflect and reinforce that society, the architectural profession/s can adopt a critical practice to expose and comment on the implicit structures of power. A transgressive spatial practice might transform culture by revealing structures of power and authority, challenging accepted norms and received wisdom while being continuously self-reflective and oppositional – architecture as provocateur. Thus the concept of 'transgression' can stimulate innovation and generate insight into architectural understanding, design practice and concepts of space.

In order to be transgressive, one might need to adopt an attitude, to operate beyond accepted norms, to be prepared to find oneself in unfamiliar and uncomfortable territory and (perhaps) to face uncomfortable consequences. Transgression is a term which offers something of a permission for *wandering* and *wondering,* across boundaries, to see what can be learned. Presented with economic and social uncertainty, along with challenges from other professions and a broad culture of conservatism, architecture is in danger of losing its prized status as one of the pre-eminent visual arts. In order for architecture to remain relevant, to position and reinvent itself in changing times, it must move across perceived disciplinary limits and explore an expanded field. The architecture of transgression opens new possibilities; the act of transgression can be seen as an opportunity.

Inversion

> There is nothing more difficult to take in hand, more perilous to conduct, or more uncertain in its success, than to take the lead in the introduction of a new order of things.

Machiavelli, *The Prince*[10]

This Transgression 'project'[11] has generated a very plural, porous notion of the term. When stripped of its negative associations (including suggestions of sin, taboo and illegality) transgression becomes a matter of adventure and exploration. The project has come to focus on the verb 'to transgress' (as a process) rather than the noun, (the transgression itself). The original call for papers for the conference, issued in December 2012, generated 104 submissions from 16 countries and six continents. It was gratifying that such large numbers, from such a diversity of institutions, not only shared the ethos of our enquiry but were willing to actively participate in it. Transgression, it appears, has become respectable – or at least a term within which 'respectable' people are willing to position themselves. Equally remarkable was the diversity of interpretation and the range of work that could potentially be grouped within, or embraced by, the term. Transgression is no longer, indeed, the province of Shelley's undead creation, Joseph Conrad's Kurtz or Foucault's human monsters; rather, it is a conceptual territory where academics and innovative spatial practitioners can test and subvert established boundaries and limits.

The myriad academics who helped contribute to the process of knowledge gathering (of which we could accommodate just a few in this volume) all share a common interest and alliance in the transgressive *process* of their work. They are all united by their desire or practice of working across disciplines in order to transgress the boundaries of their own academic discipline (or artistic endeavour). All of these transgressors are unified in working in a field that has (as yet) no name. There are various attempts by chapter authors in this book to name and/or define their post-transgression state: *expanded field* (Walters), *actor-networks, rhizomes* (Petcou and Petrescu), *performative collectivities* (Altay); *critical practice* (Sandin), *shared agencies* (Tyszczuk), *compound elements* (Rice), *hybridity* (Crisman; Bridgland and Walker). In truth, none of these terms quite describe the full compass of work outlined by the contributors of this book. What we are seeing is a set of practices, positions and attitudes generated by a hetero-tropic set of actors, agents, materials and practices. This expanded field, or zone, cannot become a discipline. It will likely remain, instead, a dirty, messy, chaotic weave of processes capturing the shift from a static end-product towards a state of emergence and contingency.

Four themes

This book is organised according into four key themes that have emerged in relation to transgression: *boundaries, violations, place* and *art practice*. These four parts contain a number of peer-reviewed chapters from conference speakers on issues exploring: transgression, global processes, transformative praxis and emergent trends in architectural production. The contributors examine alternative and radical ways of practising architecture, re-imagining of the architectural profession and expand the realm of what might constitute architecture, the built environment and urbanism. Separating these sections are four 'interventions' – these are shorter articles from each of the conference's keynote speakers, each addressing different concerns and adopting different approaches and attitudes on the theme of transgression. The four interventions begin with Bernard Tschumi who revisits some of his provocative 'adverts' (produced in the 1970s) that dealt with transgression and how they now relate to contemporary issues. The second intervention by Constantin Petcou and Doina Petrescu explores their architectural practice (through atelier d'architecture autogérée) via the examination of one of their latest projects – an ambitious mixed programme that attempts to radically challenge and re-negotiate a range of concerns including architecture, economics, governance social issues, carbon-footprints and means of production. Didier Faustino practises across the world, often adopting and appropriating art-practice methodologies as part of his work. Faustino's transdisciplinary approach is suffused with the notion of 'fragility' and temporality. The final intervention is by Can Altay, an Istanbul-based artist, architect and educator. He works collaboratively on a range of diverse issues and explores one specific project 'Rogue Games' which blurs the realm of sports-halls, games, art galleries and play. This work deliberately attempts to range across disciplines, institutions and received ideas concerning social norms, habitual uses of space and negotiations/conflict in quasi-public realm(s).

Part I: Boundaries

To cross boundaries is a key definition of transgression and is the defining theme for the first three chapters of this volume. Each of the chapters examines the notion of boundaries in different ways. Tyszczuk examines how the impacts of human-generated climate change have transgressed the 'planetary boundary' for resources. As we enter this new *carbonised* geological era the chapter considers what response(s) we, as designers and architects, might make to mitigate these harmful effects. The separation between natural, human-made and/or artificial environments, it is argued, can no longer be discerned; there is only one, all-encompassing, synthesised planetary environment to inhabit. In some ways this chapter sets a subtext for the rest of the book: at the beginning of a new millennium, the planetary-scale processes of capitalism, mass-migration, urbanisation, technological advances, extreme deprivation, climate change and population growth transgress ecological, social, cultural and ethical boundaries: whither architecture? A very different perspective on boundaries is adopted by Holm who adopts a psychologist's viewpoint to examine our individual relationship/s with the environment. Employing Lacan's trope of three psychological traits: the 'neurotic', the 'pervert' and the 'psychotic' – Holm examines how these boundary conditions affect the position of the subject in relation to spatiality. Fontana-Giusti's chapter explores boundaries from a spatio-historical perspective. Excavating the diaries of Le Corbusier's travels as a young man, Fontana-Giusti traces the significance of this geographical and psychological journey on Le Corbusier. In his 'Journey to the East', Le Corbusier enters new territories and experiences penetratingly different cultures and norms; returning back, not radically new, but profoundly altered.

Part II: Violation

Violation can be a radical and extreme form of transgression. The violation might be of: the law, social mores and norms, religious codes or taboos. Rice examines 'informal architecture' in which more than a billion people now inhabit the burgeoning slums, favelas and shanty towns across the planet. The living conditions within informal cities violate myriad ethical and moral standards of what is considered habitable in the 'West'. Informal architecture stands outside of the traditions of architecture as practised and studied within the 'architecture profession' yet affords a number of radical and potentially emancipatory lessons. Informal architecture is also predicated on a violation of law; the United Nations, for example, defines informal architecture or settlements as buildings 'to which the occupant have no legal claim, or which they occupy illegally'.[12] Vais continues exploring the relationship of transgression and the law through a case-study of Romanian development. Urban development over the past few decades has been informed by legislation and, in turn, legislation is informed by development in a mutually constitutive process. Violations of the law by property developers keen to maximise profit have led to ad hoc and ill-advised changes to legislation. What we see is an evolving 'lawscape' in action; that is, legislation unravelling, changing, modifying, transgressing, preceding and suffusing spatial development in Romania. Violation can also be achieved through less extreme means by treating something sacred or inviolable with irreverence, playfulness or disrespect. Bridgland and Walker's chapter explores this softer notion of violation in the temporary encampments of the British travelling fair – specifically the Newcastle Hoppings in the UK. There are numerous minor violations in the playful and carnivalesque behaviour at this temporary and transitory event. However, the more significant violation (at least in the sense of that most likely to end in the demise of the fairground) is that of the law. Damage to the site by the fairground and the concomitant economic and capital losses attributed to this are threatening the closure of this long-lived event.

Part III: Place

The succeeding chapters of the book deploy empirical studies of 'place' as the device through which to investigate the notion of transgression. 'Place' often implies the existence of a distinct boundary condition which delineates and perhaps harbours specific, heterogeneous cultures and local ecosystems. A much used (and perhaps overused) term 'place' continues to find relevance despite challenges from the homogenising processes of global capitalism and media, mass-migration, the kinetic elite, rapid telecommunications and multinationalism. Brown invokes dominant narratives and commentaries of Japanese architecture to investigate what, if anything, place and national culture might signify. There are tendencies to romanticise and oversimplify the notion of place in Japanese architecture. However, Brown eschews these in favour of pursuing an investigation of Taira Nishizawa's architecture as comprising a complex, hybrid and multiple network of identities – which somehow manage to retain, but not become overwhelmed by, qualities of 'Japan-ness'. Crisman uses the potential arising with a dislocation from 'place' as a learning tool. Crisman relocates architecture students from America to India as a catalyst for re-examining the norms, cultures and habitus associated with place-centred studio cultures. In this instance, it is the 'difference' in place that facilitates profound changes in student's learning practices. McAllister and Donnelly explore the role of literature in ancient folklore and contemporary culture in Ireland. Playing with the metaphor that landscapes can be considered as texts (or perhaps, more accurately, hyper-texts) that can be read, written and imbued with meanings and values. Medieval Gaelic poets roamed Ireland reading, writing and recording the landscape; these '*filid*' are compared to contemporary writers, specifically crime-fiction authors, who imbricate interweave the troubles of Ulster's recent past in fictional portraits. These contemporary representations transgress the borders of reality and fantasy as Ireland is re-appropriated and history is re-written in quasi-historical portrayals. The chapter considers the role of fiction(s) as agents in the production and re-production of 'place'. Coleman, on the other hand, explores the very physical construction of the Scottish Parliament to consider both the specificity of place and Utopia (non-place). This building project is infamous for its breathtaking financial and timescale overrun; however, Coleman revalorises this waste and financial loss as a transgressive practice that resists the reduction of value as economic capital. The transvaluation of such excess is situated within notions of what a parliament might be and its role within a fledgling nation-state qua Utopia. The accounts of 'place' attempt, in part, to 'translate' lessons, principles and practices from the 'real' world into discursive theory. This process of translation chronicles much of what could be attributed as the 'methodological' principles contained in this book.

Part IV: Art Practice

The final three chapters interrogate 'art practice' in relation to architecture. Each chapter, while sharing the theme, adopts a different approach to what constitutes such practice. Sandin looks at art practices which directly and explicitly challenge dominant institutions and/or societal codes. Artists operating in this field take as their starting point: the breaking, shattering or smearing of the boundaries of their intended targets – whether they be social, cultural, institutional or legislative. These practitioners challenge the status quo through their interventionist approach(es) and aim to reconstitute and renegotiate the institutions and organisations they interact with. Walters examines the theory and praxis of artist Joseph Beuys, particularly his maxim 'everyone is an artist' through a very personal account of her own work and that of colleague/collaborator Rebecca Krinke. Walters situates her praxis within, or as part of, a transgressed institutional field. Rather than attempting to assimilate or fit-into the existing 'ologies' of academia or the 'isms' of the art world, Walters simply accepts working in dirty, messy, boundary-free space. The term 'expanded field' is employed to capture this transgressed space where the word 'field' is particularly appropriate for such a muddied location where we ought to 'act as translators and, like Hermes, ferry back messages' across inter- and trans- disciplinary worlds. The book concludes with the work of de Carvalho and Linna who develop experimental methods for gathering knowledge, partly derived from feminist art practice. Situated within a relational network of actors and agents, their work is interwoven in the practices and materialities of (among other things): a feminist tattoo collective, a drumming school and knitting/crochet gatherings. Their chapter is partly sited in the text and partly in the accompanying images (as film stills) that constitute equally important aspects for their weaving of narratives and meaning.

This book is, therefore, something of a survey of practices and theoretical positions which are framed within the term transgression. The chapters within the book do not provide a definitive method by which transgression can be achieved or applied, but they do offer insight into the ways in which varying thinkers and practitioners have used transgression either as a construct within which to position their work, or as a point of departure. It is worth noting that transgression is a temporal phenomenon – as time passes society's boundaries and limits are inevitably subjected to pressure and alteration. Borders shift, and therefore so too do the terms of transgression. Transgression, then, is an ongoing project.

Notes

1   Henri Lefebvre (1991) *The Production of Space*. (Oxford, Blackwell), page 26.
2   Michel Foucault (2003) *Abnormal: Lectures at the College de France 1974–1975* (London, Verso), page 52
3   Ibid, page 63
4   Mary Shelley (1986) *Frankenstein*. In *Three Gothic Novels* (Harmondsworth, Penguin Classics), page 364
5   Georges Bataille (1998) *Eroticism* [quoted in Tschumi, Bernard. Oppositions. Princeton, NJ: Princeton University Press. 'Architecture and Transgression', page 357].
6   Georges Bataille (2001) *Story of the Eye* (Harmondsworth, Penguin Classics), page 18.
7   Mary Douglas (1966) *Purity and Danger: An Analysis of the Concepts of Pollution and Taboo* (London, Routledge and Kegan Paul), page 35.
8   Zigmunt Bauman (2004) *Wasted Lives: Modernity and its Outcasts* (Cambridge, Polity Press), page 34.
9   Mikhail Bakhtin (1968) *Rabelais and His World*, trans. by H. Iswolsky (Bloomington, IN, Indiana University Press), pages 11–12.
10 Niccolò Machiavelli (1996) *The Prince,* trans. P. Sonnino (New Brunswick, NJ, Humanities Press), page 51.
11 On 22 February 2010 the Architectural Humanities Research Association called for 'expressions of interest' from universities seeking to host one of AHRA's international conferences. That call prompted a vigorous and ongoing conversation among research-active staff within UWE's Department of Architecture and the Built Environment (then the Department of Planning and Architecture). Staff including Louis Rice, David Littlefield, Rachel Sara, Jonathan Mosley, James Burch, Mike Devereux and Thom Gorst looked to see where their research interests overlapped or coincided. Those original conversations – which quickly began to focus on terms such as boundaries, liminality, rogue, alternative, un/authorised and territory – coalesced around agreement that transgression was precise enough to suggest the attitude and tone of our research, but loose enough to encompass the broad scope of our interests sufficiently well. This ongoing conversation on the subject of transgression has led to a series of outcomes beyond that conference and this book, including:
    • An exhibition at Bristol's Architecture Centre (accompanied by the book *Architecture + Transgression*, published by the Architecture Centre, edited by Louis Rice. 2012).
    • 'The Architecture of Transgression', an edition of *Architectural Design* (Wiley, November/ December 2013) edited by Rachel Sara and Jonathan Mosley.
    • 'Transgression: body and space', an edition of *Architecture and Culture* (Bloomsbury, November 2014) edited by David Littlefield and Rachel Sara.
12 United Nations, Department of Economic and Social Affairs, (2001) Indicators of Sustainable Development. Frameworks and Methodologies. Report number: DESA/DSD/2001/3. New York: United Nations, Department of Economic and Social Affairs, page 112.

Intervention 1

Advertisements for architecture

Bernard Tschumi

Transgression is a very big word. It is a word that is derived from literature and philosophy, and also of course rooted in religion and other social frameworks such as the law. What, though, does transgression have to do with architecture? Architecture has a very long history spanning many thousands of years, and over this period architecture has conveyed or adopted a series of ideas which are taken for granted. Architecture has become, therefore, what I would call a 'dictionary of received ideas'. This will embody a great number of clichés; but when one questions clichés, or received ideas, one must look to see if there are moments of break-down – of where things do not quite fit.

By the late 1960s one of Modernism's defining buildings, Le Corbusier's Villa Savoye near Paris, came under threat of demolition, resulting in many young architecture students demonstrating in favour of saving it. I was one of them. When I visited it, something incredible happened; the building was amazing, it was quite astonishing in its state of decay – in its state of complete dereliction from many years of neglect. It occurred to me then that perhaps architecture is not only about perfection and the realisation of an abstract concept; it is also about the sensations of the occupant, including making room for an interaction between building and feelings/body. I therefore began to press for a resolution through which the Villa Savoye could be preserved *in the state in which it was at the time*. The building stank; it was filled with graffiti; it embodied a very different *presence* than that conceived by Le Corbusier, and more emotional charge than contemporary design could achieve (Figure I1.1). Amusingly enough, the building came to be completely restored, but the restoration was so pure it was shocking, prompting a programme of de-restoration – restoration with less 'make-up'.

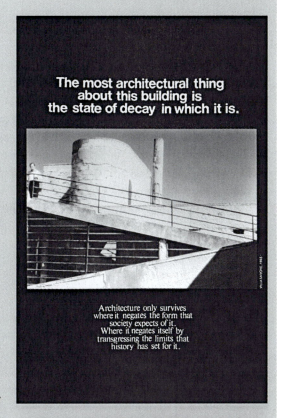

Figure I1.1
Villa Savoye advertisement: decay

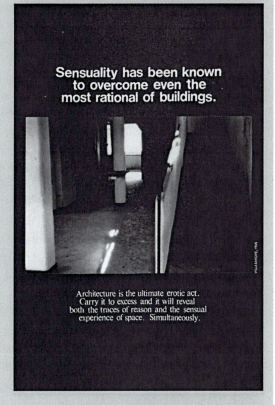

Figure I1.2
Villa Savoye advertisement:
sensuality

I quote this example to make the point that architecture is not absolute – it is relative. Architecture is related to other things that happen in it. There is no architecture unless something happens within it. Further, we know that, even for the student, architecture is filled with constraints. These constraints, these rules, these regulations (whether they are city regulations, budgets or other limits) are things we learn to deal with, to play with even. We must learn to make these constraints, dare I say, part of the project. Unless we make these limits pleasurable our lives as architects would be miserable. Much of architecture is a game where one simply takes advantage of the disadvantage; redefining the invisible opponent (the rule; the limit; the constraint) as a positive factor.

The advertisement shown in Figure I1.3 makes an analogy between certain sado-masochistic practices and the constraints facing the architect. In the 1970s I created a set of advertisements, including one depicting the Ville Savoye, for the now-defunct journal *Oppositions*, although they came to be published more widely. The intention was to demonstrate that architecture is something that belongs to everyone. Architecture is not simply a knowledge of form, it is a form of knowledge, and we share this form of knowledge with others: not only mathematicians and philosophers but anyone we might meet on the street. The advertisements were made to communicate relatively abstract ideas to a larger audience.

Traditionally, architecture's first rule is: 'Get the job!' However, I would argue that the first rule is, in fact, *to break it*. This sensibility leads the architect to do the unexpected, to surprise the client who arrives with a generic idea which provides a platform for subversion. Architecture is interesting in that it can be defined in terms of budget, square metres and programme; but it is the architect who negotiates these limits, who examines how a person might move through a building, who considers the vectors of movements which can be among the most exciting parts of a project – consider the possibilities inherent in a ramp, a stair or an elevator. Once the architect receives the brief, they should begin asking: 'how can I twist the programme? ... how can I provide extra life? ... how can I make it more than it is?' That is breaking the first rule. And it should be as pleasurable as it can be; one that is impossible to resist.

The writer and surrealist Georges Bataille cast architecture in an interesting light with his dictionary of architecture[1] which, of course, began with the letter A. Bataille (1929), however, commenced with the word 'abattoir – a slaughterhouse'.[2] Hardly a conventional way in which to begin a discourse on the subject, but Bataille's intention was to demonstrate that behind architecture exists a whole system of authority – a hierarchy – a set of disciplines which he considered problematic due to the way they structure society. In particular, Bataille set out to question the metaphors by which language adopts architectural references. In his work *The Labyrinth*,[3] Bataille discussed the strange relationship between the absolute abstraction of the one and the sensations of passing through the other; the world of abstraction versus the world of experience. I have always felt this to be a fascinating observation because it precisely defines the condition of architecture: concept and experience. In considering this further, I came to develop the notion of *death* as the ultimate abstraction juxtaposed

Look at it this way:

The game of architecture is an intricate
play with rules that you may break or accept.
These rules, like so many knots that cannot
be untied, have the erotic significance of
bondage: the more numerous and sophisticated
the restraints, the greater the pleasure.

ropes and rules

The most excessive passion
always involves a set of rules.
Why not enjoy them?

Figure I1.3
Ropes and rules advertisement

If you want to follow
architecture's first rule,
break it.

Transgression.
An exquisitely perverse act
that never lasts.
And like a caress is
almost impossible to resist.

TRANSGRESSION

Figure I1.4
Transgression advertisement

Figure I1.5
Gardens of pleasure advertisement

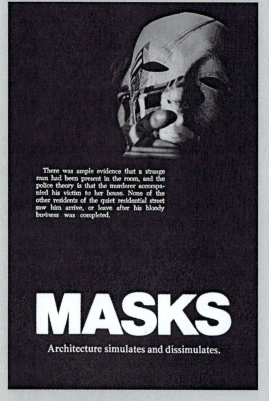

Figure I1.6
Masks advertisement

To really appreciate architecture, you may even need to commit a murder.

Architecture is defined by the actions it witnesses as much as by the enclosure of its walls. Murder in the Street differs from Murder in the Cathedral in the same way as love in the street differs from the Street of Love. Radically.

Figure I1.7
Murder advertisement

with *life* as the absolute immediacy of sensation; the boundary between the two, I came to consider, is eroticism. The idea of pleasure; the idea of desire.

Architecture shares historic links with other disciplines. Consider gardens. The gardens of the Renaissance served as the beginning of cities in the centuries that followed; the avenue of trees established the possibility of a future urban road.

I have always found such inter-disciplinary dialogues to be interesting, especially with regard to the visible and the invisible (the meanings that lie masked). The idea behind the advertisements was, in part, to help reveal to a larger audience some of the unspoken forces that lie behind the architecture.

The final advert was more violent than its predecessors. It embodied a single dramatic image from a film framed by the provocative statement: 'to really appreciate architecture you may even need to commit a murder'. The advertisement attempted to address the fact that architecture is just as much about what it does as what it looks like. Thus the architect must embrace the process of questioning. It is a questioning which makes it possible for architecture to be an activity (rather than a discipline); an activity which has a long future before it because it is so closely bound to the future of society.

This text is based on the keynote address made by Bernard Tschumi at the AHRA conference 'Transgression', Bristol, UK, 21 November 2013. The address was delivered via pre-recorded film.

Notes

1   Georges Bataille (1929–1930) *Critical Dictionary.* Originally published in the journal *Documents* (from 1929-1930) edited by Bataille.
2   Georges Bataille (1929) *Slaughterhouse*. Republished in N. Leach. N. (ed.) *Rethinking Architecture: A Reader in Cultural Theory* (London, Routledge, 1985), page 20.
3   Georges Bataille (1930) *Labyrinth*. Republished in A Stoekl, A. (ed.) *Visions of Excess. Selected Writings, 1927–1939* (Minneapolis, MN, University of Minnesota Pres, 1985), pages 171–8.

Part I
Boundaries

Chapter 1

The fly and the satellite

Transgressing 'planetary boundaries' in the Anthropocene

Renata Tyszczuk

Introduction

This chapter brings together two very different approaches to thinking about limits and boundaries that might offer some insights into inhabiting a planet of cities in planetary crisis. It offers a series of reflections on threshold conditions and transgressing planetary boundaries in the Anthropocene.

One line of thought describes humanity's home planet as having limits. It has, since the widespread emergence of environmental concerns of the 1960s, consistently warned of the hazards of transgressions. The 'planetary boundaries' hypothesis developed at the Stockholm Resilience Centre is the latest incarnation of this thinking, and its rise to prominence coincides with entry into the 'Anthropocene epoch'.

A very different approach to humanity's planetary condition is offered by reference to Michel Serres' reflections on global environmental change and world-consciousness. He discusses *world objects* – for example, satellites – and also gives the example of a transgressive species – the fly – in order to provoke imaginings of different possible trajectories within what he proposes as a limitless world-consciousness. His writing alerts humanity to the complexities of the planetary boundaries with which we must now live and think and the necessity of integrating scales and times; of considering both the 'fly and the satellite'.

The advance into the Anthropocene epoch establishes humans as a planetary-scale, climate-changing, disruptive, geological force and at the same time acts as a reminder of collective vulnerability, responsibility and state of uncertainty. Many responses have focused on effective techno-scientific management of environmental crises but there are limits to thinking in terms of 'climate calculations' in the context of global environmental change. Predictions of geo-climatic and geo-political regime shifts and a 'planetary state of emergency', demand that humanity appreciates its capacity to effect change but also that it considers the potential for far-reaching transformations in its mode of inhabiting the Earth. The 'built environment' has been prominent in the literature of transformation. This chapter considers the dominant framings of planetary and social change, and starts to probe the significance of these for thinking about urbanism and the practice of architecture. It argues in favour of notions of agency and practice which are more open, provisional, tentative and responsive than the predominantly technical pursuit of 'future-proofed' human lives and settlements.

Home Planet

> The largest apple. The most beautiful sphere or turbulent ball. The most ravishing boat, our caravel new and eternal. The fastest shuttle. The most gigantic rocket. The greatest spaceship. The densest forest. The most enormous rock. The most comfortable refuge. The most mobile statue. The complete clod of earth open at our feet, steaming.
>
> (Serres 1995, 121)

The most iconic images of humanity's home planet are the NASA photographs 'Earthrise', Apollo 8, 24 December 1968 (Figure 1.1) and the 'Blue Marble' or 'Whole Earth', Apollo 17, 7 December 1972 (Figure 1.2). These images, associated with both the space age and the environmental movement, introduce the twinned ideologies of 'one world' (human universality) and 'whole Earth' (fragile ecology). Although superficially contradictory, both global visions – the 'world without borders' and the 'delicate bounded Earth – were tied to a 'global mission' of 'human territoriality' (Cosgrove 2001, 265; 289). At the same time images of a 'static rounded Earth did much to calcify concepts of dynamic Earth systems' and for the most part, 'whole Earth gave us the illusion of the Earth as a discrete artefact, which could be managed and encoded into systems or geo-engineered' (Yusoff 2009, 1017). Since those images were taken knowledge of dynamic Earth systems and the interactions of the atmosphere, hydrosphere, biosphere, heliosphere, cryosphere, lithosphere – air, water, life, sun, ice and rock – has greatly expanded. Acknowledgement of the significant ways in which humans are changing Earth systems has unsettled existing notions of boundaries and threshold conditions and warned of planetary crisis (O'Riordan and Lenton 2013).

One expression of the planetary crisis is the concerted uptake of the concept of the Anthropocene ('the age of humans'): a new geological epoch that is replacing the Holocene.[1] In this scientific formulation humankind has become a geologic force at a planetary scale through impacts on global climate and a range of other Earth and life processes such that the collective action of the species will be found in the future geological record. The Anthropocene anticipates a materially inscribed threshold of

Figure 1.1
'Earthrise' 24 December 1968
Astronaut photograph from Apollo 8 mission

radical geological change and, whether or not it is formally accepted as a new epoch, promises to alter more than the wording in geological textbooks. It is a concept that challenges disciplinary divisions and nature–culture dichotomies and prompts the question of 'modes of existence' or what it means to be 'of this Earth' (Latour 2013a, 2013b).[2] Furthermore, the Anthropocene idea is a proleptic undertaking which identifies not only the eventual fossilization of human worlds and mass extinction of species but massive transformations in planetary geomorphology at timescales that are difficult to imagine (Zalasiewicz 1998, 2009). In other words, it is before its time. Its provocations nevertheless coincide with current concerns about the possibility of passing over thresholds or tipping points in major environmental systems leading to imminent catastrophe. The Anthropocene hypothesis thus brings new prominence to the risk and actuality of crossing significant 'planetary boundaries'.

By identifying the Anthropocene as one more stratum or 'contingent event' in a long and turbulent Earth history, humans are collectively thrown into a strange boundary-crossing historicity (Chakrabarty 2009). In the same moment as humans are asserted as an asteroid-scale force of planetary change, their agency is diminished altogether. The Earth is also reconsidered as a fearful power capable of cataclysmic intrusions into human history (Stengers 2009). Significant shifts in Earth systems and extinctions have happened before in the Earth's 4.6 billion year history, but researchers are generally in agreement that disruptions on the massive scale which are already being recorded are extremely rare. Furthermore, this scale of planetary agitation has never occurred with such enormous human populations living in tightly packed cities and settlements

Figure 1.2
**'The Blue Marble'
or 'Whole Earth', 7
December 1972**
Astronaut photograph
from Apollo 17 mission

and in such intensely monitored, regulated, and politically demarcated territories. The intersection of geophysical and ecological changes at the global scale, including climate change and biodiversity loss, in tandem with rapid urbanization, economic and cultural globalization, demands that a vulnerable humanity prepares itself practically and imaginatively for potentially sudden, catastrophic and unpredictable change.

The new generation of Earth images made of composite date and complex calculations have renewed prominence in discussions around the Anthropocene and the geological agency of humans. The most obvious ways in which humans are altering the planet is by building cities and settlements. The NASA series of images of the Earth at night are by now a familiar index of human development. Lights going on and off around the world invite thinking about shrinking post-industrial cities and suburban sprawl in the North, and the accelerated expansion of new cities and regions, their infrastructures and interdependencies (Figure 1.3).[3] These images are not only a proxy for energy-intensive fossil-fuelled human activity but also indicative of the convergence of planetary crises – political, economic, ecological: accumulated urban neglect, resource shortages, abrupt climate change, agricultural and species collapse. They reveal not only the immense scale of human capacity for destruction and construction but the

Figure 1.3
Night Lights 2012
The image of the Earth
at night is a composite
assembled from data
acquired by the Suomi
National Polar-orbiting
Partnership (Suomi NPP)
in April 2012 and October
2012

ways in which human inhabitation can all too easily be overwhelmed by forces of the Earth that cannot be either controlled or anticipated. On a planet of cities in planetary crisis, architecture and urban practices are deeply implicated in the discussions around planetary boundaries and the Anthropocene.

The consequences of accelerated environmental crisis will determine what happens next in terms of human inhabitation on Earth but also provokes questions about how humans will meet those consequences. In the midst of urgent calls for action to avert climate catastrophe (UN Habitat 2011), architecture and built environment professionals are urged to think about cities and their infrastructures in terms of resilience to crisis or the capacity to manage transformation and change. Various strategies of adaptation and mitigation are now a priority for cities, governments and markets. These include a growing interest in planetary scale design responses ranging from proposals for Earth systems augmentation through geo-engineering fixes to programmes for global 'preparedness' by the Pentagon. However, the conventions of architecture and urban planning and their emphasis on stable definitions of practice are not so well attuned to the turbulent ground that cities cling to and the radical unsettlement that this augurs. Moreover, the urgent techno-scientific focus on reducing the vulnerabilities of a rapidly changing environment-in-crisis has, paradoxically, tended to obscure the philosophical and cultural shifts to living within 'planetary boundaries' in the Anthropocene.

'Beautiful sphere ... turbulent ball' or 'the most comfortable refuge'? In an era of changes to climate, geology, assemblages of species and technologies, as well as unpredictable threats to the conditions for planetary inhabitation, architecture will also change. Architecture as transformative agency places its constructive activities and its capacity to reinvent different modes of inhabitation centre stage (Kossak *et al.* 2009). However, boundary-crossing in the Anthropocene is not simply about questioning or destabilizing the existing context of architectural practice but about allowing for practice and its pretensions to be radically altered and weakened in the process. Accepting that architectural practice is unstable and provisional is not only about inhabiting instability, but also about responding imaginatively to change and unsettlement. This is a humble practice (humility=groundedness) but no less ambitious for that.

Planetary boundaries

> We estimate that humanity has already transgressed three planetary boundaries: for climate change, rate of biodiversity loss, and changes to the global nitrogen cycle. Planetary boundaries are interdependent, because transgressing one may both shift the position of other boundaries or cause them to be transgressed.
>
> (Rockström *et al.* 2009a: 32)

The 'planetary boundaries' hypothesis proposed by Johan Rockström and colleagues at the Stockholm Resilience Centre, with its foundation in complex systems theory, or 'resilience thinking', has become an influential framework for discussing global environmental problems and solutions. It identifies nine global biophysical limits to human development: climate change; ocean acidification; stratospheric ozone depletion; biogeochemical nitrogen and phosphorus cycle levels; global freshwater use; land system change; biodiversity loss; chemical pollution; atmospheric aerosol loading. It further suggests that transgressing any of these interdependent boundaries will have catastrophic consequences. Humans are charged with imperilling 'the safe operating space for humanity with respect to the Earth system' and implored not to overstep 'planetary boundaries' newly calibrated to maintain a 'desirable' Holocene-like state for as long as possible (Rockström *et al.* 2009a). According to their research humanity has already transgressed three boundaries and is nearing others and as Rockström and colleagues acknowledge, recourse to planetary boundaries thinking allows for operating within a paradox:

> There is little doubt, however, that the complexities of interconnected slow and fast processes and feedbacks in the Earth System provide humanity with a challenging paradox. On the one hand, these dynamics underpin the resilience that enables planet Earth to stay within a state conducive to human development. On the other hand, they lull us into a false sense of security because incremental change can lead to the unexpected crossing of thresholds that drive the Earth System, or significant sub-systems, abruptly into states deleterious or even catastrophic to human well-being. The concept of planetary boundaries provides a framework for humanity to operate within this paradox.
>
> (Rockström *et al.* 2009a: 55)

The 'planetary boundaries' project follows a persistent line of thought that frames environmental crises as a planetary scale management problem within the notion of a limited Earth. In this it echoes Buckminster Fuller's programme for *Spaceship Earth* whose 'carrying capacity'[4] merged scant resources with spatial constraint in a vision of the Earth as a fragile craft (1968). This thinking also informed Fuller's project with Shoji Sadao, a city of last resort or emergency planning vision, the *Dome over Manhattan* (1960) which encapsulated a two-mile diameter section of midtown Manhattan in a climate-controlled transparent dome. Fuller offered two-handed re-assurance in suggesting that, 'the established cities will probably not adopt the doming until environmental and other emergencies make it imperative' (Fuller 1965). The data-driven survivalist discourses of the 1960s and 1970s were spearheaded by the Club of Rome's report *Limits to Growth* (1972), which was published in the same year as the first UN summit on the environment. The report attempted to visualize entangled processes of pollution, population growth, industrial output, natural resources and food. It projected visions of humanity locked into trajectories of worst-case scenarios. The only apparent escape route was to develop scientific and technological regimes of efficiency. In Fuller's terms this required a process of self-instruction for the operator of the planetarian complex of 'life support and maintenance systems'. However, despite the intensity and persistence of these calls, humans still don't have a well-proven operating manual for planet Earth.

The planetary boundaries hypothesis suggests 350 parts per million (ppm) as the safe planetary 'carrying capacity' for atmospheric carbon dioxide – the measureable parameter for the Earth system process of climate change. On 10 May 2013, the daily-average measured atmospheric concentration of carbon dioxide at the Earth Systems Research Laboratory, Mauna Loa Observatory, Hawaii was recorded as exceeding 400 ppm. At the start of the Industrial Revolution (and the proposed origins of the Anthropocene), atmospheric CO_2 was at 280 ppm. The last time CO_2 levels hit 400 ppm was in the Pleiocene (between 2.6–5.3 million years ago), when the Earth was around four degrees hotter and the oceans up to 40 metres higher than at present. The only major national newspaper in the UK to carry the story on its front page was *The Independent* – the *Financial Times* reported on corrupt banking practices, while the *Daily Mail* revealed the sale of drugs on Amazon (Simms 2013). The transgression of a planetary boundary and the symbolic ceiling of 400 ppm, long considered a figure of great jeopardy, came and went. Indeed, it may well be that the human species is becoming increasingly immune to such symbolic breaches as the processes of environmental and ecological devastation become ever more familiar.

As a response to the 'planetary boundaries' discourse, the Breakthrough Institute's report has pointed out the 'arbitrary nature of identifying non-threshold planetary boundaries and assigning them quantitative limits' (Nordhaus *et al.* 2012, 4). They argue that this challenges the claims of Rockström and colleagues that boundaries are 'non-negotiable' or that they 'exist irrespective of peoples' preferences, values, or compromises based on political and socioeconomic feasibility' (Rockström *et al.* 2009a, 35–36). Rather, the complex societal challenges of planetary stewardship suggest that 'no global boundary can be meaningfully determined' (Nordhaus *et al.* 2012, 5). Poverty campaigner Kate Raworth and colleagues at Oxfam have introduced a critique – or at least a substantial amendment – of the planetary boundaries thesis which is rooted in human needs. They have argued for 'a safe and just space for humanity' to achieve human rights and well-being, as well as equitable distribution of resources (Raworth 2012).

The 'planetary boundaries' framework involves concerted scientific effort and a call to action, but the corresponding thresholds requiring action at regional and local scales are harder to define. Furthermore, planetary boundaries thinking cannot be detached from a fraught international and domestic politics regarding rights and obligations related to pollution and natural resources. As Mike Davis points out, although climate diplomacy assumes a common interest, there is little precedent in history for the kind of solidarity needed to deal with the 'dramatically unequal impacts' of climate change, which are expected to be most severe for the world's poorest and most vulnerable people. Even though, he argues,

> there is no planetary shortage of 'carrying capacity' if we are willing to make democratic public space, rather than modular, private consumption, the engine of sustainable equality.
>
> (Davis 2010).

Davis further warns of the abandonment of global mitigation in favour of selective adaptation on Earth, the carrier:

> instead of galvanizing heroic innovation and international co-operation, growing environmental and socio-economic turbulence may simply drive elite publics into more frenzied attempts to wall themselves off from the rest of humanity. Global mitigation, in this unexplored but not improbable scenario, would be tacitly abandoned – as, to some extent it already has been – in favour of accelerated investment in selective adaptation for Earth's first class passengers. The goal would be the creation of green and gated oases of permanent affluence on an otherwise stricken plane.
>
> (Davis 2010)

Planetary crisis of agency

Zygmunt Bauman has defined the contemporary 'crisis of agency' as a crisis of governance and the disjunction between power and politics in a globalized world: 'the growing volume of power that matters … has already turned global; but politics has remained as local as before' (Bauman 2012). The Anthropocene complicates things further. It raises enormous questions for the many human institutions taken for granted in the more stable world of the Holocene. In a world of geo-political and geo-climatic turbulence, ethical, legal, spatial and environmental norms are necessarily under scrutiny. Moreover, humanity's inadvertent entry into the Anthropocene epoch signals a paradox: humans are described as an immense geological force and at the same time their possibilities for action are diminished. The time of the Anthropocene signals a planetary crisis of agency. As Bruno Latour puts it,

> How can we simultaneously be part of such a long history, have such an important influence, and yet be so late in realizing what has happened and so utterly impotent in our attempts to fix it?
>
> (Latour 2014: 2)

A planet of cities in planetary crisis describes a world with increasingly unfixed geographies, changing coastlines, climate-induced degradation, resource scarcity, fragile borders, contested states and displaced peoples. It demands rethinking, redrawing and rebuilding of existing boundaries and settlements and a radical re-organization of governance and environmental justice. Under conditions of intensifying globalization the most precarious thresholds have long been considered social or political. Imaginaries of spatial mobility, border crossing, and the transgression of boundaries have relied on notions of long-term stability: humans move across a relatively immobile Earth. But as the geographer Nigel Clark asks,

> What if the most crucial borders turn out to be not so much the lines which demarcate one political unit from another across our planet's frenetically criss-crossed surface, as those boundaries which separate one 'regime' or 'state' of the Earth system from another? To put it another way, what if the most critical thresholds are the ones that define strata rather than those which delineate territory?
>
> (Clark 2013)

Even if the collisions of human agency with non-human and more-than-human agency are acknowledged, the entanglements of geo-climatic and geo-political regime change signal the prospect of intensified upheavals on a planetary scale. In a potentially more agitated context, international climate change negotiations over carbon emissions targets may well become increasingly antagonistic.[5] Furthermore, politics can only offer up the laws, rules, procedures, visions, treaties, conventions and protocols that have developed in response to conflict and territorial appropriation during the 11,700 year-long Holocene period of relative stability (Clark 2013). What new forums and agreements would be appropriate for the wholly new and increasingly turbulent conditions of the Anthropocene?

World-objects

> Here is a hazy ball surrounded by turbulence: Planet Earth as satellites photograph her: Whole
>
> (Serres 1995,120)

From Buckminster Fuller's 'Geoscope' to Al Gore's 'Digital Earth',[6] 'capturing' the Earth as a virtual globe incorporating all known data has been a persistent objective. Knowledge of dynamic Earth systems and calculations of climate change variations have relied on increasingly sophisticated 'whole Earth' technologies and their vision of the world. The accumulation of Earth data carries political purchase in the debate around anthropogenic induced climate change and in securing political responses tied to accounting procedures. Planetary boundaries thinking has been made possible through the acquisition of data by satellites, as presented for example in the range of 'Global Maps' on the NASA 'Earth Observatory' website.

For philosopher Michel Serres, 'world-objects' are technological objects that have exceeded their literal space of occupation:

> By world objects I mean tools with a dimension that is commensurable with one of the dimensions of the world. A satellite for speed, an atomic bomb for energy, the Internet for space, and nuclear waste for time.
>
> (Serres 2006)

Through satellites – world-objects – researchers have become adept at monitoring, mapping and re-animating the movements of weather, bodies of sea temperature, earthquakes, ice flows, intensities of carbon dioxide accumulation and the way in which human interventions, particularly on the urban scale, have an impact on global environmental change. As Serres has noted,

> The Earth needs only to be observed by satellite, at night, for these dense spots to be recognized ... skyrocketing demographic growth becomes concentrated and stuck together in giant units, colossal banks of humanity, as powerful as oceans, deserts or icecaps.
>
> (Serres 1995, 16–17)

Yet can the gap be closed between data driven representations and the ground condition of human experience? The challenge is to find ways of articulating, responding to – and remaining *capable* – in the face of such enormous shifts in scale.

Satellite imagery makes familiar the before-and-after effects of the accelerated growth of cities and artificial islands, of the erosion and displacement of land forms, of wildfires, deforestation and flooding, and of zones of conflict and mass destruction.[7] Satellites can show the dependency of cities and regions upon infrastructure and their dramatically changed contours after extreme events. Their monitoring can signal an alert regarding massive agricultural transformations and the global perturbation of the nitrogen cycle wrought by the need to nourish expanding cities. Satellites allow the viewer to follow disasters in real time via enhanced images beamed around the world. As Laura Kurgan observes, although global imaging technologies, with their origins in military surveillance, are now intended to convey 'close up at a distance' a supposedly democratic, distributed and public view, 'evaluating this new visibility and negotiating its reality is a lot less obvious' (Kurgan 2013, 24). Such images also serve as a reminder of the inadequacy of human agency when faced with the unpredictable incursions of hybrid human-technological-geological agencies into human affairs.

On Friday, 11 March 2011, the Tōhoku earthquake and tsunami was followed by three meltdowns in the Fukushima Daiichi nuclear power plants. Expert analysis and calculations stand alongside eyewitness accounts. The earthquake moved Honshu (the main island of Japan) 2.4 m east and shifted the Earth on its axis by estimates of between 10 cm and 25 cm. There were 16,000 deaths accounted for, 129,225 buildings which had totally collapsed, a further 254,204 buildings 'half collapsed', and another 691,766 buildings partially damaged by the combined effects of earthquake

Figure 1.4
Ishinomaki Bay, Japan in the aftermath of the Tōhoku Earthquake and Tsunami
Agricultural fields and settled areas are submerged by muddy waters. Astronaut photograph ISS026-E-33647 taken on 14 March 2011

and tsunami. In northeastern Japan, 4.4 million households were left without electricity and 1.5 million without water. However, even with human ability to conduct the most stringent calculations, generate the most comprehensive data, construct the most animated renditions of the turbulence of Earth systems, and create the most agile communication systems, is it possible to know at a distance what it is to endure the pain and loss of an overturned ordinary existence and to experience the dramatic rearrangement of a human life? (Figures 1.4 and 1.5). Michel Serres describes the human planetary condition as 'living in a permanent earthquake':

> For, as of today, the Earth is quaking anew: not because it shifts and moves in its restless, wise orbit, not because it is changing, from its deep plates to its envelope of air, but because it is being transformed by our doing. Nature acted as a reference point for ancient law and for modern science because it had no subject: objectivity in the legal sense, as in the scientific sense, emanated from a space without man, which did not depend on us and on which we *depended de jure* and *de facto*. Yet henceforth it depends so much on us that it is shaking and that we too are worried by this deviation from expected equilibria. We are disturbing the Earth and making it quake! Now it has a subject once again.
>
> (Serres 1995, 86)

This is an unsettled time. Humanity is unsettled by the relationship with the world that it finds itself in, and the knowledge that it appears to be changing it, probably for the worse, and at a planetary scale. And, yet it has no idea what the significant boundaries really are. Although there are world-objects, of world-wide scale, Serres reminds us how impossible it is to adequately represent and determine, let alone

Figure 1.5
Ishinomaki Bay, Japan in the aftermath of the Tōhoku Earthquake and Tsunami
Image captured by the Advanced Spaceborne Thermal Emission and Reflection Radiometer (ASTER) on NASA's Terra satellite on 14 March 2011

contain, such planetary states of fluctuation especially if, as geological agents, humans are implicated in earthly turbulence.

Worldly dislocation

Michel Serres' writings recognize not only shifts in scale and points of reference, but the entangled scales and shared agencies with which humans must now live and think. Serres' topological imagination draws attention to both the fly and the satellite and 'the necessity of integrating scales' (Connor 2008: 16). The collapsing of micro-histories of human experience, planetary timescales, world-objects and diverse species constitutes a 'crazy dance', rather than any pre-supposed universality. In *Atlas*, Serres' account of world-consciousness, the fractious continuity of connections across the local and global is brought to life with the description of the irrational and seemingly random flight of a fly:

> It passes in hurried zigzags, choppy, discontinuous, changes course unpredictably, suddenly traverses the whole of the room, from one extreme point to its most distant opposite, in intervals of flight that are brief, medium-sized or long, as though generated by the throw of a dice, halts, rotates for a long period in a tight circle, comes up against close or contiguous obstacles, glass, mirror, lamp, table, buzzes imprisoned, swerves into a tiny island, sets off again
>
> … and now, look, it flies out through an open window, and enters a car or a plane, so that suddenly it is on the other side of the Earth, where it

resumes this dance that looks so crazy, but which reveals, miraculously, the reason and wisdom of the world. Yes, it really defines a locality, a here and now, marking out in its flight its frontiers, weaving an island of singularity, and seeming to abide in its chosen niche. But then, suddenly, it carries news of this particular there to distant and unexpected horizons, where it resumes weaving, threading, nesting a new place ...only to be off again. It localizes, of course, but also, indubitably, delocalizes. What invisible web does it weave, what network, what map does it mark out?

The atlas itself.

(Serres 1994, 102–103, cf. Connor 2008)

Bumping into things, landing on shit, invading the eye, buzzing to a singed death, the fly's haphazard movements evoke encounters with the world in its immeasurable and incalculable dimensions. Serres offers an invitation to think of the world in terms of topological mappings, that involve twisting, dispersing, folding movements and in terms of relations that are dynamic, perturbed, indefinite and open. According to him humanity has now left behind space, being-there and finitude, altogether:

unfinished, we have become infinite. Without niche or cradle, house or road, without borders or limits. Incomplete, certainly, imperfect, to be sure, but launched into an unpredictable time and space, in an open universe.

(Serres 2003, 82)

Serres finds promise in acknowledging this worldly dislocation. In a situation where all human constructions (physical, political, societal) are undermined by assertions of eventual fossil-fuelled demise, a different mode of involvement in the world is suggested, of 'construction at the limits of fragility' (Serres and Latour 1995, 120). In conversation, Serres and Latour recognize the fragile synthesis of the multitude of phenomena and processes that constitute the world. And as Bruno Latour observes,

The new subjects subjected to the vagaries of their own interconnected collisions are not trying to negotiate contracts but to engage in a sort of parley much more primitive than the market place or the court of law.

(Latour 2014: 6)

What are the dynamic and turbulent relationships within which planetary scale thinking and action are shaped? The Anthropocene hypothesis draws attention to a history of human attempts to overcome human finitude to the point where humans have thought of themselves as capable of inhabiting and legislating the world on their terms alone. This power is now recognized as ushering in conditions of frailty and finitude that threaten human existence (Connor 2010). At every turn it seems therefore as if humanity is confronted by the paradox of limits. How should it respond to this predicament of being exorbitant and indefinite? How does architecture change? In a cultural field increasingly aware of potentially catastrophic environmental change how can accepting the responsibility for intervention be also transformative of architectural practice and thought? Is it enough to make emergency plans, set limits on resource use, confront deficits, adopt mitigation and adaptation strategies, discuss zero, net or positive gains? Is there also a way of integrating and transgressing species, materials, scales and temporalities? Is it possible for architecture to apprehend living with a dynamic and agitated Earth that all the while resists being known, contained or demarcated?

Thinking about 'planetary boundaries'– as an attempt to inscribe humans within the limits of their own making – implies that at the same time humanity acknowledges a state of *worldly dislocation* and all that goes with that. But this inevitably leads to more difficult questions: What kinds of 'constructions' are possible both within a politics of constraints and at the limits of fragility? How can these make sense of a human agency that is weak and yet uncurbed in its capacity for entanglements and relations in the world. What would it mean for architectural practice to adopt planetary scale thinking that acknowledged such hybrid human–non-human agencies and yet resisted claims to a 'whole Earth' perspective?

Planetary state of exception

The Al-Zaatari refugee camp in Jordan was first opened on 28 July 2012 to host Syrians fleeing the violence of the civil war, which had erupted in 2011. On 4 July 2013, the camp population was estimated at 144,000 refugees, making it the world's second largest refugee camp (after Daadab in Kenya) and Jordan's fourth largest city. The very harsh climatic conditions in the region have not only exacerbated the conflict in Syria, conspiring to make it a 'climate-change war of sorts' (Solnit 2013) but have also made it all the more difficult to create good living conditions in the camp.[8] What most people know of this 'makeshift city in the desert' (Chulov 2013) is made apparent through satellites (Figure 1.6). It is possible to monitor the expansion of the camp, locate the camp manager or city 'mayor', take a 'tour of the camp' and zoom in and 'meet the residents'.[9] On the ground, Al-Zaatari is a 'dismal and edgy place' with constant military presence: 'the guards of all the inefficiencies'. It is also where 'urban planners have taken a stake' as with no end in sight to the conflict, the camp is being made more permanent (Chulov 2013). Location and scale-related decisions informed by satellite imagery have been instrumental in organizing the conditions of emergencies, wars and disaster management. However, instant global access to images and information relating to new catastrophes or disasters as they unfold is all the more disturbing, perhaps, for recalling lessons that have still not been learned.

The recent convulsions of earthquakes, tsunamis, flooding, wildfires, drought and conflict across the world demonstrate the convergence of two different earthly mobilities: people moving across the Earth's surface through economic or forced migrations *and* the shifting ground beneath our feet (Clark 2012, 23). The

Figure 1.6
Al-Zaatari refugee camp, Jordan
Satellite image data acquired 30 May 2009, 27 September 2012 and 19 July 19 2013

complex interweavings of climate, lives, economies and politics forces increasingly unpredictable global states of emergency. And as Nigel Clark points out,

> It may well be that over the coming decades it will become increasingly difficult to distinguish environmental migrants or refugees from their economic or political counterparts, and to separate the disaster relief camps from the detention centres and other sites of internment.
>
> (Clark 2012, 27)

The state of emergency that characterizes Western culture's response to crises (hybrid natural–human catastrophes and political upheavals) is related to Agamben's 'state of exception' with its spatially and temporally defined boundaries. Agamben's study of the state of siege talks of:

> gradual emancipation from the wartime situation to which it was originally bound in order to be used as extraordinary police measure to cope with internal sedition and disorder.
>
> (Agamben 2005, 5)

It describes a process, which not only expands government powers but suspends all legally established constitutional laws – where nothing matters except the will of sovereignty (Agamben 2005). The camp is the space that is opened when the state of exception becomes the rule. There it is a case of being fenced in, staying temporary for an indeterminate time, subject to constant negotiation of living conditions and the tacit promise of an alternative future. To inhabit a camp is to experience an ongoing, imminent, future mass-disaster, with uncertain thresholds and irreconcilable timescales for action or recovery. Human planetary inhabitation shares the predicament, and the legal and spatial precariousness of the refugee camp. In other words, the current global condition could be considered a planetary state of exception.

Al-Zaatari, the most provisional of cities, is a reminder of the need to develop not only shelters but also practices and theories of law, politics, economics and social relations in directions that can better support human wellbeing through frequent catastrophes. This means finding ways of steering away from increased securitization and the logic of the camp as the default response to planetary states of emergency. Given the context of a climate that humans are actively changing, catastrophic environmental change and unsettlement may well become more familiar as the so-called Anthropocene epoch unfolds. The challenge therefore is to find ways to live more equitably, more hospitably and more respectfully on a crowded planet. At the same time there is a need to recognize that much of the world's population has already endured scarcity, catastrophe and the sudden upheavals of environmental change. The local experience of hazard-prone populations is therefore essential in broadening the scope of what is considered expertise in the face of global disaster. The turbulent nature of human relations in times of escalating crisis implies the need to be better equipped to cope with experiences of estrangement and deprivation whether closer to home or further away. It therefore makes sense to ask how it might be possible to extend infrastructures of hospitality across space and time for those that need it most. Many of the adaptive strategies for present-day cities and infrastructures will not offer solutions. Instead they will be experiments, which are necessarily precarious and provisional: 'If hospitality on an episodically inhospitable Earth presents the most demanding of design problems, it also asks of us, from time to time a hasty redraft of even our best laid plans' (Clark 2012, 23).

Hotel for Humanity

How does a planet of cities respond to planetary crisis? Given that the very territories of human occupation are not simply contested but radically contingent, how is it possible to avoid becoming 'complicit in a *de facto* triage of humanity'? (Davis 2010). Michel Serres invites his readers to cast critical eyes on the ways in which humans take ownership of space and the ways in which space is befouled, polluted or contaminated as a mark of ownership. All political and legal structures have been based on the right to acquire and hold property and territory, usually at the expense of others. In *Malfeasance*, Serres' account of dealing with mess – in both senses – he questions the appropriate limits of ownership when he designates Earth, as the 'Hotel for Humanity':

> The world which was properly a home, becomes a global rental, the Hotel for Humanity. We no longer own it; we only live here as tenants.
>
> (Serres 2011, 72)

Serres advocates the 'non-ownership' of collective public goods, which concerns not only the natural spaces, territories and resources of the Earth, but also those spaces of free and open public discussion. Global rental is above all an exploration of living together, of human solidarity in the midst of the spatially and temporally extended dynamics of the world. Following Serres, this involves changing the emphasis of inhabitation, from one of appropriation, property management and technologies of exclusion on a planet of boundaries and ultrastructures to what could be imagined instead as a precarious tenancy – with all its attendant ambiguities and obligations. Staying a while in the Hotel for Humanity would also involve an indebtedness to those who came before, and a thought for those that may still seek to inhabit the Earth later:

> a greater sensitivity to the precariousness of past human life in the face of volatile Earth processes might help drive forward the still nascent and fragile commitment to intergenerational justice.
>
> (Clark *et al*. 2013, 112)

The global rental therefore requires a responsiveness to both a complex folded dynamic terrain (politics, economics, ethics), human histories 'on the ground' and the global temporalities of irreversible Earth processes. It suggests the importance of thinking provisionally in human, more-than-human and, more-than-planetary scales. Being 'at home' is never really safe, and in a less-than-ideal world there are many instances when earthly turbulence leaves Earth-dwellers unsettled, perturbed, traumatized, in need of support. What new forms and infrastructures of inhabitation and hospitality does this involve?

Camp or hotel? The most pressing design challenges of the Anthropocene are about ensuring that architectures, shelters, infrastructures, settlements and cities are not only resilient and adaptable but also welcoming to displaced and disenfranchized peoples. Technological advances and improved design can only go so far, and as Clark attests in his discussion of disaster responses, 'open doors function as the most immediate architectural innovation' (Clark 2012, 28). In the Anthropocene, a time that marks itself by intensified human intervention as much as by a surpassing of the human, how does architecture change? How might architectural practice think about itself differently if the surprising earthly dynamics that episodically pull the ground from under humanity's feet are attached to the usual physical vulnerabilities it has learnt to deal with? 'Taking responsibility' as architects and built environment practitioners will involve a good deal of resourcefulness and readiness to the radical adaptations and shifts to inhabitation that climate change may yet demand. And if planetary boundaries have already been transgressed then perhaps all that can be hoped for now is an equitable means of providing refuge, shelter and support. This inevitably involves finding ways of dealing with unfamiliar patterns of living in the midst of unforeseen dimensions of change.

> What would it mean to be worldly, when the world itself has become extraterrestrial, when we have become so exorbitant?
>
> (Connor 2010, 44)

Perhaps maintaining a planetary foothold is as much as humans can hope for. The world consciousness ushered in by acknowledgement of the Anthropocene covers a spectrum that involves both the all-seeing pretensions of satellites and the skittish improvised movements of the fly. Humanity's interconnected collisions and encounters might therefore not be solely concerned with trying to re-negotiate existing contracts in the world, that revolve around issues of appropriation and ownership, or even with intervening in pre-determined settings. In the Anthropocene, architecture needs to find ways of practising and thinking at planetary scales that can accommodate the exorbitant, that is, situations that are off-track and unexpected. It therefore needs to acknowledge an agency that is both weak and excessive. In this respect, 'worldliness' may not be about setting ever more stringent boundaries and limits (or worrying about crossing them), but instead about a more provisional, hospitable and generous engagement in the process of re-making – and not owning – the worlds that humanity lives in now.

Acknowledgements

The work on this chapter forms part of the project, *Provisional Cities*, funded by a British Academy Mid-Career Fellowship (2013–2014).

Notes

1   The term Anthropocene was first introduced in 2000 by the Dutch atmospheric chemist and Nobel Prize winner Paul J. Crutzen and by Eugene F. Stoermer in a publication of IGBP and later expanded on in an article by Crutzen in 2002 in the journal *Nature*. As yet there is no official start date for the Anthropocene-proposals include the beginning of industrialization around 1800 or the atomic bomb tests of 1945 which also signal the start of the 'great acceleration' (Steffen and Crutzen, 2003; Steffen *et al.*, 2011). The formalization of this term by the International Commission on Stratigraphy and the International Union of Geological Sciences would mark the official end of the Holocene. The current target date for this decision is 2016 (Zalasiewicz *et al.* 2011; Subcomission on Quaternary Stratigraphy 2012).
2   Bruno Latour, 'Facing Gaia: A new enquiry into natural religion', The Gifford Lectures, February 2013. The Anthropocene was the subject of Latour's fourth lecture: 'The Anthropocene and the destruction of the image of the globe'. http://www.ed.ac.uk/schools-departments/humanities-soc-sci/news-events/lectures/gifford-lectures/archive/series-2012-2013/bruno-latour/lecture-four
3   For NASA Earth Observatory on the study of urbanization and city lights see for example, http://earthobservatory.nasa.gov/Features/NightLights/
4   The concept of 'carrying capacity' used by ecologists to define the maximum number of representatives of a given species that a habitat can support without permanently corrupting the environment and endangering the life of the species. It is closely linked to the notion of sustainable development and the discourse around ecological limits.
5   Since 1992, and in spite of the formation of the UNFCCC (United Nations Framework Convention on Climate Change), COP (Conference of the Parties) negotiations have not managed to achieve legally binding global agreements on carbon emissions. At COP 13 in Warsaw, November 2013, during talks about 'loss' and 'damage' in the aftermath of Typhoon Haiyan, climate negotiations became 'increasingly fractious'(Vidal 2013).
6   Buckminster Fuller described plans for his 'Geoscope', a geodesic sphere used for observing dynamic world data in *Education, Automation*, (1962). The idea of 'digital Earth' was proposed by former US Vice President Al Gore, in a speech given at the California Science Centre, Los Angeles, California, 31 January 1998: 'The digital Earth: understanding our planet in the twenty-first century.' http://digitalearth.gov/VP199B0131.html
7   See for example, the NASA website, 'Images of change'. The website information reads: 'Each week our State of Flux gallery features images of different locations on planet Earth, showing change over time periods ranging from centuries to days. Some of these effects are related to climate change, some are not. Some document the effects of urbanization, or the ravage of natural hazards such as fires and floods. All show our planet in a state of flux.' http://climate.nasa.gov/state_of_flux
8   Syria experienced a period of drought with 75 per cent of farmers suffering total crop failure which resulted in massive displacement of rural populations to the urban areas. Syrian cities were already unstable and experiencing economic insecurity as a result of conflicts in the region. A combination of 'social, economic, environmental and climatic changes ... eroded the social contract between citizen and government in the country, strengthened the case for the opposition movement, and irreparably damaged the legitimacy of the Assad regime.' (Werrell and Femia 2013, 24)
9   See for example, the interactive map on BBC News website: 'Zaatari refugee camp: Rebuilding lives in the desert' 3 September 2013. http://www.bbc.co.uk/news/world-middle-east-23801200

Bibliography

Agamben, G. (2005) *State of Exception* [*Stato di Eccezione*], trans. Kevin Attell. London: University of Chicago Press.

Bauman, Z. (2012) 'Times of interregnum', *Ethics & Global Politics*, 5(1): 49–56.

Bauman, Z. (2013) Lecture 'Crisis of agency, or living through the times of interregnum' http://www.vanleer.org.il/en/event/crisis-agency-or-living-through-times-interregnum

Chakrabarty, D. (2009) 'The climate of history: four theses', *Critical Inquiry*, 35: 197–222.

Chulov, M. (2013) 'Zaatari camp: makeshift city in the desert that may be here to stay', *The Guardian*, 25 July. http://www.theguardian.com/world/2013/jul/25/zaatari-camp-makeshift-city-jordan

Clark, N. (2011) *Inhuman Nature: Sociable Life on a Dynamic Planet.* London: Sage.

Clark, N. (2012) 'Moving and shaking: mobility on a dynamic planet', in Tyszczuk, R., Smith, J., Clark, N. and Butcher, M. (eds), *Atlas: Geography, Architecture and Change in an Interdependent World* (pp. 22– 9). London: Black Dog Publishing.

Clark, N. (2013) '400ppm: Regime Change in geo-social formations', '400 ppm', discussion forum convened by Kathryn Yusoff, July 2013, *Environment and Planning D: Society and Space.* http://societyandspace.com/material/discussion-forum/400ppm/

Clark, N, Chhotray, V and Few, R. (2013) 'Global justice and disasters', *Geographical Journal*, 179(2): 105-113.

Connor, S. (2008) 'Wherever: the ecstasies of Michel Serres', lecture given at 'Digital Art and Culture in the Age of Pervasive Computing', Copenhagen, 14 November. http://www.stevenconnor.com/wherever/wherever.pdf

Connor, S. (2010) 'I believe that the world', in Nünning, V., Nünning, A. and Neuman, B. (eds) *Cultural Ways of Worldmaking: Media and Narratives* (pp. 29–46). Berlin and New York: De Gruyter.

Cosgrove, D. (2001) *Apollo's Eye: A Cartographic Genealogy of the Earth in the Western Imagination.* Baltimore, MD: Johns Hopkins University Press.

Crutzen, P.J. (2002) 'Geology of mankind', *Nature* 415, (3 January), 23.

Crutzen, P.J. and Stoermer, E.F (2000) 'The Anthropocene', *IGBP [International Geosphere-Biosphere Programme] Newsletter* 41: 17–18.

Davis, M. (2008) 'Living on the iceshelf: humanity's meltdown' 26 June. http://www.tomdispatch.com/post/174949

Davis, M. (2010) 'Who will build the Ark?' *New Left Review* 61, January–February unpaginated. http://newleftreview.org/II/61

Fuller, R. Buckminster (1962) *Education, Automation: Comprehensive Learning for Emergent Humanity.* Baden, Switzerland: Lars Muller Publishers.

Fuller, Buckminster (1965) 'The Case for a Domed City', St. Louis Post Dispatch, St. Louis, Missouri, September 26; pp. 39–41; see Eco Redux; http://www.ecoredux.com/archive_project03_01.html

Fuller, R. Buckminster (1968) *Operating Manual for Spaceship Earth.* Baden, Switzerland: Lars Muller Publishers.

Kossak, F., Petrescu, D., Schneider, T., Tyszczuk, R. and Walker, S. (eds) (2009) *Agency: Working with Uncertain Architectures.* London: Routledge.

Kurgan, L. (2013) *Close Up at a Distance: Mapping, Technology and Politics.* New York: Zone Books.

Latour, B. (2013a) *An Inquiry into Modes of Existence. An Anthropology of the Moderns*, trans. C. Porter. Cambridge, MA: Harvard University Press.

Latour, B. (2013b) 'Facing Gaia: six lectures on the political theology of nature', Gifford Lectures on Natural Religion, Edinburgh, 18–28 February. http://www.bruno-latour.fr/sites/default/files/downloads/GIFFORD-SIX-LECTURES_1.pdf

Latour, B. (2014) 'Agency at the time of the Anthropocene', *New Literary History,* 45: 1–18. http://www.bruno-latour.fr/sites/default/files/128-FELSKI-HOLBERG-NLH-FINAL.pdf

Meadows, D.H., Meadows, D.L., Randers, J. and Behrens III, W. W. (1972) *The Limits to Growth.* New York: Universe Books.

Nordhaus, T., Schellenberger, M. and Blomqvist, L. (2012) *The Planetary Boundaries Hypothesis: A Review of the Evidence.* Washington, DC: Breakthrough Institute.

O'Riordan, T. and Lenton, T. (eds) (2013) *Addressing Tipping Points for a Precarious Future*, The British Academy. Oxford: Oxford University Press.

Raworth, K. (2012) 'A Safe and Just Space for Humanity: Can We Live Within The Doughnut?', Oxfam Discussion Papers (Oxford: Oxfam) http://www.oxfam.org/en/grow/policy/safe-and-just-space-humanity

Rockström, J. et al. (2009a) 'Planetary boundaries: exploring the safe operating space for humanity', Ecology and Society 14(2): 32–64. www.ecologyandsociety.org/vol14/iss2/art32;

Rockström, J. et al. (2009b) 'A safe operating space for humanity', Nature 461: 472–5.

Rockström, J. et al. (2009c) 'Supplementary Information'. www.stockholmresilience.org/planetary-boundaries

Serres, M. (1994) Atlas. Paris: Julliard.

Serres, M. (1995) The Natural Contract. Ann Arbor, MI: University of Michigan Press.

Serres, M. (2003) L'Incandescent. Paris: Éditions le Pommier.

Serres, M. (2006) 'Revisiting the Natural Contract'. 1000 Days of Theory. www.ctheory.net/articles.aspx?id=515

Serres, M. (2011) Malfeasance: Appropriation Through Pollution?, trans. A-M. Feenberg-Dibon. Stanford, CA: Stanford University Press.

Serres, M. and Latour, B., (1995) Conversations on Science, Culture and Time. Ann Arbor, MI: University of Michigan Press.

Simms, A. (2013) 'Why did the 400ppm carbon milestone cause barely a ripple?', The Guardian, 30 May, http://www.theguardian.com/environment/blog/2013/may/30/carbon-milestone-newspapers.

Solnit, R. (2013) 'Bigger than that: (the difficulty of) looking at climate change', 6 October. http://www.tomdispatch.com/blog/175756/

Steffen, W. and Crutzen, P. (2003) 'How long have we been in the Anthropocene era?', Climatic Change 61(3): 251–7.

Steffen, W., Grinevald, J., Crutzen, P. and McNeil, J. (2011) 'The Anthropocene: conceptual and historical perspectives', Philosophical Transactions of the Royal Society A, 369: 842–67.

Stengers, I. (2009) Au temps des catastrophes: résister à la barbarie qui vient. Paris: Les Empêcheurs.

Subcomission on Quaternary Stratigraphy (2012) 'What is the Anthropocene ? – current definition and status'. http://quaternary.stratigraphy.org/workinggroups/anthropocene/

UN Habitat (2011) 'Global Report on Human Settlements 2011, Cities and Climate Change: Policy Directions', United Nations Human Settlements Programme. http://unhabitat.org/publications/cities-and-climate-change-global-report-on-human-settlements-2011/

Vidal, J. (2013) 'Poor countries walk out of UN climate talks as compensation row rumbles on', The Guardian, 20 November. http://www.theguardian.com/global-development/2013/nov/20/climate-talks-walk-out-compensation-un-warsaw

Werrell, C.E. and Femia, F. (2013) The Arab Spring and Climate Change, Climate and Security Correlations Series. Washington, DC: Stimson. http://climateandsecurity.files.wordpress.com/2012/04/climatechangearabspring-ccs-cap-stimson.pdf

Yusoff, K. (2009) 'Excess, catastrophe and climate change', Environment and Planning D: Society and Space, 27: 1010–29.

Zalasiewicz, J. (1998) 'Buried treasure', New Scientist 158(2140) 27 June.

Zalasiewicz, J. (2009) The Earth After Us: What Legacy will Humans Leave in the Rocks? Oxford: Oxford University Press.

Zalasiewicz, J. et al. (2011) 'Stratigraphy of the Anthropocene' Philosophical Transactions of the Royal Society A 369: 1036–55 .

Chapter 2

Space and its assembled subjects

The neurotic, the psychotic, and the pervert

Lorens Holm

Ikea and the neurotic, the psychotic, and the pervert

Ikea is in the details, those fiddly little connector pieces that come in a bag.[1] If a neurotic, a psychotic, and a pervert were to assemble their spaces the way we are increasingly exhorted by the self-help industry and the neoliberal ideology that drives it, to assemble our psyches (I can be whatever I want! I can assemble myself!), the neurotic would take longer to finish than the suggested times because s/he would read the instructions thrice to get it right, sort all the bits into piles, and would worry that it is not finished even though everyone else thinks it is. The pervert would finish in record time, maybe even beat it (clever bugger!), but s/he would do something naughty with the arrangement of panels, like find a way to leave 'Allen' in the panels or protruding a bit, or build the carcass inside out, something that would 'fetishize' it. The neurotic and the pervert know to focus on the fastening system with the 'male' Allen key and those double threaded screws that insert into the little holes. The psychotic would miss the point of flat pack and attempt to make space by trying to fold the panels. Because this did not work (try folding an Ikea birch veneer hollow core sandwich panel), s/he would begin the process of rearranging the panels; s/he would produce endless variations, each a scintillating glimpse of a possible world, none of which would keep the rain out. Think of Vitruvius – the law giver – and his temples: Doric, Corinthian, Ionic. Same elements – different geometries of arrangement. The psychotic just doesn't 'get it'.

Figure 2.1
The law of the subject
The law of the
subject is the law of
space. In this 'how
to do a perspective'
instructional picture,
Dürer shows the eye of
the artist fixed to a view
point, and his image of
the view of the model
projected from this
point onto the screen.
There is a ship in the
background. Deleuze &
Guattari would call this
perspective apparatus
an assemblage of
machines: drawing
machines attached
to seeing machines
attached to inscription
machines attached to
being seen machines.
(Albrecht Dürer,
'Draughtsman drawing a
reclining woman' in *The
Painters Manual*, 1525)

The law and the neurotic, the psychotic, and the pervert

What is at stake is the relation of each subject to the law. The pervert and the neurotic both know the law. The pervert derives pleasure from subverting, inverting, converting, reverting, unnerving it. The neurotic agonizes about whether s/he complies with it. The psychotic does not know what law is. The psychotic knows its out there, may even be able to fool people by imitating it but s/he has no working relation to it. S/he never stops arranging panels because 'getting it right' involves conforming to a law or a principle that fixes them, and it is precisely the order of the law – what Lacan called the symbolic order – that does not work for him/her. That's why the psychotic is the most difficult to explain. We all know worry, we all know naughty. What is difficult to contemplate is someone in no stable position in the symbolic world of sense and non-sense. For the psychotic, the blue of the sky does not signify the benign father shining in through a carefully constructed window, nor does it signify Giedion's cosmos that puts a scale to our temples and our knowledge, and guarantees their sense. For the psychotic, the blue of the sky is the simple and incontrovertible fact that the panels do not cohere to do what they are supposed to do: articulate his/her space from that which is other, outside, elsewhere.

The law of the subject and how the psychotic breaks it

The neurotic, psychotic, and pervert are the *dramatis personae* of the law, but what law? What is the law of the subject, what law binds the subject to space, and thereby guarantees the subject's integrity? In his *Dictionary of Lacanian Psychoanalysis*, Evans states that for Lacan, the neurotic, the psychotic, and the pervert denote psychical structures, not symptoms. They constitute the three possible relations of the subject to what Lacan calls *the field of the Other* (essentially the field of signifiers and their rules of engagement; the subject is a signifier). In psychoanalytic terms, there are laws for the assembly of Ikea furniture and Vitruvian temples; there are laws of assembly for subjects.[2] What we are going to argue is that the psychoanalytic subject is a spatial

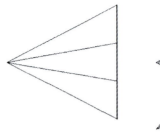
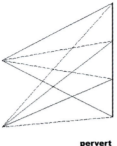

neurotic   pervert   psychotic

Figure 2.2
Subject positions
The three subject positions diagrammed as three relations of the subject to the environment mediated by a symbolic threshold or screen. The vertical line denotes the subject's image, what would appear on the picture plane.

assembly. Architecture is first and foremost about space-making, and in architectural discourse, the law of the subject is the geometry that binds the subject to space by positioning him in it. Arguably, psychoanalytic discourse presupposes the Cartesian subject who constructs the world from an inner point of consciousness and peers at it through a threshold of doubt. This subject was anticipated by Brunelleschi's demonstration of perspective: in the demonstration, Brunelleschi asked his subject to view the world through a peephole he had drilled through his picture of the world. Thereafter, the spatial canon of architecture was marked by the threshold; space is conceived as a projection through a screen from a single point by a viewing subject. Perspective and its screen seem therefore to describe the relation of a subject to space, and also to describe the spatial structure of the subject. They are already double. The neurotic, psychotic, and pervert are called subject positions in psychoanalytic discourse because they mark positions within the field of the Other; and whether or not the field of the Other is spatial (we are going to argue that it is), or that space is symbolic (again, yes), position is ineluctably spatial and symbolic. This paper will build upon the affinity between the subject, the field of the Other, and architectural space to develop spatial diagrams that define the positions of neurotic, pervert, and psychotic in relation to the space of architecture.[3]

If we strip the perspective diagram to its essentials, we obtain the three subject positions (Figure 2.2). In the leftmost diagram, which we take to be canonical (the normally neurotic position), a triangulating geometry fixes the subject in relation to a vertical line. At risk of being overly reductive, this is the law of space, in the simplest terms, at least in the western tradition. The diagram is a simplification of the perspective apparatus consisting of view point, cone of vision constituted by lines of sight, and picture plane. The vertical line indicates the subject's image of space, to which the triangulating geometry fixes him, but it could indicate the relation of the subject to his environment more generally, or rather to the codes – spatial or otherwise – that symbolize the environment to the subject. Any code imposes a symbolic matrix upon the world, which parcelizes the world and positions its subjects. Without this grid, day and night flow continuously into each other as a continuing and never-repeating miracle.[4] That the code should be indicated by a surface which forms a screen between subject and world says something about the surfaciality [sic] of signification which is beyond the scope of this chapter to do more than allude to. We have three possible relations to space. The subject suffers the tyranny of position that our spatial model imposes upon him, a tyranny exploited by devices like the Panopticon, this suffering producing the symptoms we would expect when wandersome desire is repressed in the name of compliance with the law; or the subject plays with position and enjoys breaking the rules about position; or the subject is, if not exactly alienated from position, unable to find it, identify it uniquely, and find himself at it; which may be dizzying, terrifying, or exhilarating and the ground for invention.

Deleuze and Guattari are at pains to point out, this model is not the law of the subject, it is simply the law of the neurotic subject. If these diagrams have a way of capturing the psychotic position as well, they are capturing it from a neurotic's point of view. Every discourse is written for a subject – Deleuze and Guattari (1994: 61ff) call them *conceptual personae*, not subject positions – and they argue that the psychoanalytic canon was written for the neurotic.[5] Deleuze and Guattari (1977: 2) would rather leave the neurotic on the couch worrying about the meaning of his actions, and take the schizophrenic for a walk in the material world where storms and sunlight slice through him. The figure of the neurotic comprises a punctal inside (think of all that navel-gazing) in relation to a projective outside, he is the architectural figure of the façade concealing/revealing an interior. The schizophrenic is all outside, all surface, all material.[6]

If the threshold is the spatial figure of psychoanalysis and architecture and their neurotic subject, the figure that Deleuze and Guattari invoke for their material philosophy is the fold. The fold is the form of the material world not carved up by threadbare philosophies, concepts, categories, hierarchies, theories. Deleuze and Guattari link folding with the schizophrenic because the schizophrenic runs riot with these symbolic distinctions. The parametric movement, whose aim is to construct through their architecture a world of continuous variation without thresholds, has chosen Deleuze and Guattari as their guiding light. No symbolic distinctions, only material continuities. No facading; only folding. Following our argument about position, we can see in fold-space an attempt to develop an architecture that eschews position, or at least eschews formal categories and box spaces in favour of the continuous surface where difference is not marked by the threshold but by an even gradient of qualities.[7]

Although Deleuze and Guattari (1977) are indebted to psychoanalytic discourse, they reject it – in particular the Oedipal drama – as a vestige of nineteenth-century bourgeois prejudices about the family that celebrates the neurotic. They hail the schizophrenic as the action hero of a twentieth century dominated by technology and capitalism because his incessant construction speaks to the potential of creativity, to the shifting flows that characterize capital, labour and desire, and finally, to the psychotic's capacity – like capital and technology – to gatecrash (i.e. reterritorialize) symbolic barricades. Creative destruction replaces creation. Everything solid melts into air. Capitalism has replaced meaning with value. Don't ask what something means, ask how much it costs. They describe the schizophrenic as a desiring machine. About a machine you ask not what it means but how it functions, what it does.[8]

Psychoanalytic detour

Freud attributes psychosis to a failure, during the Oedipal stage, for the child to internalize the authority of the father and make it his own. In the text of Lacan, this authority is signified by what he calls the *name-of-the-father*, the signifier of the father. In a semiotic event that has the structure of metaphor (the replacement of one signifier by another, Lacan calls it the paternal metaphor), this signifier of authority replaces the real love of the mother in the unconscious of the subject (2006: 465). The symbolically empowered subject practises in the name of the father, in the way a sheriff practises in the name of the law.

In their dictionary of psychoanalysis, Laplanche and Pontalis (1973: 370) describe psychosis as a 'primary disturbance in the libidinal relation to reality', and the psychotic's delusion as an 'attempt to restore the link to objects'.[9] Lacan (2006: 445–88) explains this break with the reality of objects as an effect of *foreclosure*, the foreclosure of the name-of-the-father. (Foreclosure is one of several terms in psychoanalytic discourse poached from property law, which reflects the contractual and territorial nature of subjectivity).[10] *Forclusion* (English, foreclosure) is Lacan's translation of Freud's *verwerfung* (repudiation in the *Standard Edition*), 'the mechanism … by means of which the ego detaches itself from the external world' (1993: 153) . The foreclosure or lack of this signifier leaves a hole in the symbolic order for the subject. 'Psychosis consists of a hole, a lack, at the level of the signifier' (1993: 201). The psychotic subject suffers a semiotic failure: he is unable to summon this signifier of the father, the authority of which guarantees the subject's power and efficacy in the symbolic world, because it never replaced the real love of the mother. Where the symbolic order should function like a screen that opens onto a significant and signifying world, there is instead a hole.[11]

The symbolic order, which links subjects to space, the subject to itself, is broken for the psychotic. The psychotic never assimilates or internalizes the law to make it his own, the way the rest of us do. This failure of introjection leads to an excess of projection. Like the neurotic subject (i.e. like most of us), the psychotic subject probably has an image of the world, it's just that his image is no different to him than all the images of other subjects out there. The image has no proper or stable relation to him. It is the psychotic's inner world that does not make sense to him. It is not joined up into a coherent narrative thread of thought and action. Without Ariadne's thread to lead him through a labyrinthine inside to a blazing blue outside, which makes it understandable, makes it bearable, paradoxically, the world seems real to him. Lacan (1993:13) has a way to understand this: '…whatever is refused in the symbolic order, in the sense of *Verwerfung*, reappears in the real'. The psychotic subject never stops trying to assemble an outer world because his inner world is disintegrating. '… a hole that it opens up in the signified, sets off a cascade of reworkings of the signifier …' (2006: 481).[12] The psychotic attempts to compensate in the real what should be happening in the symbolic. But he never stops reworking, rearranging, reassembling; the project is not completable because he is building, not in the wrong place, but in the wrong register. It is his symbolic or inner world, not his real or outer world, that needs building.[13]

The diagram (Figure 2.3) that Lacan publishes of the visual field in the *Four Fundamental Concepts of Psychoanalysis* is a map of the subject (1981: 106). It shows

Figure 2.3

Figure 2.3
Lacan's diagram of the subject in the visual field
The spatial subject has a correspondence to Dürer's perspective apparatus. The so-called illusion of space consists in the fact that the subject's image – what the subject imagines itself to be – never corresponds to the image that others have of it. Dürer's draughtsman sees himself to be the one whose masterly drawing of a model confirms him as an artiste; we and his model see him as the one who is pretending not to look up a woman's skirts.

at the apex of the second triangle. The two triangles are here superimposed, as in fact they are in the functioning of the scopic register.

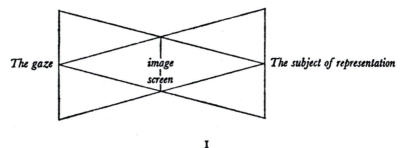

I

I must, to begin with, insist on the following: in the scopic field, the gaze is outside, I am looked at, that is to say, I am a picture.

how the subject is constituted of a viewing position, image/screen, and object, bound by an internal geometry. The gaze or *objet a* – more a position than an object – shows the position an object has to be in, relative to the subject and its images, in order for that object to be an object of desire. Desire is about position. Projected on the screen is the subject's fantasy of the object: not simply the image of the object, but the image of the subject fulfilled by the object. Of course, it does not correspond to the image that others have of the subject (in Dürer's instructional picture, the image of the artist from the point of view of the model). The fantasy of the subject is that s/he is made whole or complete or beautiful again by attaining the object; but what others see and respond to is simply the same wreck that s/he always was. In so far as these images are communicated to the subject (body language, speech, photographs, whatever), they are also represented upon the screen for the subject. The subject's internal geometry manages this shifting dislocation of images – the advertising industry has made an art of closing the gap – and links this montage to the subject. Although Lacan does not describe it thus, the diagram shows the structure of the field of the Other in a spatial register where signifiers are flows of images: the relation of self and other are played out on the screen as a jostling of images. The perspective demonstration of Brunelleschi attempted to close the gap between the subject's and the Other's image, a gap that every architecture – when it builds a space – attempts to close as well. This closure is itself a fantasy: the fantasy of an objective world.

We can understand the spatial effect of psychosis, by putting it in relation to Lacan's diagram. To my knowledge, Lacan never brings his work on psychosis and his visual field diagram together, but we have to because we are architects and we deal in form, space and geometry, not speech. How does space become disorganized for the psychotic? Spatial mastery is about maintaining one's position in the internal triangulating geometry of the visual field, fixed before one's images. The neurotic will be tormented by the internal geometry that never quite succeeds in bringing the self image in conformity with the images of others. The pervert will play with alignment and misalignment (we can imagine that little *objet a* thing wobbling around). They both inhabit the difference – the images never align – but the one enjoys it where the other doesn't. If this internal geometry, which binds subject to screen, becomes unstable and begins to unravel, we would expect the subject to lose the capacity to distinguish self-image from the images of others. The psychotic subject would continue to have images – he would not become deaf, dumb and blind – but he would have no more affective relation to his own images than to anyone else's. Images would not come to the subject tagged inside (mine) or outside (from others). The screen and its images would become indistinguishable from the artefacts of others, like photographs or paintings. What is lost in the symbolic register, returns in the real. The letter becomes litter.[14] Architecture recreates this internal geometry in the material world; and we would expect the psychotic builder – of architecture or Ikea – to build compulsively.

The space of the psychotic neurotic and the pervert

How is space a constituent of the symbolic order? The perspective image is not a simulacra of space (we don't see in perspective), but a model of spatial experience.[15] It is the model by which we signify or encode spatial experience. It is important to get clear the symbolic status of perspective and to distinguish it from real space, whatever that may be. If real space, the space of natural law, has certain properties, like a capacity for position and transparency to light, perspective gives these properties significance for the subject by codifying them as spatial relationships. It emphasizes position, geometry, and transparency over other aspects of our relation to space. It positions the subject in space as a viewer before an image of a view. The subject is shown as a point of reception of images. Of all the ways that we could be in space, we are in it the perspectival way. The lesson of Lacan's diagram for the visual field is that the modern subject emerges from the Oedipal drama by internalizing the perspective model of space, enabling him to use spatial metaphors: having a point of view, taking a position, seeing the light, getting inside something, being out on a limb, crossing thresholds and bridges when we get to them; all of which allow the fully constituted subject to navigate the spatial world, position himself within it, and make sense of it. Chief among these metaphors is the Cartesian metaphor of the subject as a hidden point of thought and doubt from which the world extends.[16]

We can speculate about what would happen if the subject fails to internalize the perspective model for space, and the consequent lack of what we might call spatial authority. If the chief consequence is the incapacity of the psychotic subject to position himself, we would expect this to emerge as an inability to master spatial metaphors, an inability to have stable relations to his objects of desire, and by a diminished sense of identity, to the extent that identity and difference depend upon position (*I am here and you are there*). The psychotic may be taught to use spatial metaphors (Lacan thought that the only treatment for the psychotic subject was to bolster its imaginary register as a compensation for a broken symbolic one), but we would expect it to be an imitation of spatial mastery without a strong attachment to these metaphors as working tools

Figure 2.4
The position of the psychotic
For the schizophrenic subject, there is no 'I' as I knows it, because there is no single point of signification about which I finds itself. The psychotic subject has a self-image, and it is 'out there', but for the psychotic, it is no different from anyone else's image out there. The aspiration of an architecture constituted by folds is to create surfaces which have qualities, but on which there are no thresholds, like the continuous surfaces of geology . We would expect that in a thorough-going folded architecture, there would be *de facto* subject positions, but as is the case with geological space, they would have no particular significance.

the dispersed I

an image that I cannot call my own

the psychotic I does not come to a point or is not located

corresponding to the lived experience of a spatial life. S/he will always be alienated from space in the way that the neurotic who suffers it, and the pervert who plays with it, is not. In his paper, 'Mimicry and legendary psychasthenia' (1935), Roger Caillois (1984: 30) describes the spatial condition of the psychotic. They can see the space they are in but cannot locate themselves in it. Space is dark and invasive. Space seems to slice through them. In this testimony, we observe space failing to do the three things that we expect of it: to position us, to delineate the contour of the body, and to articulate the threshold of the psyche, that divides inside from outside – upon all of which the integrity of the spatial subject and its body depends.[17]

The diagram for the psychotic subject (Figure 2.4) shows the lines of sight/light, but they now no longer function to fix him/her to a position by converging at a single point. We can speculate about this peculiar condition of parallel or stratified vision. We could speculate about how a world of parallel vision might be a world constituted of a seamless and isomorphic surface across which the subject glides unhindered in any direction. Imagine the work of those nomads, Superstudio. In more familiar architectural territory, it has its counterpart in certain forms of architectural representation, in particular, elevation and axonometric drawings. We regard these images as somehow more objective, because they are not restricted to a point of view; or perhaps more real, because they contain all points of view. There is a sense in which the psychotic is the only subject positioned in the world, and not distanced from it by the symbolic clutter that represses the neurotic or is eroticized by the pervert.

We can map the three subject positions onto the post-structuralist avant-garde practices that emerged in the late 1960s, which sought – in buildings and texts – to redefine the humanist subject. By subject we mean both the architect and the inhabitant: anyone who can be said to have an architectural practice, either by designing or inhabiting buildings. Rem Koolhaas argued that Le Corbusier was psychotic; Bernard Tschumi that all architects are perverts or at least should be; Peter Eisenman that the human subject has no claim on position in architecture. We can assume that they are not commenting on the temperaments of their colleagues but on how they position their practices within the field of architecture.

In his *Ropes and Rules* 'postcard', Tschumi (1994a: 100ff) invokes the figure of the pervert in order to explain the predicament of architecture. No other creative

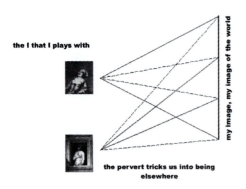

the I that I plays with

the pervert tricks us into being elsewhere

my image, my image of the world

Figure 2.5
The position of the pervert
'The rendezvous of Bellevue is on the tip of the rock'. Lequeu's image pops up everywhere, always out of place. The pervert plays with the rules of space, according to which the I is supposed to be a single point of signification and projection. Lequeu plays with the spatial codes of position the way the pervert plays with the social codes of dress.

practice is as rule-bound as architecture: its history of treatises that lay down the law; its professional memberships, qualifying courses and examination; statutory controls, building regulations, Highways Act, Health and Safety at Work Act, Disabilities Act, Town & Country Planning Acts; fully constituted professional and statutory oversight bodies. The rules 'have the erotic significance of bondage'. In 'Architecture and Transgression', Tschumi (1994b: 65–78) raises the question of enjoyment. The pervert eroticizes the rules, in order to enjoy his/her predicament. Jean-Jacques Lequeu is an obvious nominee for the pervert position, not merely because of his association with de Sade, not merely because the French Enlightenment was the episteme in which the restricted reason of Descartes, bound by doubt, is erected as law (reason in a dialectic relation with containment); but because he is always deliciously out of place in his own work. He keeps popping himself up as a leering whore festooned with phalluses, all over his own architecture, an architecture which wrecks all the rules of language, proportion, and assembly of parts (cf. 'Rendezvous de Bellevue'; Figure 2.5).

If the pervert eroticizes the rules in order to play with them, the neurotic represses his desire in order to obey them. Eisenman's practice is probably in the neurotic position. Although his work challenges the canon of architecture, he has done it by constructing another rule book, the rule book of deconstruction. The scalings and recursive operations that define projects like *Moving Arrows, Eros, and Other Errors*

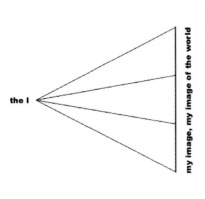

the I

my image, my image of the world

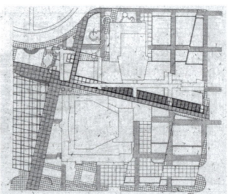

the neurotic I comes to a point of signification in a symbolic inside

Figure 2.6
The position of the neurotic
The neurotic subject finds itself at a point in space. I come to a point which I signify within a symbolic matrix called space. The neurotic is constituted of a single point of signification from which an ego is projected like an image.

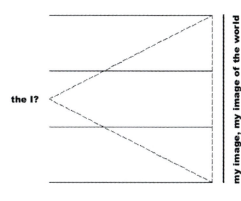

the neurotic or obsessive I: either
too much or too little code

Figure 2.7
**The position of the
paranoid. Le Corbusier
in the interior of Villa
Church at Ville d'Avray**
We don't know if
this is a neurotic Le
Corbusier trying to
get into position by
recreating Brunelleschi's
demonstration of
perspective; or a paranoid
Le Corbusier who
overcompensates for his
loose grip on signifiers of
self and space, by over-
coding for position and
thresholds. In *Delirious
New York*, Rem Koolhaas
argued he was the latter.

(Romeo and Juliet, Verona 1985) and *Cannaregio Town Square* (Venice 1978), and
the shifting frames and grids of the *IBA Social Housing* (Berlin 1985) and the *Wexner
Centre* (Columbus Ohio 1989), in their different ways interrogate the assumptions that
architecture makes about the position and centrality of its subject (its anthropocentrism,
its commitment to presence). Eisenman's project is to reconstruct deconstruction for
architecture, what we might call an obedience to the text of *père* Derrida. Eisenman
and the critics who wrote about Eisenman, guarantee the authority of his work, by
putting it in relation to the authority of another.

For Koolhaas, psychosis raises the question of how the subject relates to
reality by producing more of it. Where Tschumi focuses on enjoyment and Eisenman on
authority, Koolhaas focuses on production: arguably, producing more reality is what any
creative act does. The psychotic is a form of symbol-producing machine in overdrive,
and new reality is produced by concretizing its symbolic produce. In *Delirious New
York*, Koolhaas attributes Dali's Paranoid Critical Method (PCM) to Le Corbusier, for
reasons which seem themselves to be symptoms of PCM. PCM is a form of psychosis
in practice in which 'limp unprovable conjectures… [are] supported by the "crutches"
of Cartesian rationality' (Koolhaas 1994: 236). Preposterous propositions are ossified
as reality by an ultra-rational logic that seeks confirmation everywhere. His reason for
attributing to Le Corbusier what is Dali's, is the fact that both modernist and surrealist
went to Manhattan and hated it because it was more modern/surrealist than they
were (Koolhaas 1994: 235). Le Corbusier is fond of reinforced concrete because it is
a material metaphor for PCM.[18] It is formed in 'irrational' shapes, it is supported by
a rational grid of steel, and it concretizes to become an 'irrefutable' fact in the world
(Koolhaas 1994: 249). For Koolhaas – like Lacan – psychosis is a structural dysfunction
in the subject's relation to reality. In Koolhaas' terms (1994: 241), when there is too
much symbolism (i.e. symbolism is overused and worn out), and hence there is not
enough reality, or rather not enough access to it, the paranoid critical method is a way
of generating more of it.

The law of architecture and its transgression

I would like to return to the spatial subject. If the first love of architecture is space, and its first commitment, staking its claim on space, then we would expect its most serious transgressions would take the form of trespass. Architecture – like the neurotic – has an investment in territory, and this is inscribed in its language of curtilages, properties, covenants, estates real or otherwise, party walls and fences, rights of access, rights to light, views, sun angles. The trespasser is in a place s/he should not be. A neurotic architecture is about erecting the boundaries that separate one space from another and organizing the relations between them. That the distinction, inside/outside is both fundamental and symbolic, should be clear from Alberti's dictum that the first act of architecture is to inscribe the plan on the surface of the Earth and thereby delineate inside from outside. Cain killed Abel because he violated this line by crossing it at a point where he should not have. We should expect to find the most potent transgressions at the threshold, the detail where inside/outside press up against each other without touching (erogenous zones). The all-time perversion is Michaelangelo's Porta Pia, which welcomes you *out* of Rome. We expect most transgressions to pass almost unnoticed, in the detail where wall frames window or door. Or in the other liminal gestures that map onto inside/outside, like private/public.

It is too quick to associate subject positions with transgression: for instance, the neurotic never transgresses, the pervert does it occasionally, and the psychotic always. If we follow Tschumi's thought, architecture is essentially transgressive. There are neurotic, psychotic and perverse ways to transgress. The neurotic will trespass when s/he has to, in order to get to the other side. The pervert will trespass to derive pleasure from it. And we can always ask: transgression by who, or for whom? For others, the psychotic subject may appear to be the ultimate transgressor: talking nonsense with an insistence that others find threatening; all those images of outsider art, buildings so festooned with ornament that the canonical hierarchies of architecture – notably the hierarchy between structure and ornament – seem to no longer exist. But for the psychotic, the psychotic is not the transgressor. For the psychotic, there is no law, or at least no clear path to attaining it, and hence no possibility of transgression. It is not possible for the psychotic to be here where he should not be, rather than there, because he is always, no *where*.

Archanalysis

I am neurotic. Can I get it right? Can I position myself as master of my own discourse? Let's try … The three diagrams in Figure 2.2 are the most important part of this paper, a contribution to our knowledge of architecture and how it structures subjectivity. There were three steps:

1   I reduced the perspective diagram to its essentials: a point and a line. In the spatial canon of architecture as it is codified by perspective, this

corresponds to a point of projection and a screen, the point of view of a subject, and its view through a window.

2   I argued that this stripped down diagram could be used to define the relation of the subject to the law. *Law* is meant in its most general sense, to denote not simply the legal code but any and all codes by which we symbolize our world to ourselves or to others, what Lacan refers to as *the field of the Other*. This field is represented as a line; the subject as a point in relation to it. It functions as a screen because it gives the subject access to the world as a significant world. At this point, the diagram says little more than the fact that there is a code by which we represent the world and each of us has a relation to it. The line extends to infinity, and one thing each subject does is mark out a portion of the symbolic world that is within its purview.[19]

3   By modifying the diagram, we are able to codify three positions. Only once we have more than one diagram, is it possible to articulate differences. The first diagram defines the neurotic relation to the field of the Other. It is normative only in the sense that it is closest to architectural conventions for space. The other two diagrams define psychotic and pervert relations, which are departures from this convention: in place, out of place, no place. Note that the line does not disappear for the psychotic; the field of the Other is there for others – this is the neurotic's view of the psychotic's predicament. The psychotic simply ceases to fix him/herself to it.

It should be clear from our brief foray into architecture that the diagrams in Figure 2.2 and its elaboration in Figures 2.4–2.7 must be developed if they are to fulfil their potential to revivify post-structuralist discourse:

1   The diagrams indicate the potential for architectural thought to inform psychoanalytic thinking.

2   The diagrams indicate how a building positions its subject in space; and how architecture positions a particular practice or a particular building within its field.

The diagrams need to be refined beyond their degree zero state, in terms of their form and interpretative power. No attempt has been made to apply them to specific buildings or space conceptions; no attempt has been made to elaborate them to account for subdivisions within the three clinic structures.[20]

Historical postscript

We are ineluctably spatial, and every attempt to make architecture is an attempt to remake ourselves. Our three subjects are building themselves even when they build their Ikea boxes. To refashion ourselves is a humanist ideal and a sci-fi nightmare; and in order not to reduce it to the glib choices of DIY culture and Ikea fantasies, we have to theorize ourselves and theorize our space in ways that allows us to build ourselves.[21]

I used a diagram derived from a discourse (i.e. perspective) that puts subjects in space to develop the relation of a subject to any discourse, including space itself. Along the way, it is used to develop the internal structure of the subject. We are our most important artefacts. Psychoanalytic thought is simply one of the more radical humanist discourses for reflecting on our artefacts. What is radical, perhaps transgressive, about this coupling of psychoanalytic to architectural thinking is that it has a category-wrecking logic that allows it to think the subject *in* space, and *as* space, and in varying relations *to* space; and thereby resolutely to conflate the distinction between inner and outer worlds, resolutely to put an entity as immaterial and as nowhere as the psyche in relation to a practice as material and as here as architecture. Psychoanalytic discourse has the power to rethink our relation to the space that architecture makes, a relation that seems almost impossible to articulate nowadays, except in the techno-monetary terms of development. In the psychoanalytic thought of Lacan, the neurotic, the psychotic, and the pervert map out the different possible relations of the linguistic subject to the symbolic field of culture and society, to the law, to others. Architecture addresses this *field of the Other*, in so far as that space is symbolic, and its subject is the spatial subject, the localized or de-localized *I*. Architecture is the symbolic field *par excellence*, where social, political and cultural practices can be assessed, decoded, anticipated.

When we attend to the architectural fact that space positions the subject in its field, we see that as inescapable, as quotidian, and as ubiquitous as it may be, this fact has effects upon the subject. Position, point of view, screen, these components may be shadowed by optics, but they are components of the assembled subject, without which the subject as we know it would not be possible. Perspective is a way of assembling ourselves; and if it unravels we unravel with it. The 'I am here' is a question of our capacity to signify locality and not simply the default mode of natural law, although our symbols stand before the harsh light of natural law. We don't exactly choose – 'hmmm should I be here at this point where I find myself, or should I be distributed today' – but we construct these relations, or they us, nevertheless. To the extent that this geometry defines the subject, the psychotic resists subjectification. The psychotic inhabits a world unencumbered by positions, or at least a world where they do not seem to work. Hence Deleuze and Guattari predicated this world of real material continuity upon the figure of the schizo, hence their attention to its material and machinic subjectivity. And although our language of the *assembled* self seeks an affinity with their discourse, we can still ask of them to articulate the position from which they speak.

If the psychotic glimpses a real world beyond the spatial assembly that screens it, it is not perhaps the first time it has been named in architectural discourse. The outside that architecture posits of the subject, is here posited by architects and historians of the spatial world itself. In *The Eternal Present*, Giedion (1964: 520ff) touched on this outside when he developed the three space conceptions that organize his history. The Archaic, Classic, and Modern conceptions turn out not to be different types of space, but different ways of conceiving man's relation to the cosmos. In Giedion's text, architecture's material threshold between one space and another shadows another threshold – a screen – between the spatial subject and the immensity of its unknown outside. Space screens the subject from the world. Likewise, Aldo Rossi (1976: 31) touched on this function of architecture to symbolize the spatial subject's relation to what is outside space in his paper 'The blue of the sky'. In the Modena Cemetery, the monument to the dead took the form of a roofless floorless building with frameless windows. It is not a ruin (it is not picturesque). It is unfinished. It lets the sky in. It glimpses the material, not the symbolic, demise of architecture before the immensity of the sky. Whenever we conceive of architecture as an act of building ourselves, we do it before the immensity of this outside. We are all, always, rebuilding our space and ourselves as space, under the blue of the sky.[22]

Notes

1   Ikea, like God, is in the details. I Mac, I Pod, I Phone, I Kea.
2   See the entry for 'Structure' in Dylan Evans, *An Introductory Dictionary of Lacanian Psychoanalysis* p, 194. The neurotic, the psychotic and the pervert denote the principal nosographic categories in psychoanalysis. Everyone is either neurotic, psychotic, or a pervert. What Freud called normal is a form of neurotic. The role of psychoanalysis is not to change us from one to the other – it cannot do that – but to enable us to live fruitful lives whichever we are. Hence, Slavoj Žižek could write a book called *Enjoy your Symptom: Jacques Lacan in Hollywood and Out.*
3   Louis Sullivan said the law of architecture was *form follows function* in his essay 'The tall office building artistically considered' (1896). '...form ever follows function, and this is the law'.
4   Lacan, *The Psychoses*, pp. 148–9. '...symbolic nihilations – the human being detaches itself from the day.' And 'very early on, day and night are signifying codes, not experiences.'
5   Gilles Deleuze and Felix Guattari, *What is Philosophy?* pp. 61–83 (translation of *Qu'est-ce que la philosophie?* (Paris 1991) by Graham Burchell and Hugh Tomlinson). Every philosophy has *conceptual personae* that precede it and make it possible. They are both author and muse of the philosophy. 'The conceptual persona is the becoming or the subject of a philosophy, on a par with the philosopher,...' (p. 64) They exist 'on the plane of immanence of philosophy....' (p. 66) 'Conceptual personae ... are irreducible to psychosocial types ... the stranger, the exile, the migrant, ... the homecomer.' (p. 67) The plane of immanence is the surface of nonsense from which a philosophy emerges like Venus emerging from the sea.
6   This figure of the schizophrenic on a stroll is from the beginning of Deleuze and Guattari, *Anti-Oedipus: Capitalism and Schizophrenia* p. 2 'A schizophrenic out for a walk is a better model than a neurotic on the couch'. *Surfaciality* is a variant of Deleuze and Guattari's *faciality.*
7   For an account of parametric architecture by one of its leading spokesmen, see Greg Lynn, ed., *Folding in Architecture*, in particular Lynn's Introduction and his paper 'Architectural curvilinearity: the folded, the pliant and the supple', in which he outlines its features, theories, and histories. Included are projects by Gehry, Hadid, UN Studio, Monica Ponce de Leon and Nader Tehrani of Office dA, Eisenman, Coop Himmelb(l)au. See also Sophia Vyzoviti, *Folding Architecture: Spatial, Structural, and Organizational Diagrams*, which is a studio manual that begins with paper-folding as a thinking-through-making exercise. Lynn and Vyzoviti reference Gilles Deleuzes, *The Fold: Leibniz and the Baroque*. Deleuze and Guattari, and Lynn seem to forget that Lacan's first professional interest was psychosis, and that he used topological figures like the Mobius strip to think his way out of Freud's container metaphors and oppositional dichotomies like inside/outside. In mathematics, the picture plane extends to infinity and back in the form of a Mobius strip.
8   The phrase *creative destruction* is coined by Joseph Schumpeter in his analysis of Marx in *Capitalism Socialism and Democracy*. It refers to the way capitalism, according to Marx, reconfigures the processes of production from within and devalues existing wealth. The phrase everything solid melts into air is borrowed from Marshall Berman, *All That is Solid Melts into Air* which is taken from the *Communist Manifesto* by Marx and Engels. In Berman's text it refers to modernism and its self-destructive nature.
9   The 'psychosis' entry in Laplanche and Pontalis, *The Language of Psycho-Analysis* pp. 369–72. The relation to real objects is qualified as *libidinal*, which, here, should be understood as any relation that is driven, interested, motivated, in a word significant to the subject. Lacan distinguishes the reality of objects which is essentially symbolic and non-essential, from the real, which is essential and has the quality of what philosophers call brute fact. The sky is blue because it is blue. Reality is within the compass of perception and conception; the real is what escapes these boundaries. The real wreaks havoc with categories, logics, comprehension.

10   Jacques Lacan, 'On a question prior to any possible treatment of psychosis' in *Ecrits: The First Complete Edition in English* pp. 445–88. Other land law terms include Freud's *besetzung*, translated by Strachey as *cathexis*, which means *interest, investment, occupation* (by troops), *charge* (of electricity).

11   See for instance Lacan, 'On a question prior to any possible treatment of psychosis' pp.465–66 'I will thus take *Verwerfung* to be "foreclosure" of the signifier. At the point at which the Name-of-the-Father is summoned … a pure and simple hole may thus answer in the Other'; p. 470, 'It is around this hole, where the subject lacks the support of the signifying chain, and which need not be ineffable to induce panic, that the whole struggle in which the subject reconstructed himself took place' ; p. 481, 'It is the lack of the Name-of-the-Father in that place which, by the hole that it opens up in the signified, sets off a cascade of reworkings of the signifier from which the growing disaster of the imaginary proceeds, until the level is reached at which signifier and signified stabilize in a delusional metaphor.'

12   Al Alvarez draws on the concept of psychosis in his introduction to *The New Modern Poetry* when talks about a poetry that displays an outer technical mastery that masks an inner disintegration of self. Freud called it a 'patch on reality'. For Freud's patch see 'Neurosis and Psychosis' p. 151, in *The Standard Edition of the Complete Psychological Works of Sigmund Freud Book XIX (1923–25) The Ego and the Id and Other Works*.

13   Lacan, *The Psychoses* p. 13. The real, for Lacan, is the material world stripped of its significance. It is hard to imagine what that would be, even what it would feel, look, or taste like. See my 'Psychosis and the ineffable space of modernism' for an elaboration of the term name-of-the-father and the idea of compensating in the real for foreclosure in the symbolic.

14   Russell Grigg, 'Language as Sinthome in Ordinary Psychosis' p. 58 'The word becomes a thing; the letter transmutes into a litter, we might say.'

15   Vision is binocular, discontinuous, fluttersome, partial, localized, spherical; not monocular, continuous, infinite, planar. Panofsky called perspective a symbolic form. Giedion called space a conception, a principle of constancy. See Panofsky, *Perspective as Symbolic Form,* and Giedion, *The Eternal Present* and *Space Time and Architecture*

16   In my book, *Brunelleschi, Lacan, Le Corbusier: Architecture Space and the Construction of Subjectivity* I argue that Brunelleschi's demonstration has the structure of an Oedipal drama. This subject who has internalized perspective as a symbolic structure has been subsequently theorized in Western philosophy; Descartes plan of the dual subject (mind/body, inside/outside, conscious/unconscious) has become one of the key templates for western discourses of the human subject. It is in the *Discourse on Method* (1637) that Descartes posits his model of the doubting subject from which a world is constructed. This thought experiment is visualized in his *Dioptrics* (included in the *Discourse*).

17   Roger Caillois, 'Mimicry and legendary psychasthenia' p.30 *'I know where I am but I do not feel as though I am at the spot where I find myself*. 'To these disposed souls, space seems to be a devouring force … not similar to something, but just similar'. *'Dark space envelops me on all sides and penetrates me much deeper than light space.'* 'Life takes a step backward.'

18   Cf. Rem Koolhaas, 'Europeans: Biuer! Dali and Le Corbusier Conquer New York', pp. 235ff. To the extent that Koolhaas identified with Le Corbusier, he is talking about his own practice. For instance, in some projects, Koolhaas disconnects the rules for architectural form-making from the rules for architectural representation. In the Bibliothèque de France competition Koolhaas uses an ultra-rational approach to plans and sections, according to which the block is cut at every metre horizontally and vertically like a giant block of meat asleep upon a microtome; the disregard of plan and section conventions, leads to a new way of thinking about the block, its oneiric organs, its stacks. That Koolhaas identified with Le Corbusier should be clear from the number of Corbu-like photographs of Koolhaas in the internet.

19   This symbolic field is the precondition of structuralist–post-structuralist discourse. Its foundational status is not recognized in phenomenology, which is the other discourse most frequently drawn upon by architects and theorists of architecture. Psychoanalysis and phenomenology begin from the experience of the individual subject, but phenomenology treats experience as originary, and psychoanalysis recognizes the degree to which experience is always already bound to the subject in a symbolic inter-subjective world. To the pre-Socratic wonderment with which phenomenology approaches the world of scintillating qualities, psychoanalysis brings the grid of reason, its syntax, its conceptual apparatus, its clinical categories.

20   These basic psychoanalytic nosographic categories have subdivisions, which are subject to debate within different schools of psychoanalytic theory and practice. Within the neuroses Lacan distinguishes obsessional neurosis and hysteria, within psychosis: paranoia, schizophrenia, and manic-depressive psychosis.

21   If Lewis Mumford's oeuvre could be reduced to a single message it would be that man makes himself when he builds his technological outer world. Man is natural and his nature is technology. See for instance Chapter 10 'The megamachine' in *The Myth of the Machine: the Pentagon of Power*.

22   See Sigfried Giedion, *The Eternal Present: The Beginnings of Architecture: A Contribution on Constancy and Change* pp. 493–526, esp. pp. 520ff. See also Aldo Rossi 'The blue of the sky' 'The

blue of the sky' is the title of the descriptive text to Aldo Rossi's winning competition entry for the Modena Cemetery in 1971. The text never refers to the blue of the sky. I assume the title refers to the Sanctuary, the cubic building that has no floors window frames or roof. '[T]his is the house of the dead and, in terms of architecture, it is unfinished and abandoned and therefore analogous to death.' (p. 31). Georges Bataille's erotic novella *Le Bleu du Ciel,* published in English as *The Blue of Noon*, was a critique of leftist ideology in the face of the rise of fascism. Rossi's sanctuary fails to keep the sky out. The psychotic's Ikea project also fails to keep the sky out. The blue of the sky describes a situation where only architecture's symbolic function mediates our relation to the sky.

Bibliography

Alvarez, Al (ed.) (1962) *The New Poetry: An Anthology Selected and Introduced by A. Alvarez.* Harmondsworth: Penguin.

Bataille, Georges (2001 [1978]) *The Blue of Noon,* trans. Harry Mathews. London: Penguin. (Originally published as *Le Bleu du Ciel,* 1957)

Berman, Marshall (1983) *All That is Solid Melts Into Air: the experience of modernity.* London: Verso.

Caillois, Roger (1984) 'Mimicry and legendary psychasthenia', trans. Roger Sheply, *October* 31 (Winter) 12–32. (Originally published in *Minotaure*, 1935)

Deleuzes, Gilles (1993) *The Fold: Leibniz and the Baroque*. London: Athlone Press.

Deleuze, Gilles and Félix Guattari (1977) *Anti-Oedipus: Capitalism and Schizophrenia*. Harmondsworth: Penguin. (Originally published by Les Editions de Minuit, 1972).

Deleuze, Gilles and Félix Guattari (1994) *What is Philosophy?* trans Graham Burchell and Hugh Tomlinson London: Verso. (Originally published as *Qu'est-ce que la philosophie?* 1991).

Derrida, Jacques (1988) 'Why Peter Eisenman writes such good books', *Threshold: Journal of the School of Architecture* IV (Spring): 99–105.

Derrida, Jacques (1990) 'A letter to Peter Eisenman', *Assemblage* 12 (August): 7–13.

Derrida, Jacques and Peter Eisenman (1997) *Choral Works*. New York: Monacelli Press.

Descartes, René (1998) *Discourse on Method and Meditations on First Philosophy,* trans. by Donald A. Cress from *Discours de la methode*. Indianapolis, IN: Hackett.

Duboy, Philippe (1986) *Lequeu: An Architectural Enigma*. London: Thames and Hudson.

Eisenman, Peter (1990) 'Post/El Card', *Assemblage* 12 (August): 14–17.

Evans, Dylan (1996) *An Introductory Dictionary of Lacanian Psychoanalysis*. London, Routledge.

Freud, Sigmund (1923) 'Neurosis and psychosis', in James Strachey (ed.), *The Standard Edition of the Complete Psychological Works of Sigmund Freud Book XIX (1923–25) The Ego and the Id and other works* (pp. 147–153). London: The Hogarth Press and the Institute of Psycho-Analysis.

Giedion, Sigried (1964) *The Eternal Present: The Beginnings of Architecture – A Contribution on Constancy and Change*. London: Oxford University Press.

Giedion, Sigried (1967) *Space Time and Architecture: The Growth of a New Tradition*. Cambridge MA: Harvard University Press.

Grigg, Russell (2009) 'Language as sinthome in ordinary psychosis', *Psychoanalytic Notebooks no. 19 Ordinary Psychosis* (pp. 51–61). London: Society of the New Lacanian School.

Holm, Lorens (2010) *Brunelleschi, Lacan, Le Corbusier: Architecture Space and the Construction of Subjectivity*. London: Routledge.

Holm, Lorens (2013) 'Psychosis and the ineffable space of modernism', *The Journal of Architecture* 18(3): 402–24.

Koolhaas, Rem (1994 [1978]) 'Europeans: Biuer! Dali and Le Corbusier Conquer New York', *Delirious New York: A Retroactive Manifesto for Manhattan*. New York, The Monacelli Press. (Originally published as 'Dali and Le Corbusier: the paranoid critical method' in *Architectural Design 2–3* 1978)

Lacan, Jacques (1981) *The Four Fundamental Concepts of Psycho-Analysis*. New York: Norton.

Lacan, Jacques (1993) *The Psychoses: The Seminar of Jacques Lacan, Book III 1955–1956.* ed. Jacques-Alain Miller, trans. Russell Grigg. London: Routledge. (Originally published as *Le Seminaire, Livre III Les Psychoses,* Editions du Seuil, 1981)

Lacan, Jacques (2006) 'On a question prior to any possible treatment of psychosis', *Ecrits: The First Complete Edition in English,* trans. Paul Fink. New York: Norton.

Laplanche, J and J.-B. Pontalis (1973) *The Language of Psycho-Analysis*. London: Hogarth Press/Institute of Psycho-Analysis.

Lynn, Gregg ed. (2004 [1993]) *Folding in Architecture*. London: AD Architecture Design + Wiley-Academy.

Mumford, Lewis (1970) *The Myth of the Machine: the Pentagon of Power*, New York: Harcourt Brace Jovanovich.

Panofsky, Erwin (1991) *Perspective as Symbolic Form,* trans. Christopher S. Wood. New York: Zone Books.

Rossi, Aldo (1976) 'The blue of the sky', *Oppositions* 5 (Summer): 31–4. (Originally published as 'L'azzurro del cielo', *Controspazio*, October 1972)

Schumpeter, Joseph A. (1992) *Capitalism, Socialism, and Democracy.* London: Routledge.

Sullivan, Louis (1896) 'The tall office building artistically considered', republished in *Kindergarten Chats and other writings* (1947), New York: George Wittenborn), pp202–213; first published in *Lippincott's Magazine* 57 (March 1896), pp 403–9.

Tschumi, Bernard (1994a) 'Advertisements for architecture' (1975–78), *Architecture and Disjunction*. Cambridge, MA: MIT Press.

Tschumi, Bernard (1994b) 'Architecture and transgression' (1976), *Architecture and Disjunction.* Cambridge, MA: MIT Press

Tschumi, Bernard (1994c) 'The pleasure of architecture' (1977), *Architecture and Disjunction*. Cambridge, MA: MIT Press.

Tschumi, Bernard (1994d) 'Madness and the combinative' (1984), *Architecture and Disjunction*. Cambridge, MA: MIT Press.

Vyzoviti, Sophia (2003) *Folding Architecture: Spatial, Structural, and Organizational Diagrams*. Herengracht: BIS Publishers.

Žižek, Slavoj (2001) *Enjoy your Symptom: Jacques Lacan in Hollywood and Out.* London: Routledge.

Chapter 3

Transgression and ekphrasis in Le Corbusier's *Journey to the East*

Gordana Korolija Fontana-Giusti

> Architecture was revealed to me. Architecture is in the great buildings, the difficult and the high-flown works bequeathed by time, but *it is also in the smallest hovel*, in an enclosure-wall, in everything, sublime or modest, which contains sufficient geometry to establish a mathematical relationship.
>
> (Le Corbusier, *Voyage to the East*, 206–207)

The invisible lines of this revelation have been woven in the text, sketches and photographs of Charles-Édouard Jeanneret's 1911 voyage to the east. They have outlined this architect's future career that played itself out in the five decades that followed. This was not an ordinary career; it was a unique professional path with effects that have touched many across the globe. In relation to this path, the world has observed the emergence, flourishing and subsequent erosion of Modernist architecture. From its outset, this career has resonated with peripatetic and nomadic cords of transgression; the tunes of its register were still reverberating in the summer of 1965 when Le Corbusier edited his travel diary for publication, shortly before his death.

In this chapter I argue how the experience of this trip worked itself out as a transgression and how this transgression was the necessary condition for a particular quality that epitomised Le Corbusier's work that followed. My emphasis will not be on widely theorised topics such as the fascination with the Parthenon or the importance of certain churches. Rather, I shall focus on the prior and less acknowledged aspects of this trip, such as the effects of the indigenous arts and architecture in the countries along the River Danube. I shall support my argument by making reference to the subsequent scholarship on prehistoric civilisations such as the Vinča culture, in order to shed more light on Jeanneret, who by the time of his arrival in Constantinople had already changed his approach to arts and design.

The notion of transgression in the context of the twentieth century

The notion of transgression enters European cultural discourse in the early twentieth century. The term had already existed in medieval Latin and in the legal lexicon for two millennia, denoting the phenomenon primarily in relation to law, understood in its negative sense as the violation of legislation. However, during the twentieth century, the signification of this term acquired more complex undertones, linked predominantly to avant-garde figures such as Marcel Duchamp, Georges Bataille, Antonin Artaud and Raymond Roussel. Their (in part surrealist) writings, art and lives subsequently gained the attention of Michel Foucault (1963, 1977), Jacques Derrida (1978), Denis Hollier (1989) and others who further explored the phenomenon of transgression.

Experiencing life fully, with its contradictions, ambiguities and intricacies, was central for the proponents of the early avant-garde such as Artaud, Bataille or Roussel. These and other twentieth-century adventurers drew novel aesthetic qualities from the experiences of the new metropolitan life as we observe it in Duchamp's work such as the iconic 'Nude Descending a Staircase' (1912) where the painter explored the experience and the movement, beyond creating a simple 'retinal pleasure', Duchamp, who could also be considered the first conceptual artist, was a friend of Roussel and considered the French poet as an inspiration 'pointing the way' to the radical artists at the time. Foucault's only book-length work of literary criticism is on Roussel, while Derrida and Hollier wrote enthusiastically on Artaud and Bataille respectively. Personal curiosities and dispositions guided Bataille, Artaud and others through the new circumstances, while extreme experiences were accelerated with the advances in mechanisation, the breakout of the Great War and the first socialist revolution.

For these and other twentieth-century young radicals of any vocation such as Shackleton, the Wright brothers, Einstein or Coco Chanel, finding oneself in unfamiliar and uncomfortable territory facing difficult predicaments became part of life's challenges. Travels to distant corners of the world such as the North and the South Poles, 'sailing of the air' across the ocean, revolutionary changes in female clothing and the struggle for equal rights were all different forms of breaking the existing boundaries and thus transgression in a wider sense.

Le Corbusier and the tour as the point of transgression and genesis

In contrast to the 'Grand Tour' travellers of the eighteenth century, who searched for legacy of the classical antiquity, and distinct from the self-conscious romantic 'adventurers' of the nineteenth century, early twentieth-century itinerants such as Charles-Édouard Jeanneret plunged into a different kind of adventure. Although Jeanneret (later known as Le Corbusier) made his first trip to Italy in 1907, it was the six-month May–November 1911 journey to the east that profoundly affected him. The trip that aimed to reach Constantinople was less grand and obsessive, but, I shall argue, more absorbing, life-changing and transgressive.

The formative role of *Voyage d 'Orient* for Le Corbusier's theoretical work and practice thereafter has been broadly recognised.[1] References to art and architecture experienced on this trip appear in his writings as early as 1915 and span numerous publications, among them *L'Art décoratif d'aujourd'hui* (1925), *La Ville radieuse* (1933), *Quand les cathédrales étaient blanches* (1937) and *Le Modulor* (1949). It has been acknowledged that a number of his early villas, such as Villa Jeanneret-Perret (1912), Villa Favre-Jacot (1912) and Villa Schwob (1916), were inspired by the houses seen on the trip in terms of their internal organisation around a central hall, ample spaces, massing and blank street facades (Çelik 1992: 59).

While Zeynep Çelik provides an important argument in relation to Le Corbusier's orientalism and colonialism by additionally examining the context of Algiers, Çelik often equalises his orientalism with Islamic architecture. This might be appropriate for Algiers, but would be reductive for Le Corbusier's orientalism as it appears in his *Journey to the East,* which includes exploration of both Islamic and Christian arts and architecture. More to the point, Jeanneret is interested in an understanding of the arts *before* they were Christian or Islamic as neither was of essential significance for his investigation. It is therefore important to draw the attention to the cultural mélange of the region he visited but even more so to the role of the underlying indigenous arts of this part of the world, as they became important discoveries for Jeanneret.

Departing from Dresden via Prague and Vienna, twenty-four-year-old Jeanneret and his friend August Klipstein travelled east through the countries of Hungary, Serbia, Romania, Bulgaria, Turkey and Greece. The trip took the two men down the River Danube, a major natural and cultural infrastructure linking northern Europe with the Mediterranean world.[2] Travelling along its waters made a huge impression on the two friends, who felt the excitement of being part of the system that connected Europe with Asia and Africa.

Until this point in his life, Jeanneret was a draftsman at the office of Peter Behrens in Berlin and had not yet found his own focus in architecture. Were it not for this journey that imprinted deeply felt experiences upon Le Corbusier as a young man, his career would not have taken the radically innovative direction for which we know it. In other words, it was on this journey to Constantinople that Le Corbusier experienced his 'road to Damascus' moment.

This claim is bold and not demonstrable with mathematical precision; it is not entirely new either. According to Ivan Žaknić, the editor and English translator of the *Voyage*, the more we know about Le Corbusier and his later accomplishments, 'the more significant this "grand tour" becomes as a substantive locus and point of genesis for ideas in all domains of his creativity' (Le Corbusier 2007a: vi). Le Corbusier himself had singled out the year of the trip as the most decisive year of his professional growth (Le Corbusier 2007a: xvi).

According to Jeanneret's travel diary and numerous letters to family, friends and mentors such as Charles L'Eplattenier and William Ritter, Charles-Édouard lived through events that were overwhelming and fundamentally altered his previous understanding about architecture and decorative arts[3] (Gresleri, 1987). Jeanneret admitted that he was not able to cope with the intensity of the experiences he lived through on this journey: he writes, 'these notes are lifeless; the beauties I have seen always break down under my pen...' (Le Corbusier 2007a: xiii). The depth of these experiences determined his personal development and gave Jeanneret the necessary confidence for future projects.

Transgression and ekphrasis

My hypothesis is that Jeanneret's experience of the indigenous arts and culture encountered on this trip was a transgression, and that his related observations, contemplation, sketching and writing could be understood and qualified as *ekphrasis*, whose breadth and depth facilitated and determined the genesis of Le Corbusier's work.

Let us therefore clarify what is meant by *ekphrasis*. *Ekphrasis* is a detailed description of a work of art that is practised to enhance the contemplation and experience of the arts. This practice cultivates a person's perception, sensitivity and reflectivity through observation. It could inspire another work of art in a manner of *ut pictura ut poesis* ('as is picture so is poetry'). *Ekphrasis*, an essentially rhetorical device, was commonly used by the scholars of late Antiquity and the Middle Ages, as it was instrumental for grasping the arts in words and letters. In Byzantium, it was studied as part of the *trivium*.[4] There is no explicit evidence that Jeanneret was familiar with this concept; however, the impact of his co-traveller August Klipstein, an art history graduate with a keen interest in Byzantine art, should not be underestimated. According to Tim Benton, Jeanneret had learned a great deal from Klipstein (Benton 2013:12). Moreover, having previously visited Spain and Italy, it was Klipstein's idea to travel to Constantinople and Athens, at a time when Jeanneret dreamed of an 'idler's tour to Rome' only (Benton 2013:100). In the end, Jeanneret agreed to go to Rome via Constantinople and Athens because he needed a travel companion and the two men seemed to get along well (Benton 2013:100).

Both Klipstein and Jeanneret wrote detailed journals during the trip. We do not know whose idea was this or whether it was simply a common practice at the time. As a Byzantine scholar, Klipstein would have been familiar with the practice of *ekphrasis* and could have encouraged it, as Jeanneret's narratives became more vivid and read as 'drafted and painted' with words.[5] Charles-Édouard's writing is personal and authentic, based on his perception of the arts and life as encountered. It noticeably improves with time and we observe a gradual change and broadening of Jeanneret's perception. This enhanced and fine-tuned perception, in part due to *ekphrasis*, underpins most of Jeanneret's travel journal.

In a self-reflective manner, Jeanneret describes the training of the eye and the depth of observation by comparing sketching and photography:

When one travels and works with visual things – architecture, painting or sculpture – one uses one's eyes and draws, so as *to fix deep down in one's experience* what is seen. Once the impression has been recorded by the pencil, it stays for good, entered, registered, inscribed. The camera is the tool for idlers, who use a machine to do their seeing for them.

(Le Corbusier 2007a: xiv; my emphasis)

For Jeanneret drawing was part of a profound registering of lived experiences into his personal memory system. He strove to record everything in an organised way by using writing, drawing and photography, and by collecting objects of arts and crafts that were shipped back to Switzerland as the journey progressed. He planned this methodically, while letting his susceptibility lead the way. In this undertaking, various arts were studied in their own right and in relation to each other, allowing for *ekphrasis* to work and cross-fertilise them. Indeed this dynamic persisted beyond the trip and throughout most of his career, as Le Corbusier continued to draw from these experiences. On the importance of being drawn to action and on the primacy of sketching, Charles-Édouard wrote emphatically:

To draw oneself, to trace the lines, handle the volumes, organise the surface … all this means first to look and then to observe and finally perhaps to discover … and it is then that the inspiration may come. Inventing, creating, one's whole being is drawn into action, and it is this action which counts. Others stood indifferent – but you saw!

(Le Corbusier 2007a: xiv)

Jeanneret took many photographs, yet he overtly gave little importance to them, preferring his sketches and writing instead. But despite his apparently dim view of the camera, Jeanneret clutched one throughout the trip and took shots that have become paradigmatic. Tim Benton's *Le Corbusier: Secret Photographer* (Benton 2013) makes a seminal contribution to the understanding of Le Corbusier's photography. Benton points out that during the 1906–11 period, Jeanneret made a serious effort to master the technique and the art of photography by purchasing three cameras, a tripod and many filters. He also learned how to print and develop negatives (Benton 2013: 9). According to Benton, in the year of the voyage alone, Jeanneret went through three different styles of taking photographs. From the initial phase in which he was trying to make professional architectural photographs in Germany and Prague (April to May 1911), via photographs in a more personal style (May to September), Jeanneret ended up producing photography in the style of visual notes (October 1911) (Benton 2013: 9). Implied in Benton's statement is the assertion that Jeanneret's changing attitude towards photography hinges upon the transformative experiences of this trip. This understanding runs in parallel with and directly supports my main argument.

Figure 3.1
**Black and white
drawing of Prague
cityscape by
Jeanneret, 1911**

An art that is sensuous, authoritative and that 'gives to the body its fair share'

As mentioned, the change is evident not only in Jeanneret's style of writing and photography but also in his drawings as they became less academically studious (Prague drawings) and more abstract (Constantinople sketches) (Figures 3.1 and 3.2). How are we to explain this conversion?

The two friends' journey was dominated by their fascination for the unconsidered lands and the people they encountered. Their journey was filled with unexpected moments of exaltation and joy, as Jeanneret and Klipstein stumbled upon the simplicity of everyday life in the landscapes of Hungary, Serbia, Romania and Bulgaria. Impressed by the prolific nature of traditional arts amongst non-academically educated people, Jeanneret wrote ecstatically:

> In our travels we passed through countries where the artist peasant matches with authority the colour to the line and the line to the form, and we were green with envy! But this continued without end!
>
> (Le Corbusier 2007a: 15)

At this point it might be instructive to briefly consider the role of Worringer's influential 1907 book *Abstraction and Empathy*, as Klipstein was a protégé of Wilhelm Worringer (1881–1965). According to Rabaça and Brooks, and quoted by Benton, Klipstein had his master's book with himself, had written and quoted from it during the

Figure 3.2
A watercolour sketch
of Constantinople by
Jeanneret, 1911

travel and had apparently encouraged his companion to read it (Rabaça 2012; Brooks 1997: 235). In *Abstraction and Empathy*, Worringer makes an important distinction between the two kinds of art: a) the art that takes pleasure in making recognisable simulacra; and b) the art that suppresses that illusion in favour of something more constricted and abstract. Both can produce beauty, however, according to Worringer, the former accepts and idealises the world, while the latter is concerned and anxious about it and thus compelled to devise artistic strategies designed to minimise the sovereignty of representation. This compulsion for non-representational artistic strategies is Worringer's 'urge for abstraction' (Worringer 1997: vii–xv).[6] As evident in his sketches, writings and photographs, Jeanneret was taken by this urge.

Excited by abstract objects of traditional ceramics, woodcarvings, stone-cuttings and freshly painted peasant houses, he writes that in the pursuit of these simple abstract forms they had to 'flee from the invading Europeanisation' of big cities, into the refuge of the countryside where the great popular traditions survive (Figure 3.3).

In this 'flee' we can read the urge to transgress all that was left behind in the cities, including the work with established architects such as Behrens. Jeanneret searches for something more 'sensual', which he finds in the traditionally designed objects. He writes:

> The art of the peasant is a striking creation of aesthetic sensuality. If art elevates itself above the sciences, it is precisely because, in opposition to them, *it stimulates sensuality and awakens profound echoes in the physical being. It gives to the body – to the animal – its fair share*, and then upon this healthy base, conductive to the expansion of joy, it knows how to erect the most noble of pillars.

> (Le Corbusier 2007a: 15)

Figure 3.3
Vernacular house in Serbia,
photograph 1911

Jeanneret makes an uncanny libidinal connection between art objects and physical pleasure. What makes this statement extraordinary and transgressive is the fact that the aesthetic judgement is not disinterested (as in the tradition of Kant). Instead, Jeanneret calls for an unapologetic aesthetic pleasure that is instinctive, physical and intoxicating. He continues:

> The forms are voluminous and swollen with vitality, the line continually unites and mingles native scenes, or offers, right alongside and on the same object the magic of geometry: an astonishing union of fundamental instincts and of those susceptible to more abstract speculations.
>
> The colour, it too is not descriptive but evocative – always symbolic. It is the end and not the means. It exists for the caress and for the intoxication of the eye and as such, paradoxically, with a hearty laugh it jostles the great inhibited giants, even the Giottos, even the Grecos, the Cézannes and the Van Goghs!
>
> (Le Corbusier 2007a: 16)

Jeanneret thus boldly brings together the cool reason of geometry and the libidinal passions for forms and colours. The blaze of this passion prevailed as Jeanneret aimed for the works that were able to induce physical and authoritative pleasure. The two photographs in Figures 3.4 and 3.5 show Jeanneret's appreciation of the haptic qualities in art and design.

Figure 3.4
In the workshop at 29 rue d'Astorg, Paris, 1922
Le Corbusier holds a ceramic pot acquired from Serbia in 1911; in the background is a kilim, probably from the same trip.

Figure 3.5
Le Corbusier relaxes surrounded by works of art

Transgression by lines and the pre-historical ancestry of the vernacular art in the Danube region

Several visual notions relate to Jeanneret's transgressive experience, including the observation of lines such as the flat line of the horizon (Figure 3.6). Describing the experience of Danube from the river-boat Jeanneret writes:

> It is like being on the Amazon, so remote are the river banks and so impenetrable are their forests ... There is now nothing to see but a horizontal line.
>
> (Le Corbusier 2007a: 36)

Reading Jeanneret's notes evokes the fluvial land crowned with the immense sky that must have projected a sense of luxury, which rendered everything possible. Calm, lush scenery must have brought reassurance about life linked to the ground. In absorbing the richness of this vast landscape, its plain topographical qualities, its vegetation and its people, Jeanneret recorded:

> Why should one copy some shrivelled bud? That is so monstrous! ... Joy – it is a tree spread out like a magnificent palm, with flowers and with all its fruits. Beauty is this splendid flourish of youth, its liveliness and its variety.
>
> (Le Corbusier 2007a:18)

In a similar appreciation of the instinctive, natural and organic lines recognisable on the pots and other traditional art objects, we read:

Figure 3.6
Horizontality: the River Danube near the medieval fortress of Smederevo, a photograph by Jeanneret 1911

First and foremost among these men who do not reason is the instinctive appreciation for the *organic* line, born from the correlation between the most utilitarian line and that which encloses the most expansive volume – thus the most beautiful.

(Le Corbusier 2007a:16)

Jeanneret gradually articulates a definition of beauty that acknowledges the 'organic line'. He observed this line in the way in which earthenware developed organically from the ground into everyday life and in the manner it continued to live on the fingertips of the locals (Figure 3.7). In comparison to the flatness and striation of modern industrial design, Jeanneret considered the lines of this traditional design more purposeful, less arbitrary, and in that sense superior:

In effect these pots too are young, beaming ... with their curves expanding to the bursting point, and what a contrast they make, created as they are on the wheel of the village potter, ... whose fingers unconsciously obey the rules of an age-old tradition, in contrast to those forms of disturbing fantasy, or a stupefying imbecility, conceived by who knows whom in the unknown corners of large modern factories; those are nothing but the foolish whims of some low-ranking draftsman who draws such form for the sole purpose of differentiating it from the one he drew yesterday.

(Le Corbusier 2007a: 18)

Jeanneret saw curved lines of pots as analogous to the arcs and bends of the natural surroundings and to the voluptuous bodies of women in traditional costumes

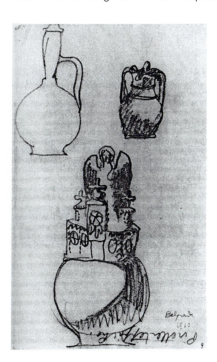

Figure 3.7
Jeanneret's sketches of the pottery from the Balkans, 1911

that he watched with interest when they unintentionally had to stay in Baja. These kinds of accidental encounters, at times combined with the soul-searching music of the gypsies (as in the occasion of a wedding that Jeanneret and Klipstein inadvertently attended), are experiences that proved to be long-lasting and relevant. The two men found the local women intriguingly different, more relaxed and strangely tuned to life.

It would not be an exaggeration to say that Jeanneret's photographs of the curvaceous women of Hungarian *pusztas* potentially bring to mind female figurines coincidentally excavated in the not-too-distant Willendorf in 1908 by the archaeologists Josef Szombathy, Hugo Obermaier and

Josef Bayer.[7] While this is a truly large time gap to cover, in my view the traditional vernacular arts that Jeanneret observed cannot be dissociated from the legacy of the previous prehistoric cultures of the Danube region (Figures 3.7 and 3.8). Contemporary Corbusian scholarship habitually does not study this aspect because of the presumed red line separating so-called pre-history and history. However, the virtue of the traditional art of pottery is in the fact that it spans this tentative line.

The advances in archaeology in central Europe during the period when Jeanneret and Klipstein travelled were significant and ought to be highlighted. Apart from finding the well-known Austrian figurine, archaeologists were working on many Neolithic sites that were part of the Danubian brunch of cultures. For example, in 1908, archaeologist Miloje Vasić made the important discovery of a prehistoric settlement of Belo Brdo close to the village of Vinča, downstream of Belgrade on the right bank of the Danube, paving a way for future discoveries of what came to be known as the Vinča culture. This civilisation from about 7,800 years ago, which spread from Hungary to Greece, incorporating most of contemporary Serbia and parts of Romania, Bulgaria, Macedonia and Bosnia, was once a highly sophisticated European culture which lasted for about 1000 years before it diminished. In addition to the organised settlements and copper metallurgy, these people had an early form of writing and a highly developed pottery that included anthropomorphic pots and small sculptures.[8] There was at the time a considerable general and scientific interest in the archaeological excavations conducted; Jeanneret and Klipstein were most probably aware of them. Although Jeanneret did not warm to Belgrade, he paid a visit to its newly established Ethnographic Museum, which he liked, and where he was exposed to the latest findings and related scholarship.[9] He writes how they decided to make a detour to Knjaževac in order to explore the pottery:

> In a quiet corner of the city there is an exquisite ethnographic museum, with carpets, clothing, and pots – beautiful Serbian pots of the kind we will go looking for in the highlands of the Balkans around Knjaževac.
>
> (Le Corbusier 2007a: 43)

In his overall quest for the primary and universal quality in the arts, Jeanneret did not follow a strictly rational or academic approach. The stimulating sensuality of the shapes and colours of pots and other objects constantly affected him as he often extracted, recorded and abstracted forms that he enjoyed (Benton 2013:13). The use and application of these forms recorded in the sketches is subsequently evident in Le Corbusier's paintings, design and architectural projects, including the Dom-ino house (Figures 3.10 and 3.11).

We can therefore construe that Jeanneret's knowledge of vernacular art was based on some scholarly knowledge passed to him by friends and mentors, but mostly it was acquired on the trip by observation and direct experience. In this way Jeanneret's 'urge for abstraction' worked through the ekphrastic contemplation of the freshly discovered 'art of the peasant'. This attitude gradually became Le Corbusier's

Figure 3.8
Pots owned by Le
Corbusier acquired in
Serbia, 1911

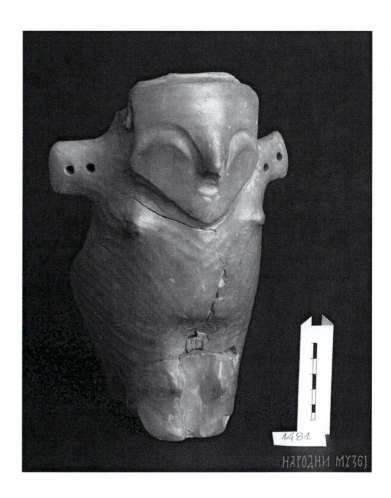

Figure 3.9
Prehistoric
anthropomorphic pot
from Vinča, near Belgrade

Figure 3.10
Interior of the house in
Kasaniak, sketched 1911

Figure 3.11
The proposal for the
interior of the Dom-ino
house, 1915

own strategy for approaching art and design, where the processes of abstraction and
ekphrasis stimulated sensuality and awakened the body by giving it pleasures.

But abstraction also worked at another level: on the macro *Weltanschauung*
(world-view) level, where it was the way in which one coped with the complexities and
anxieties of the world. Jeanneret indeed displayed his personal pleasure and joy in
the process related to the arts, but he showed a certain oblivion of the socio-political
context, as he remained silent about the political tensions that existed in this region
prior to the breakout of the 1912 and 1913 Balkan Wars and the 1914 Great War.

The 'savage' and the unlocking of the universal quality of art

Jeanneret's language, which includes terms such as 'sensuality', 'physicality', 'expansion of joy' and 'erection' of the 'most noble of pillars' reveals Jeanneret as an open, experimental explorer who embraced life with passion. From his excitement over colourful crafts, via the study of the pots and sketches of the vernacular whitewashed houses, he came to Bosporus to appreciate the spaces of the imperial Stamboul. The perspectival study drawings are gone, while sensuous, inspirational often abstracted sketches take over. The new drawings make observations on a deeper level, beyond the framed and academically taught perspectival copying. Jeanneret observes the inner and outer structure of the overall urban phenomenon and its topographical relation to the sea, the sun and the sky. He cherished the life-changing hold that the trip provided, enabling him to see things differently, to transgress and to speak a new language of empathy and universality of the arts. He evoked the tactile qualities of the traditional art that led him to this realisation:

> Thus this traditional art, like a lingering warm caress, embraces the entire land, covering it with same flowers that *unite or mingle races*, climates and places. It has spread out without constraint, with the spiritedness of a beautiful animal.
>
> (Le Corbusier 2007a: 16; my emphasis)

These exaltations clearly echo beyond the Heimatschutz movement to which Jeanneret was initially responsive[10] (Benton 2013:15). He penetrated deeper than the urban followers of this movement by uncovering the traits of arts and culture *in situ* in the ancient crafts of Pannonia and the Balkans. This awareness enabled him to reach fundamental strata of the arts where written language, history and categories such as style appeared irrelevant. He writes:

> Considered from a certain point of view, folk art outlives the highest of civilisations. It remains a norm, a sort of measure whose standard is man's ancestor – the savage, if you will.
>
> (Le Corbusier 2007a: 16)

The discovery that universal pleasure in art is linked to the qualities of the art of the savage was transgressive. Understanding these principles led Jeanneret to search for and find the same underlying universal traits in the Balkans, in Stamboul and elsewhere beyond this trip in places such as Brazil and India.

Jeanneret's contribution to the formulation of modern abstract art was also in the fact that he gradually ceased to use the term 'primitive', previously widely used. He replaced it with the term 'peasant'. This meant that the term 'abstract' became dissociated from the term 'primitive', which was still the case in Worringer. In this way, the terms 'abstract' and 'abstraction' were emancipated. Consequently, the concept

Figure 3.12
**Charles-Édouard
Jeanneret, Istanbul,
1911**

of abstract art emerged in its own right. It was soon to be linked not to the past, but almost exclusively to the future, progress and modernist experimentation. This is the important legacy of Jeanneret and of his trip to the East.

History has often been patronising towards and reluctant to consider the indigenous art of this part of Europe. Indeed, since the Romans this area was considered marginal – a *limes*. By identifying the importance of these previous cultures for Le Corbusier's work and therefore for Modernism generally, I also suggest the relevance of the prehistoric cultural heritage of this part of the world which twentieth- and twenty-first-century archaeological scholarship has confirmed. This aspect deserves further elaboration, which goes beyond the scope of this chapter.

In relation to transgression, it is important to state the following: Jeanneret was able to capture previously non-theorised conditions of arts due to his acquired openness, empathy and the sense of abstraction that he and Klipstein developed on the way. This experience amounts to a cultural transgression or something very close to it.

Jeanneret generated radically different language in art and architecture, containing elements of his own invention such as the new relation to the horizon and horizontality, the juxtaposition of straight and organic lines, the pockets of beaming colours in their dialogue with the light source, the physical pleasure of emphatically abstracted forms and the new awareness of the complex geometry and topography of urban spaces. These are the elements of the new grammar invented through an ekphrastic reflection on the transgressive experiences of this trip. They are evident in Le Corbusier's projects such as Villa Savoye and the chapel in Ronchamp, where this approach produced powerful infringements and innovative solutions.

Notes

1 The latest significant contemporary book on this subject is *L'invention d'un architecte: Le voyage en Orient de Le Corbusier* (2013). Le Corbusier prepared the book *Voyage en Orient* in July 1965; it was published posthumously in 1966 by Jean Petit. Although in 1965 Le Corbusier was a recognizable citizen of the world and a household name, curiously he still insisted that the experiences of young Charles-Édouard should be recorded. This suggests the importance he gave to this early travelogue. The book has subsequently been translated into Italian as *Le Corbusier Viaggio in Oriente* (1984). It appeared in English as *Journey to the East* (1987/2007).

2 See among other general literature the book by C. Magris (1999).

3 Note that when Le Corbusier speaks about 'the decorative arts', he does not refer to the arts that include ornaments and decoration but to the 'design' of objects.

4 For more on *ekphrasis* see Curtius (1990), 302–47. The *trivium* refers to the medieval curriculum consisting of three arts: grammar, dialectics and rhetoric. In late antiquity it was a method of systematic thinking for deriving certainty from any information coming into the mind via the five senses. See more in Curtius (1990).

5 People who practised *ekphrasis* often saw themselves as 'painters with words'. Historical examples include Philostratus and Callistratus, who aimed to reproduce paintings and statues and to instruct the reader both in art appreciation and in the entire story, of which the artefact was only a part. Curtius, *ibid.*.

6 Worringer's 'urge to abstraction' is related to Riegl's 'will for art', *Kunstwollen*, as Worringer was a student of Alois Riegl (1858–1905). Otto Rank (1884–1939), a Viennese psychoanalyst and a student of Freud, cites Worringer as 'taking Riegl up to the verge of psychological insight where art forms can be interpreted parallel to forms of belief in the soul'. See Rank (1989). Worringer is also credited for coining the term 'expressionism'.

7 Paleolithic Venus of Willendorf was excavated by a worker, Josef Veram, in 1908 at the excavations carried out by archaeologists Josef Szombathy, Hugo Obermaier and Josef Bayer. It is kept at the Natural History Museum in Vienna. Pusztas are big empty spaces of Pannonian plain; a sort of steppe of vast wilderness of grass and bushes; the name comes into Hungarian from Slavonic languages. In Serbo-Croation, Polish and Bulgarian *pust* means – bare, empty.

8 The Vinča sign system is a proto-writing that existed before the others appeared in Mesopotamia or Egypt. This sign system is believed to be the basis for both the Linear A and Linear B that later emerged in Greece. For more on this, see the reports on the 1961 archaeological works in Tărtăria, Romania. See also Vasić (1936); Chapman (1981); and Winn (1973, 1981). On later Vinča culture scholarship that includes the excavations in Lepenski Vir, see Srejović (1969, 1971, 1972, 1978).

9 The Ethnographic Museum of Serbia in Belgrade was opened in 1904 after the proposal and the theoretical base conceived by Stojan Novaković, a leading Serbian historian of the nineteenth century and a member of the Serbian, Yugoslav and Russian Academy of Arts and Sciences. The museum contained traditional pottery, textile, jewelry, metal and glass objects. Most of the content was subsequently destroyed in the First World War, but the museum was restored.

10 Like the Arts and Crafts Movement in Britain, this movement was eager to restore the charm of old towns and villages and related arts and crafts in Germany and Switzerland.

Bibliography

Amirante, R., Kutukcuoglu, B., Tournikiotis, P., and Tsiomis, Y. (2013). *L'invention d'un architecte: Le voyage en Orient de Le Corbusier*. Paris: Edition de la Villette.

Artaud, A. (1994 [1938]). *The Theater and Its Double*, trans. Mary C. Richard. New York: Grove Press.

Barthes, R. (1972 [1962]). 'Metaphor of the eye', in *Critical Essays*, trans. R. Howard, 239–48. Evanston IL: Northwestern University Press.

Bataille, G. (2001 [1928]). *The Story of the Eye*. San Francisco, CA: City Lights.

Benton, T. (2013). *Le Corbusier Secret Photographer*. Zurich: Lars Müller Publishers.

Bozdoğan, S. (1988). 'Journey to the east: Ways of looking at the orient and the question of representation', *Journal of Architectural Education JAE*, 41(4): 38–45.

Brooks, H.A. (1997). *Le Corbusier's Formative Years: Charles-Edourd Jeanneret at La Chaux-de-Fonds*. Chicago, IL: Chicago University Press.

Çelik, Z. (1992). 'Le Corbusier, orientalism, colonialism', *Assemblage*, 17 April, 58–77.

Chapman, J. (1981). *The Vinča Culture of South-East Europe: Studies in Chronology, Economy and Society* (2 vols), BAR International Series 117. Oxford: BAR.

Chapman, J. (2000). *Fragmentation in Archaeology: People, Places, and Broken Objects*. London: Routledge.

Curtius, E.R. (1990). *European Literature and the Middle Ages*, 3rd edn, trans. W.R. Trask, Bollingen Series XXXVI. Princeton, NJ: Princeton University Press.

Deleuze, G. and Guattari, F. (1988 [1980]). '28 November 1947: How do you make yourself a body without organs?', in *A Thousand Plateaus: Capitalism and Schizophrenia*, trans. B. Massumi, 149–67. London: The Athlone Press.

Derrida, J. (1978). 'La Parole soufflée', 'The theatre of cruelty' and 'The closure of representation', in *Writing and Difference*, trans. A. Bass. London: Routledge.

Farrère, C. (1943 [1907]). *L'Homme qui assassina*. Paris: Flammarion.

Foucault, M. (1977). 'A preface to transgression', in *Language, Counter-memory, Practice: Selected Essays and Interviews*, ed. D. F. Bouchard. Ithaca, NY: Cornell University Press.

Foucault, M. (2004 [1963]). *Death and the Labyrinth: The World of Raymond Roussel,* trans. C. Raus. London: Continuum.

Gresleri, G. (1987). 'Viaggio e scoperta, descrizione e trascrizione' ['Travelling and discovering, description and transcription'], *Casabella* 51(531–32): 8–17.

Hollier, D. (1989). *Against Architecture*. Cambridge, MA: MIT Press.

Korolija Fontana-Giusti, G. (2012). 'The urban language of early Constantinople: The changing roles of the arts and architecture in the formation of the new capital and the new consciousness', in Stephanie L. Hathaway and David W. Kim (eds), *Intercultural Transmission in the Medieval Mediterranean*, 164–202. London: Continuum.

Le Corbusier (1933). *La Ville radieuse*. Boulogne-sur-Seine: Editions de l'Architecture d'aujourd'hui.

Le Corbusier (1937) *Quand les Cathédrales étaient blanches.* Paris: Librairie Plon.

Le Corbusier (1949) *Le Modulor*. Boulogne-sur-Seine: Editions de l'Architecture d'aujourd'hui.

Le Corbusier (1984). *Le Corbusier Viaggio in Oriente*. ed. G. Gresleri, trans. M. Gresleri-Coppola. Venice: Marsilio Editori and Paris: FLC.

Le Corbusier (1987 [1925]). *The Decorative Arts of Today*, trans. J. Dunnett. Cambridge, MA: MIT Press.

Le Corbusier (2007a [1966/1987]). *Journey to the East*, trans., ed. and annotated by I. Žaknić. Cambridge, MA: MIT Press.

Le Corbusier (2007b [1923]). *Toward an Architecture,* trans. John Goodman. Los Angeles, CA: Getty Research Institute.

Magris, C. (1999), *Danube: A Sentimental Journey from the Source to The Black Sea*, trans. P. Creagh. London: The Harvill Press.

Olcayto, R. (2013). 'It's time to question the classic Corb backstory'. *Architects Journal*. Retrieved 19 November 2013 from http://www.architectsjournal.co.uk/comment/its-time-to-question-the-classic-corb-backstory/8644080.article.

Rabaça, A. (2012). 'Documental language and abstraction in the photographs of Le Corbusier'. *Jornal dos Arquitectos* 243: 102–9.

Rank, O. (1989). *Art and Artist: Creative Urge and Personality Development,* trans. C. F. Atkinson, New York: Norton.

Renan, E. (1899). *Prière sur l'Acropole, compositions de H. Bellery-Descfontaines graveés par Eugène Froment*. Paris: E. Palletan.

Riegl, A. (1985 [1901]). *Late Roman Art Industry*. Rome: Giorgio Bretschneider Editore.

Srejović, D. (1969). *Lepenski Vir*. Beograd: Srpska Knjizevna Zadruga.

Srejović, D. (1971). 'Die Anfänge des Neolithikums im Berich des mittleren Donaurames', *Actes du VIIIe Congres International des Sciences Préhistoriques et Protohistoriques* (3): 252–62, Beograd.

Srejović, D. (1972). *Europe's First Monumental Sculpture: New Discoveries at Lepenski Vir*, ed. M. Wheeler. London: Thames & Hudson.

Srejović, D. (1978). 'Néolithisation de la région des Portes de Fer', *Godišnjak*, 16: 21–9.

Tanju, B. (2000). 'Charles-Édouard Jeanneret's Journey to the east', in *Seven Centuries of Ottoman Architecture: A Supra-National Heritage,* 78–85. Istanbul: Yapi-Endustri Merkezi Publications.

Vasić, M. (1936). *Preistorijska Vinča I–IV* [*Prehistoric Vinča I–IV*]. Belgrade: Državne Štamparije Kraljevine Jugoslavije.

Winn, S.M.M. (1973). *The Signs of the Vinča Culture*. Ann Arbour, MI: Michigan University Microfilms.

Winn, S.M.M. (1981). *Pre-writing in Southeast Europe: The Sign System of the Vinča culture.* Calgary, AB: Western Publishers.

Worringer, W. (1997). *Abstraction and Empathy: A Contribution to the Psychology of Style*. Chicago, IL: Elephant Papers.

Intervention 2

R-Urban

A participatory strategy of transgression towards a resilient city[1]

Constantin Petcou and Doina Petrescu

Recently, growing global awareness has led to increased calls for collective action to confront current and future challenges, such as global warming, depletion of fossil fuels and other natural resources, economic recession, population growth, housing and employment crises, growing social and economic divides, and geopolitical conflict.[2]

While governments and institutions seem to be taking too long to reach agreement and to act, many initiatives have started at the local level.[3] These initiatives are nevertheless confronted with the difficulty of changing current economic and social models based on global-scale economics, which are premised on increasing consumption and the exclusion of those who cannot consume. How can we support initiatives that oppose current consumption drive? How can we begin to act? What tools and means can be used, what transgressive approaches are needed to push the boundaries of the existing practices and institutions? How can progressive practices be initiated while acting locally and at a small scale?

These are some questions we asked within R-Urban, a project initiated in our research-based practice, atelier d'architecture autogérée (aaa), as a bottom-up framework for resilient urban regeneration. After three years of research, we have proposed the project to various municipalities and to grassroots organizations in cities and towns. We conceived it as a participative strategy based on setting up local ecological cycles that activate material (e.g., water, energy, waste, and food) and immaterial (e.g., local skill, socioeconomic, cultural, and self-building) flows between key fields of activity (e.g., the economy, habitation, and urban agriculture) that exist or are implemented within the existing fabric of the city. R-Urban started in 2011 in

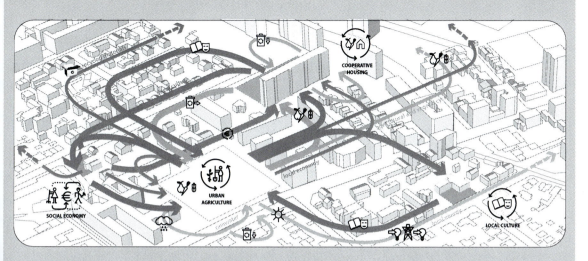

Figure I2.1
R-Urban ecology: locally closed cycles, complementary and transversal

Colombes, a suburban town of 86,000 inhabitants near Paris, in partnership with the local municipality and a number of organizations, and involving a range of local residents. The project is intended to gradually create a network around three 'pilot units', each with complementary urban functions, bringing together emerging citizen projects. This bottom-up strategy explores possibilities of enhancing the capacity for urban resilience by introducing a network of resident-run facilities.[4]

R-Urban, drawing strength from very active civic life and from Colombes's cultural and social diversity, started by launching several collective facilities, including recycling and eco-construction projects, cooperative housing, and urban agriculture units, that are working together to set up the first spatial and ecological agencies in the area. Their architecture showcases the various issues they address, such as local material recycling, local skills, energy production, and food growing. The first three pilot facilities – Agrocité, Recylab, and Ecohab – are collectively run and catalyse existing activities aiming to introduce and disseminate resilient habits and lifestyles that residents can adopt and practise at the individual and domestic levels, such as retrofitting dwellings to accommodate food growing and energy production.

Agrocité is an agro-cultural unit comprising an experimental micro-farm, community gardens, pedagogical and cultural spaces, and a series of experimental devices for compost heating, rainwater collection, solar energy production, aquaponic gardening, and phyto-remediation. Agrocité is a hybrid structure, with some components running as social enterprises (e.g. the micro-farm, market, and cafe) and others being run by user organizations (e.g. the community garden, cultural space, and pedagogical space) and local associations.

Recyclab is a recycling and eco-construction unit comprising several facilities for storing and reusing locally salvaged materials, recycling and transforming them into eco-construction elements for self-building and retrofitting. An associated fab lab[5] has been set up for resident use. Recyclab will function as a social enterprise.

Ecohab is a cooperative eco-housing project comprising a number of partially self-built and collectively managed ecological dwellings, including several shared facilities and schemes (e.g. food growing, production spaces, energy and

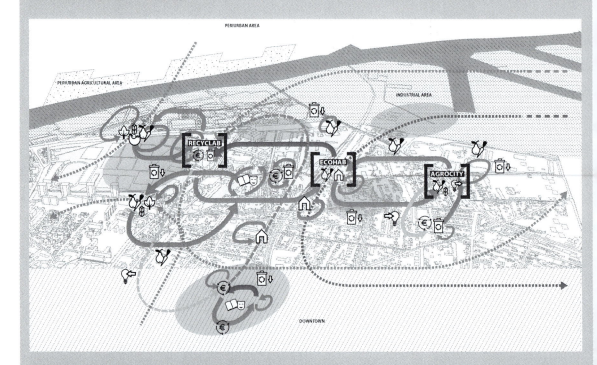

Figure 12.2
**R-Urban Colombes:
local and regional
dissemination**

water harvesting, and car sharing). The seven dwellings will include two social flats and a temporary residence unit for students and researchers. Ecohab will be run as a cooperative.

The R-Urban collective facilities will grow in number and be managed by a cooperative land trust, which will acquire space, facilitate development, and guarantee democratic governance.[6]

Flows, networks, and cycles of production–consumption will form between the collective facilities and the neighbourhood, closing chains of need and supply as locally as possible. To overcome the current crisis, we must try, as French philosopher André Gorz (2008: 13) states, 'to produce what we consume and consume what we produce'.

R-Urban interprets this production–consumption chain broadly, going well beyond material aspects to include the cultural, cognitive, and affective dimensions. The project sets a precedent for the participative retrofitting of metropolitan suburbs, in which the relationship between the urban and the rural is reconsidered. It tries to demonstrate what citizens can do if they change their working and living habits to collectively address the challenges of the future.

'R'

'R'-Urban relates directly to the three 'R' imperatives discussed in any ecological approach – i.e., Reduce, Reuse, and Recycle – and suggests other iterations, such as Repair, Redesign, and Rethink. In addition, the term indicates explicitly that R-Urban reconnects the 'urban' and the 'rural' through new, more complementary and less hierarchical kinds of relationships. The 'R' of R-Urban also reminds us that the main goal of the strategy is 'Resilience'.

'Resilience' is a key term in the context of the current economic crisis and resource scarcity. In contrast to sustainability, which focuses on maintaining the status quo of a system by controlling the balance between its inputs and outputs, without necessarily addressing the factors of change and disequilibrium, resilience addresses how systems can adapt and thrive in changing circumstances. Resilience is a dynamic concept that does not have a stable definition or identity outside the circumstances that produce it. In contrast to sustainability, which tends to focus on maintaining the environmental balance, resilience is adaptive and transformative, inducing change that offers huge potential to rethink assumptions and build new systems (Maguire & Cartwright, 2008). Although the current resilience discourse should not be embraced uncritically, without acknowledging the sometimes naïve and idealistic comparison of social to biological systems and their capacity to adapt to engender wellbeing, the concept of 'resilience' has the potential to include questions and contradictions addressed in political ecology terms.[7] Resilience must be thought about not only in terms of 'transition', as proposed by movements like Transition Town, but also in terms of 'transgression': the dynamic adapting involves quick reassessing of rules and limitations and changes and transformations within the support infrastructures, the value systems, the behaviour patterns etc.

R-Urban is thus not about 'sustainable development' but about societal change, and political and cultural reinvention, addressing issues of social inequality, power, and cultural difference. The resilience of a social system also implies the capacity to preserve specific democratic principles and cultural values, local histories and traditions, while adapting to more ecological and economically mindful lifestyles. A city can only become resilient with the active involvement of its inhabitants. To stimulate the democratic engagement of the largest number of citizens, we need tools, knowledge, and places for testing new collective practices and initiatives and for showcasing the results and benefits of a resilient transformation of the city. In this, architects have a role to play. Rather than acting merely as building designers, they can be initiators, negotiators, co-managers, and enablers of processes and agencies.

Concentrating on spatial agencies and pilot facilities, R-Urban tries to supply tools and spaces that will manifest citizens' existing resilience initiatives and practices. Spatial design processes contribute to expressing ecological cycles in tangible ways and help facilitate citizen experiences of making and doing. Democratic governance principles are as such associated with concrete hands-on actions whose consequences are visible and measurable. More than just adaptation, resilience is for R-Urban a transgression based on urban activation, innovation, and creativity.

Parallel to its pilot facilities, which form a new ecological urban infrastructure, R-Urban puts in place new political and democratic tools. These tools are co-created with other partners and concerned citizens, being transferable and multipliable. As noted by the Marxist philosopher John Holloway in *Change the World without Taking Power* (2002), the numerous movements seeking ways to overcome the current crisis are somehow locked in oppositional struggles with the state, understood as a political instrument of coercion. Holloway believes that fetishizing the state and/or capital traps most people within existing power systems, preventing them from striving for radical change. He concludes that if we want to escape and transgress the current societal blockage, we should not fight to take power but for alternatives to power, for the dynamics of social self-determination. These dynamics must necessarily be anchored in everyday life: 'the movement against-and-beyond is a movement that emerges from everyday life' (authors' translation; Holloway, 2006, p. 17). This is what characterizes R-Urban: a transgressive process of resilience that starts at the everyday life level.

Micro-social and micro-cultural resilience

Unlike other initiatives that deal exclusively with sustainability from a technological and environmental perspective, R-Urban advocates a general 'change of culture', understood as a change in how we do things, in order to change our future. The future is culturally shaped as much as the past is, because culture gives us 'the capacity to aspire' (Appadurai, 2004). One might say also 'the capacity to transgress' the order in place, to push boundaries and go beyond existing habits. This transgression always starts at a micro-social level.

R-Urban proposes new collective practices that, in addition to ecological footprint reduction, contribute to reinventing proximity relationships based on solidarities (i.e., ways of being involved and deciding collectively, sharing spaces and grouping facilities, and rules and principles of cohabitation). In neoliberal societies, urban lifestyles have progressively abandoned various forms of solidarity that were perceived as inadequate or outdated. However, these relationships of reciprocity constitute the very basis of social progress. In his analysis of the connections between the economy and politics (inspired by Tarde's sociology), philosopher Maurizio Lazzarato (2002) critically describes the civilization of 'progress' as 'a constantly renewed effort to replace reciprocal possession with unilateral possession' (authors' translation; p. 354). It is precisely these relationships of reciprocity and solidarity that are missing from today's urban environment. The model proposed by R-Urban aims at restoring these solidarity relationships through processes that implicitly produce sociability, shared spaces, common values, and affective relationships.

Transformation must occur at the micro scale with each individual, each subjectivity, and this is how a culture of resilience is constructed. As Rob Hopkins puts it, 'resilience is not just an outer process: it is also an inner one, of becoming more flexible, robust and skilled' (Hopkins, 2009, p. 15). The transgression towards a resilient city starts with many individual and collective transgressions. These include processes of reskilling, skill sharing, social network building and mutual learning. These micro-social and micro-cultural practices, which are usually related to individual lifestyles and practices (e.g., growing food and collecting waste, sharing a car, and exchanging tools and skills with neighbours), prompt attention to details, singularities, and the capacities for creativity and innovation that operate at the level of everyday life. R-Urban maps in detail this local capacity to invent and transform but also, in parallel, the administrative constraints that block it, proposing ways of bypassing these constraints through renewed policies and structures. This also involves forms of transgression within the professional practices and institutions and the ways of understanding architecture and urban planning as open source processes and within the role of specialists and professionals as agents of change.

Pioneering R-Urban

R-Urban is on the way. Over the next few years, we will nurture the diverse economies and initiate progressive practices within the R-Urban network in Colombes. We will reactivate cultures of collaboration and sharing. We have designed R-Urban to be a slow and easy to appropriate and replicate process of transgression. We will be testing it for a while, before leaving it to proliferate by itself. Will it succeed? Will it remain transgressive? For how long? These are questions to be answered in a few years. For the present, it is a visionary attempt to encourage more democratic and bottom-up processes of resilient regeneration in a suburban context; it is a process designed specifically to be appropriated and followed up by others in similar contexts.

No radical change will happen in current society without the involvement of the many. Change needs to be multiplied and disseminated rhizomatically, involving a multitude of processes of self-emancipation of people who choose to change their current lifestyle. As suggested by Holloway (2006, p. 2), 'if we want to take seriously the idea of self-emancipation … we need to look at people around us – the people at

Figure I2.3
Agrocité, agro-cultural civic hub, Colombes, June 2013

Figure I2.4
Recyclab, recycling and
eco-construction civic
hub, Colombes, June
2013

work, in the street, in the supermarket – and accept their own way of being rebellious, despite their external appearance. In a self-emancipated world, people shouldn't be taken for what they seem. They are not contained by their assigned identities, which they overpass and break into pieces, going against-and-beyond them'.

R-Urban is for the people who are now 'at work, in the street, in the supermarket'. It is up to them to take the effort further, 'against-and-beyond-themselves', toward a radical change of society. It is a participatory collective transgression towards a resilient city.

Figure I2.5
Agrocité, alternative
economy market,
November 2013

Notes

1 This chapter has evolved from initial versions published by Tyszczuk, Smith, Clark, and Butcher (2012) and Bradley and Hedren (2014); it is reprinted with permission of the editors and publishers.
2 One of the first occasions marking the emergence of this global awareness was the first UN Conference on the Human Environment in Stockholm (1972), followed up by the Nairobi (1982), Rio (1992), Johannesburg (2002), and Rio+20 (2012) meetings. In recent years, such summits have multiplied and diversified in both scope and participants. The Copenhagen Climate Change Conference of 2009 recently exemplified the blockage resulting from the growing conflicts between and opposing interests of major international actors (e.g., governments, corporations, and NGOs), a blockage that paralyses decisions at the global scale.
3 Transition Towns, Incredible Edible, Continuous Productive Urban Landscapes (CPULs), and Ecovillage Networks are a few such initiatives that have started at the local scale and developed into extended networks.
4 For more information, see http://r-urban.net
5 'Fab lab' is short for 'fabrication laboratory', a small-scale workshop equipped with various fabrication machines and tools that enable users to produce 'almost anything'.
6 For more information about the R-Urban cooperative land trust, go to http://r-urban.net/en/property/
7 We are joining here with those political ecologists who criticize the superficial understanding of politics, power, and social construction promoted in resilience rhetoric (see, for example Hornborg, 2009, pp. 237–265).

References

Appadurai, A. (2004) 'The capacity to aspire', in V. Rao and M. Walton (eds), *Cultural and Public Action*. Stamford, CT: Stamford University Press.

Bradley, K and Hedren, J. (2014) *Green Utopianism: Strategies, Perspectives and Micropractices*. London: Routledge.

Gorz, A. (2008) *Manifeste utopia [Manifeste Utopia]*. Brest, France: Edition Parangon.

Holloway, J. (2002) *Change the World Without Taking Power*. London: Pluto Press.

Holloway, J. (2006) 'Un mouvement "contre-et-au-delà": À propos du débat sur mon livre *Changer le monde sans prendre le pouvoir*'. *Variations: Revue internationale de théorie critique*, 18(04), 15–30.

Hopkins, R. (2009) 'Resilience thinking'. *Resurgence*, 257, 12–15.

Hornborg, A. (2009) 'Zero-sum world: Challenges in conceptualizing environmental load displacement and ecologically unequal exchange in the world-system'. *International Journal of Comparative Sociology*, 5(3–4), 237–262.

Lazzarato, M. (2002) *Puissance de l'invention: La psychologie économique de Gabriel Tarde contre l'économie politique* [*Powers of Invention: Gabriel Tarde's Economic Psychology Against Political Economy*]. Paris: Les Empêcheurs de penser en rond.

Lefebvre, H. (1991) *The Production of Space*. New York: Blackwell.

Maguire, B. & Cartwright, S. (2008) 'Assessing a community's capacity to manage change: A resilience approach to social assessment'. Retrieved 14 February 2013 from http://adl.brs.gov.au/brsShop/data/dewha_resilience_sa_report_final_4.pdf

Tyszczuk, R., Smith, J., Clark, N. & Butcher, M. (2012) *ATLAS: Geography, Architecture and Change in an Interdependent World*. London: Black Dog Publishing.

Part II
Violation

Chapter 4

Informal architecture/s

Louis Rice

In a time when architecture has been so distant from the political ground and the social fabric that shapes it, the critical observation of these [informal] settlements ... is a risk worth taking.

(Cruz, 2005: 34)

One billion informal occupants

By the middle of this century, the majority of the world's urban population will be housed in what are variously referred to as: slums, favelas, barrios, shanty-towns, informal cities, arrival cities, invisible cities, self-made cities and shadow cities (Davis, 2006; Dovey & King, 2011; Hernández *et al.,* 2010; Neuwirth, 2005; Saunders, 2012; United Nations, 2009). (For simplicity this chapter conflates all of these typologies under the term 'informal architecture'). At the start of the previous century there were barely any in existence on the planet but at the turn of the millennium one billion people occupied these urban spaces (UN-Habitat, 2006). Within the next decade this will rise to two billion people, a number that continues to rise and rise. The scale of this new development is breathtaking in its scale, every week another million people arrive (United Nations, 2007). Each year, it is the equivalent of building a city the combined size of London, Paris, Rome, New York, Tokyo, Beijing and Sydney.

Through its sheer size alone, this urbanism can barely be ignored any longer. The teeming metropolises of informal development form 'a mountain range of evidence'

(Koolhaas, 1994: 9) which can be considered as a laboratory of experimental informal architecture. There are millions of different buildings, types of construction, mix of uses, social groupings, religious codes, modes of governance and myriad urban forms. Much might be learned from such informal development, although at the beginning of this millennium this research is simply focused on trying to understand and describe the informal city, let alone attempt to 'fix' or 'solve' them. As many commentators have already noted, the informal city defies easy classification and categorization (Dovey, 2012; Lepik, 2013); accordingly, this chapter begins by examining the constitution of informal architecture without attempting to impose any *a priori* categories. Architecture here is not solely concerned with the building as an object; but as we shall see, architecture that transgresses social, material, economic, ecological, ethical and political boundaries.

The chapter begins with four empirical accounts of informal architecture/s that capture some of their everyday qualities, materials, processes and constituents. The chapter then situates these accounts within broader literature concerning informal architecture.

Empirical study 1: Bangkok, Thailand

A large advertising hoarding in Bangkok looms over an informal settlement. Under the gaze of three photoshopped hair models, adjacent to a large highway intersection, sits a small neighbourhood of illegally built housing. The houses are nestled around a widening of the city's old water-canal system. The waterway is used as a place to fish, bathe, swim, do laundry, wash dishes and it also acts as an open sewer and waste disposal unit.

The housing is fairly basic; timber-frame structures (occasionally augmented by additional steel supports and struts) sit in, or adjacent to, the water. Attached to

Figure 4.1
Informal architecture on the waterfront

which are profiled metal sheets and/or timber panel boards along with other found and recycled materials. Overhanging metal roof panels allow space for laundry to be dried, places to sit during the rain, and additional storage area for sundry items. Amidst the buildings and walkways are a variety of large trees and some low-lying shrubs and bushes (some of which are used for their edible fruits, nuts or other bio-produce). Electrical power is accessed by informally tapping into the city's formal power grid. Street lighting is afforded by the glow of the twenty-storey high advertising hoarding that is illuminated throughout the night. Satellite dishes are affixed to some of the houses so the residents can (illegally) view channels such as Sky Sports on demand. The scene is fairly typical of many instances of informal architecture: the condition of sanitation is appalling; the condition of the housing is basic; the condition of the telecommunications is excellent. High-tech and low-tech, organic and natural, synthetic and artificial, new and old, recycled and reclaimed are hybridized.

Empirical study 2: Mumbai, India

A woman stands outside a wall comprised from a range of heterogeneous materials: plastic water containers, old rags, cookers, wooden logs ready for burning, pram wheels ripe for upcycling, acres of blue tarpaulin, timber panelling, rope ties, cord restraints, ladders to access the roof, parked motorbikes, fabric curtains to demark and protect the entrances, lines of washing, folded blankets, chapati drying in the sun, old chairs covered in rugs, some food bubbling away atop a coal-burning stove and a range of things one cannot discern from this picture (but are invariably present): bacteria, oxidization and dirt. This wall forms the very essence of an active frontage – literally and metaphorically.

Figure 4.2
Compound elements

Where the elevation starts, the building ends and the street begins is difficult to discern. It is also difficult to describe the multiplicity of functions, roles and purposes that comprise this architectural element (i.e. 'wall'). What is it by function: a storage facility, security zone, territorial marker, larder, kitchen, living room, garage, car park, front door, window, laundry, dining room, builders' yard, illegal squat or, to talk architecturally, the front elevation (south-facing)? Part of the reason why the architectural term 'wall' is no longer sufficiently accurate to apply in this instance, and why the list of functions is so long, is due partly to the kineticism of its constitution. The construction of this 'wall' is in a state of flux; it is constantly being added to or taken from; parts of it are burned, eaten, become clothing, sat on, dried, hung up, strung out, twisted round, squashed into and myriad other *activities*. A wall of activities – is this a contradiction in terms? A wall, that most immutable and unchangeable of architectural elements, that is simultaneously fabricated from activities.

One set of washing forms the 'elevation' (until the laundry is dry, whereupon it is removed from the elevation) and a different set of washing subsequently constitutes a new elevation. A panel of wood that formed the 'elevation' is dismantled for a while and used as a makeshift worktable. Some of the tarpaulins that cover the 'roof' of the space are moved to form a canopy to protect the entrance from the rain showers in monsoon season (but replaced in the dry seasons). Potentially useful items are found each day and brought back and form another addition to the architectural entity; waiting for a more appropriate application for these sundry items. The 'building' is a swarm of activities *and* profusion of materialities; trying to define exactly what the habitable environment 'is' is difficult as it is neither and both simultaneously. It is some 'other' hybrid entity.

At the micro-level, the use of the architectural term 'wall' does a disservice to the richness, constitution and complexity of such informal physical, social and natural environments. Perhaps it is fairer to merely describe this milieu as some form of 'compound'. The first reason is, as the dictionary defines, a compound is 'a thing that is composed of two or more separate elements'; which captures more accurately this state of construction. Second, this wall-element stretches around the home and forms a compound (in the second meaning of the term). The second meaning of 'compound' is an area enclosed by a border, as for example, in 'military compound', 'secure compound' or 'luxury compound'. The defining aspect of a compound is its edge condition, rather than what it contains. Informal architecture in this instance elides both of these definitions into one spatio-temporal condition. Informal architecture is not constituted by mono-functional walls (and roof) rather it is a compound element, consisting of a range of material, social and natural actors.

Empirical study 3: International airspace.

Informal architecture utilizes the entire gamut of materiality in its lexicon of construction; no material is ruled out as unsuitable. Satellites and open sewers are found in the same space. 'Informal architecture' might encompass nothing more than a thin plastic sheet

Figure 4.3
Informal architecture(s)
amidst the formal city,
as seen from a Boeing
747 window (economy
class)

for a dry place to sleep. At other times, a cardboard box becomes a miniscule dwelling (sometimes for an entire family) – a kind of 'Laugier hut' for the twenty-first century. Both of these forms of informal architecture share a pragmatism and ease of construction. The plastic sheet is 'constructed' by a person literally rolling themselves up in the sheet; the cardboard box can be climbed into, or lain on. More complex architectures are also produced; shelters are erected from profiled metal panels, the metal often reclaimed from oil drums and other waste products. Profiled metal sheets are quick to erect, readily available and easy to handle, however they are very noisy in the rain and are rather prone to rust. Profiled metal sheets used to be the *ne plus ultra* of informal architecture, however this has been usurped by blue tarpaulin. 'Weather dissenters' (Sloterdijk, 2009) looking down from their Boeing 747's now gaze across acres of these soft, blue roofscapes. This burgeoning blueness is a global phenomenon and is recasting many cities under a wash of 'International Slum Blue' (a reference to Yves Klein's 'International Klein Blue'). Tarpaulin has many advantages over other building materials: waterproof, pliable, flexible and lightweight but the principal advantage is financial – tarpaulin is incredibly cheap. The reason 'blue' is the colour of choice is mostly down to economics: blue tarpaulin is usually a thinner grade of material and hence cheaper to produce; blue dye is also cheaper than bleaching the raw materials. Cost is not the only logic behind this choice of colour; blue is also used by the UN for disaster and emergency shelters due to the colour being relatively resistant to deterioration by the sun and to its contrast with the colours of natural materials, which makes it easier to spot dirt and decay. This explains blue tarpaulin's ubiquity across the planet; it is evident in every continent regardless of climate and stretches across all cultural, economic and political boundaries.

Empirical study 4: Bandra, India

The paradox evidenced at the micro-scale of informal architecture, that is, the socio-material heterogeneity of 'wall/compound' construction can also be found at the macro-scale. A multiplicity of programmes, functions, materials, corporeality, activities and performance emerge throughout the daily life of much informal urban space. Urban sites are backfilled with a variety of uses: 'the Lagos superhighway has bus stops on it, mosques under it, markets in it' (Koolhaas, 2001, 686). Solà-Morales (1995) refers to this as 'mixity' – a dense mix of uses, activities, functions and practices hybridized into a single space. This mixity is enacted through a compound of activities and the materials required to facilitate these activities to occur. A single 'space' can change function several times a day and/or share multiple functions simultaneously. Instant

Figure 4.4
**Informal architecture
(with railtracks)**

architectures are effected that may last for a few moments or hours or perhaps may endure longer.

In the depths of a large informal settlement, a narrow alleyway is used as: a (small) factory, a cafe, hairdressers, living room, open market, place to sleep, dining area, storage and footpath – all at the same time. To enable these activities to occur: carpets are dragged out to sit on; hammers, spanners, bolts and nails are brought into the alley; fires are made; scissors/combs and mirrors fashion *al fresco* hairdressing salons; blankets are laid out and impromptu beds are effected out of junk materials. Sociality and spatiality blend into each other. In this empirical study, one afternoon a tired worker takes a break and lies down on a plump sack (full of plastic scraps that are awaiting processing and recycling) to use as a makeshift mattress; shortly afterwards another tired worker uses the body of the now recumbent sleeper as an *ad hoc* pillow. The plastic scraps that now form makeshift bedrooms also obstruct the alley; pedestrians can squeeze past or hop over but it prevents motorcyclists and car drivers from using this as a road – or at least slows them down considerably. The plastic scraps/bedding have inadvertently become a 'sleeping policeman' (the English term for a 'speed-bump') a material intervention that acts to affect human behaviour (Latour, 1992). Rather than trying to maintain all of these entities according to *a priori* classifications, it is far easier to relax/remove the boundaries and permit more fluid transgressions. The sleeping worker (i.e. human) has been transformed into a pillow (i.e. material) as a kind of compound element in this architectural milieu (where humans become materials). In a reverse process, scraps of plastic become sleeping policemen (i.e. materials become human). Industrial materials become soft furnishings, alleys become bedrooms, lunchtime becomes bedtime and temporary factories are infused with dreams. The limits of societal, architectural, spatial and temporal boundaries blend, merge and fuse; in this single situation there is metamorphoses of action, experience, sound, mixity, smells, meaning and performance.

Activity spills out from the informal city and permeates into the formal city. This sometimes overruns the urban spaces of the formal city, which are appropriated temporarily for informal uses. For example, railways are used for a number of different informal purposes. Temporary markets and cafes with goods and wares sprawling across the train-tracks. When a train passes by, all the goods are quickly removed from the rails and the space momentarily transforms back into its official usage (Dovey, 2012). As soon as the train passes, the market reclaims the available space. Laundry is also dried along these railway tracks which works particularly well for this function as the train tracks are often exposed to the sun, the passing trains generate wind and air movement (thus increasing the drying process) and the stones used under sleepers are perfect devices for holding the washing in place. The other important function railway lines serve: *a place for junk*. Crossing through the city, the railway lines serve as huge garbage facilities with all types of waste deposited here (including human waste). A corollary of this is the proliferation of recycling of that waste. Through the day (and sometimes at night) individual scavengers or teams of people work to sift through the junk and convert it back into quasi-precious materials. These linear refuse sites evidence the prodigious recycling activities that occur as part of the broader informal economy.

Almost everything thrown away by the nearby inhabitants (and the materials thrown from the passing trains) are recycled. Entire communities and several generations of families have conquered the sites of dumps with their entrepreneurial dexterity.

Informal urban spaces share the similar constitution of 'compound-ness' found at the micro level, but also at the macro scale. Instant urban conditions are effected by their users, space is appropriated for a bewildering number of different uses simultaneously that function in complex and kinetic ways. Even those 'formal' spaces that bisect informal cities are retrofitted with these compound conditions. The 'architect' is more analogous to a relational set of actors: humans, materials, ecology, politics, territories, economics, society and technology hybridized together in a kinetic system of negotiations, conflicts and dissent.

Processual architecture

The four empirical case-study accounts approached the examination of informal architecture through its configuration as an 'end-product'. That is, in each of the studies, the inhabitations were mostly already built to a substantial degree (albeit there was still a large degree of flux and change in evidence). In order to understand this 'end-product' further, it is helpful to explore the processes through which informal architecture is borne, produced and enacted. This subsection attempts to understand and capture the production of informal architecture 'in action'.

Mass migration from rural areas into urban centres of population creates a shortage of housing; this leads in part to overcrowding and to the construction of new 'housing' (Dovey, 2012). Given much of the migration is driven by economic desperation, these new habitats are constructed incredibly cheaply, quickly and shoddily. Informal architecture is often on appropriated land that is taken by force by, what are pejoratively referred to as, 'invaders' (Brillembourg & Klumpner, 2013); or 'pirates' (Hernández et al., 2010; Davis, 2006). Spatial territory is quickly barricaded with makeshift hoardings or fencing and converted into some form of inhabited encampment. Initially these structures might be partial and tentative – little more than the delimitation of space as more readily defendable territory. These structures are physically held together with cords, ropes, restraints, straps, nails and myriad other ad hoc connectors that bind, wedge, stick, lash, bung, tether and shackle. At all times these physical structures are bound socially; partly out of necessity as a location of habitation, but also as a tactic for 'occupation'. The building would be demolished without the tenants/squatters and it is their presence in conjunction with the material structure that generates a unified territory of resistance. Over time these encampments are modified, expanded, altered, partially demolished and/or upgraded by their occupants to suit individual needs. However the ambiguous legal ownership of land often prohibits tenants from investing too much time and money into property upgrading for fear of eviction at some later point.

Migrants construct their own residences on whatever space they can, using whatever materials are available or at hand. Davis (2006: 19) describes how informal architecture is 'largely constructed out of crude brick, straw, recycled plastic, cement blocks and scrap wood' almost all of which is appropriated from the remains (and left-over space) of the formal city. Many of the migrants modify their own (former) expertise into a means of production for their housing. For example basket-weavers deploy their craft to effect makeshift structures in the city such as small tents woven from reeds and organic produce brought when they migrated from the rural areas; metal-workers modify oil drums and tin sheets into encampments; carpenters develop structures from discarded pieces of wood. Sometimes these constructions become relatively durable, in the sense that they are fabricated from reinforced concrete and bricks.

(*Illegal*) squatting of existing buildings is also employed as a tactic of occupation; such as the appropriation of derelict spaces, disused factories, offices and commercial properties. Invaders 'hack' into existing buildings to gain unauthorized access and make *ad hoc* modifications. Over time the new inhabitants have made modifications and hacks to the original building. 'The term hacking is often simply understood as the process of improving and rebuilding … via unconventional means' (Baraniuk, 2013: 36). Throughout these squatted buildings there are ongoing alterations, updates, demolitions, interventions and insertions enacted by the residents. Spatial-hacking such as this enables informal architecture to modify, recode and rebuild with (to prolong the technological metaphors) the latest apps, upgrades and plug-ins. A startling illustration of which is the 'The Tower of David' a 45-storey building in Caracas. This skyscraper was initially designed to be the headquarters for a large petrochemical company and (partly) built during the previous economic boom but abandoned during an economic crash. The building was left partially unfinished by the original developer: some elevations were fully clad in curtain walls of mirrored glass (ready for air conditioned interiors); other elevations were left only as the raw concrete structure, the building abandoned before all the curtain walling could be installed. The invading inhabitants took the building by force and have subsequently created the world's tallest squatter settlement (Schmid, 2013). Initially the inhabitants used the existing structure as a space in which to make temporary encampments. The 'unfinished' elevations have since been completed by the three thousand inhabitants who have taken up residence there; each of the many families and social groupings have produced different elevations to meet their requirements. The building now boasts a church, cafes, hairdressers, shops, a gym, grocery stores, a tailors, stationery shop, basketball court and these are partially expressed in the inchoate elevations. The 'finished' elevations, which were comprised of mirrored curtain walling, have also been modified by residents. Some of the glass panels have been removed to allow greater airflow through the building. This is an example of a more 'sustainable' informal architecture through the provision of natural ventilation brought about by the occupiers' actions. The elevation now has an ambiguous state: the finished elevations are becoming unfinished; the unfinished elevations are becoming finished; it is perhaps no longer relevant to attempt to apply these terms. The elevations are neither finished or unfinished, finishing nor finishable. The elevations are in a liminal state – part of the ongoing, processual development of this inhabitation.

The production of informal architecture involves iterations of construction to compose and form new architecture/s; simultaneously the situation becomes more complicated and complex. The process of occupying space, consolidating territory and generating a more robust habitat is a temporal event. In these modes of occupation and production of space there is a processual quality to the architecture. These processes are not exclusively social events, for example, they are not protests or crowds of people at rallies (who eventually disperse); nor are these actions wholly physical/material. Instead there is a mutually constitutive inter-relationship. Occupation is both a spatial *and* social process (as well as political). Informal architecture does not have a finish-point or apotheosis to which repairs and renovations are directed. Informal architecture is always 'under construction' – it is in a constant state of upgrading, alteration, repairs and modification. Space is coded, decoded, recoded and encoded through these actions. Informal architecture is open-ended in its evolution. Modifications are part of a (potentially) endless series of iterations that compound the initial situation contingent to emergent contextual processes.

Resistance

Whilst informal architecture is sometimes portrayed as a domain of the weak, unfortunate and powerless, there is an alternative rendering of the situation.

> We must cease once and for all to describe the effects of power in negative terms: it 'excludes', it 'represses', it 'censors', it 'abstracts', it 'masks', it 'conceals'.
>
> (Foucault, 1991: 194)

As Cruz (2005: 34) points out 'we cannot forget that they are the product of resistance and transgression'. Informal architecture is the embodiment of resistance against the dominant/ruling elite. Even the UN (2001: 121–2) defines informality through this transgressive resistance: 'land to which the occupant have no legal claim, or which they occupy illegally'. Informal architecture often arises from deliberate acts of defiance against official institutions and governmental organizations. The invasions are tactical manoeuvres enacted spatially that subvert hegemonic power structures. Rancière (2010) refers to such tactics as dissensus; where transgressive acts, dissent against the norm/elite and conflictual relationships offer the potential for emancipatory action. The formal city and its attendant systems 'of discourses, institutions, architectural forms, regulatory decisions, laws, (and) administrative measures' (Foucault, 1980: 194) are not only challenged through the production of informal architecture; but are transformed, distorted, renegotiated and modified. Informal architecture forces a decoding and recoding of the formal city.

Perhaps it is obvious to state, but this resistance is not restricted to social or political acts; they are not rallying in the streets outside the government's headquarters or surrounding the presidential palace with protestors. This resistance movement is embodied in the material and physical realm of informal architecture and enacted through its production and re-production. This spatial, social and political resistance through occupation is often portrayed as a quasi-military act. The language used by commentators derives from those used by the army: 'tactics of invasion' (Cruz, 2005: 33); 'invasion' (Brillembourg & Klumpner, 2013: 145b); 'endless war on the streets' (Davis, 2006: 202). Informal architecture and each of its constituent structures, houses and spaces, form a guerrilla army of resistance. This is an army of materiality; battalions of junk materials, recycled scrap, brigades of metal sheets, tarpaulin, faeces, dirt, hoarding, laundry, fabrics, rope ties and woven canopies. The fabric of the informal city is a political and military act in itself. Social organizations within informal architecture(s) run their own economies, civil movements, transport systems, health facilities, sports sites and other civic and cultural facilities. There is resistance against police and other enforcement agencies; squatters often create their own security forces. Some informal architectures operate outside of all forms of governmental control; they exist entirely outside the law (Agamben, 1998). Informal architecture has resisted multiple attempts for its destruction and attests to its durability and resilience as a form of resistance. The presence of informal architecture attests to the possibility for resisting, challenging, transgressing and subverting dominant politico-spatial power relations.

The limits of (informal) architecture

Before commenting further on informal architecture it is important to reiterate their problems and issues. There are many positive and innovative aspects to informal architecture, however it is clear there are serious flaws and drawbacks. The conditions in slums are appalling in many ways: poor sanitation, hygiene and health infrastructure causes relatively high mortality rates, particularly amongst children (United Nations, 2009). Pollution and contamination levels are often at dangerous levels. Human excrement is a particularly difficult waste product to dispose of, often the only solution is to use plastic bags and throw these out of the window. Fire can be devastating as the dense footprint facilitates rapid spread of fire with few opportunities for escape combined with difficult access for firefighters. Safety can also be an issue, some locations are controlled by criminal gangs, often fuelled by drug traffic and other organized crime (Mowforth & Munt, 2008). In certain neighbourhoods, even the police may not enter safely and the military intervene, portrayed vividly by Davis (2006: 206): 'helicopter gunships stalk enigmatic enemies in the narrow streets of slums districts, pouring hellfire into shanties'.

Koolhaas insists that 'people can inhabit anything' (1996) which is a tantalizing polemic, yet evidently untrue. We cannot inhabit *anything* although informal architecture steers close to the limit (and sometimes beyond). The appallingly high death rate evinces the fallacy of this polemic statement. There are some locations where inhabitation is attempted that exceed the biological limits of human existence – i.e. many desperate people die, or become seriously ill, testing the limits of architecture. It goes almost without saying that these extreme locations exceed the ethical limits of what is considered habitable. Yet regardless of deliberations concerning what humans 'should' do, or how humans 'ought' to live, almost no location is deigned unsuitable 'in practice'.

Informal settlements occupy the spaces on the brink of what is habitable (by humans) – conditions on 'the limits of architecture' (Schmid, 2013: 387). Contaminated sites, dumps and places of pollution, considered uninhabitable by the residents of the formal city, are aggregated into the informal city (Koolhaas, 2003) Precipitous mountains of mud, unstable hills, subsiding land and other 'hazardous locations' considered too steep to build on by city planners and civil engineers, become the site for informal architecture (United Nations Human Settlements Programme, 2003:19). Similarly, river floodplains and tidal zones are prevalent locations sometimes producing settlements that literally ebb and flow with the tides (Dovey & King, 2011). Thousands of homes are washed away annually and with them intolerably high death rates; in Pakistan alone 18 million people were affected by floods in 2010 and 'most have returned home to destroyed homes' (BBC, 2011). Fatalities expose the raw truth behind life in informal architecture, it can be a dangerous and precarious existence. Koolhaas was close in his statement, but perhaps more accurately it should have read: 'people can inhabit anything – or die trying'.

Informal architecture has chronic issues, but even the act of *researching* informal architecture is problematic. 'Learning' from the informal city is beset with innumerable difficulties that are often not present when researching the formal city. Slums as research destinations are sometimes criticized as colonialist, unethical and/or a form of 'research tourism' (Mowforth & Munt, 2009). 'Accessing' the slums is relatively difficult as researchers are invariably visitors rather than constituent actors and most slums are located in the 'global South' yet most research institutions are not (Peritore, 1999). Informal architecture has no (or few) institutions to represent itself, its histories and narratives are written from the outside by outsiders. Many of the researchers are more akin to ghostwriters of informal architecture. Cruz (2005: 34) warns: 'it is clear that, very easily, one risks romanticizing and, patronizing their fragile conditions'; a point echoed by Dovey (2012: 363) 'urban informality is too often either demonized as the virus that must be removed or romanticized as the plight of the poor'. Rather than casting a verdict on which theorists are correct or whether a certain point is right or wrong, the pertinent concern is that these judgements are being made at all. These judgements form yet another series of 'materials' from which informal architecture is constituted. The 'compound' that already comprises myriad materials, activities and processes is also suffused with ideology, semiotics, risk, romance, demons and ethics.

Conclusions

> The architecture of informality is to undertake the task of informalizing architectural practice and a rethinking of professional ideology, architectural theory and education.
>
> Dovey (2013: 86)

A note on methodology

The chapter is primarily focused on learning from informal architecture. However, the chapter is partly methodological in focus through its attempt to construct/register the process of 'translation' from a built environment (in this instance from myriad slums, shanty towns, informal settlements and favelas) into an architectural theory. A new lexicon is required to translate between formal architecture and informal architecture: a language that can imbricate the social, political and natural networks into material and spatial domains. Some theorists have attempted to capture these ambiguous worlds, for example: quasi-objects (Serres, 2007); hybrids (Latour, 1993); assemblages (Deleuze & Guattari, 1988); cyborgs (Haraway, 1991); actor-networks (Law & Hassard, 1999); dispositif (Foucault, 1980) and foams (Sloterdijk, 2004). This chapter does not attempt to delve too deeply into this emerging terrain of linguistics and neologisms, other than note the embryonic state of its existence. The methodological aim is not to attempt to apply an existing theoretical framework or readymade conceptual model as a means for analysing informal architecture; nor is it to use a theory to design architecture; nor to invent a theory to use for investigation. The aim is to unearth/register the process through which the existing informal 'real' world can be translated into a conceptual model (and in this instance towards a predominantly *architectural* theory).

Towards an informal architecture

The existing terminology for formal architecture is relatively good at describing a static, immutable material world of bricks, glass and steel. However it is of limited use when attempting to interpret informal architecture as it lacks a vocabulary that can ascribe its myriad qualities. Standard architectural elements such as a wall or roof do not suffice in the description and/or analysis of the constitution of informal construction. For example, there is a lacuna of devices that can be employed to interrogate the action-*icity* of informal architecture; i.e. a description of compound elements that come and go, dissolve, emerge, encrust, effervesce and are constantly 'under construction'. 'Other' entities need to be enrolled into the constitution of informal architecture.

The notion of 'compound' has emerged (*a posteriori*) through this research to help describe the constitution of an architecture of informality. Elements of spatial and territorial inhabitation are compounds of materiality, sociality, semiotics and politics. It is this 'space' of events and actions that defines and constitutes informal architecture. Coterminous to the notion of a compound element (something composed from a hybrid of different entities) is that of the boundary condition which amalgamates heterogeneous internal contents. Perhaps paradoxically, such compounds are unified by their boundaries and limits, not by their contents. Both of these conceptions of compound focus on informal architecture as the 'object' of study, rather than the means of production and performance of that object. However, informal architecture is inherently processual. Its materiality is imbricated with actions, activities and flux. Informal architectures are formed and *per*-formed through social practices, biological agents, natural entities and political action suffused with proliferating meanings, semiotics and resistance. These interpretations of the notion of compound are found at a variety of scales, from the micro scale of informal architecture, at the scale of the body, the hand, the architectures of sitting, lying and standing – all the way through to the macro scale: neighbourhood, urban and now at a global scale. This global phenomenon attests to the power of informal architecture to resist the hegemonic forces at play. Whilst still strongly embedded within global capitalism, there is hope that in its dissidence and transgression lies the potential for recoding a more hopeful future.

Informal architecture will be the *de facto* mode of inhabitation for the majority of humanity this century, but it is an architecture that is barely understood. Informal architecture is a perplexing, abstruse phenomenon and challenges our knowledge/s of the built (and natural) environment. As a laboratory of experiments it is unparalleled in magnitude and breadth; one billion people already testify to this most Promethean of experiments in living. The limits of architecture are being re-set everyday through the lives (and deaths) of these inhabitants.

References

Agamben, G. (1998) *Homo Sacer: Sovereign Power and Bare Life*. Stanford, CA: Stanford University Press.

Baraniuk, C. (2013) 'Civic hackers: Techies volunteer to rescue government', *New Scientist* 2923: 36–9. 29 June.

BBC (2011) 'Pakistan floods still claiming lives'. Available from: http://www.bbc.co.uk/news/special_reports/pakistan_floods/ . [Accessed 09 January2014].

Brillembourg, A. and Klumpner, H. (2013) 'i: Past', in A. Brillembourg. and H. Klumpner (eds) *Torre David. Informal Vertical Communities*, 70–129. Zurich: Lars Muller Publishers..

Cruz, T. (2005) 'Tijuana case study tactics of invasion: manufactured sites', *Architectural Design* 75 (5): 32–7.

Davis, M. (2006) *Planet of Slums.* London: Verso.

Deleuze, G. and Guattari, F. (1988) *A Thousand Plateaus*. London: Athlone Press.

Dovey, K. (2012) 'Informal urbanism and complex adaptive assemblage', *International Development Planning Review* 34 (4): 349–67.

Dovey, K. (2013) 'Informalising architecture: the challenge of informal settlements', *Archit Design* 83: 82–89.

Dovey, K. and King, R. (2011) 'Forms of informality: morphology and visibility of informal settlements', *Built Environment* 37 (1): 11–29.

Foucault, M. (1980) 'The confession of the flesh', in C. Gordon (ed) *Power/knowledge: Selected interviews and other writings, 1972–1977 by Michel Foucault,* 194–228. Hemel Hempstead: Harvester Press.

Foucault, M. (1991) *Discipline and Punish: The Birth of the Prison*. London: Penguin Books.

Haraway, D. J. (1991) *Simians, Cyborgs, and Women*. London: Free Association.

Hernández, F., Kellett, P.W., Lea, K. and Allen, L.K. (eds) (2010) *Rethinking the Informal City: Critical Perspectives from Latin America*. Oxford: Berghahn Books.

Koolhaas, R. (1994) *Delirious New York*. New York: Monacelli Press.

Koolhaas, R. (1996) 'In interview with Katrina Heron. From Bauhaus to Koolhaas' *Wired* 4 (7), available from: http://archive.wired.com/wired/archive/4.07/koolhaas.html (accessed 12 August 2013).

Koolhaas, R. (2001) *Mutations*. Barcelona: Actar.

Koolhaas, R. (2003) 'Lagos', in R. Koolhaas and V. Bregtje, *Lagos Wide & Close, An Interactive Journey Into an Exploding City.* The Netherlands: Submarine DVD.

Koolhaas, R. & Harvard Design School Project on the City (2001) 'Lagos', in S. Boeri, S. Kwinter, N. Tazi, and H.U. Obrist (eds) *Mutations,* 650–720. Barcelona: Actar.

Latour, B. (1992) 'Where are the missing masses?', in E. Wiebe and J. Law (eds) *Shaping Technology/Building Society: Studies in Sociotechnical Change,* 225–58. Cambridge, MA: MIT Press.

Latour, B. (1993) *We Have Never been Modern*. Cambridge, MA: Harvard University Press.

Law, J. and Hassard, J. (eds) (1999) *Actor Network Theory and After*. Oxford: Blackwell.

Lepik, A. (2013) 'Introduction: an experiment with three thousand participants', in A. Brillembourg and H. Klumpner (eds) *Torre David. Informal Vertical Communities*, 29–51. Zurich: Lars Muller Publishers.

Mowforth, M. and Munt, I. (2009) *Tourism and Sustainability: Development, Globalisation and New Tourism in the Third World*. London: Routledge.

Neuwirth, R. (2005) *Shadow Cities: A Billion Squatters, A New Urban World*. London: Routledge.

Peritore, N.P. (1999) *Third World Environmentalism: Case Studies from the Global South*. Gainesville, FL: University Press of Florida.

Rancière, J. (2010) *Dissensus: On Politics and Aesthetics*. London: Continuum.

Saunders, D. (2012) *Arrival City.* London: Vintage Books.

Schmid, C. (2013) 'Afterword: urbanization as an open process', in A Brillembourg and H. Klumpner (eds) *Torre David. Informal Vertical Communities,* 384–87, Zurich: Lars Muller Publishers.

Serres, M. (2007) *The Parasite*. Minneapolis, MN: University of Minnesota Press.

Sloterdijk, P. (2004) *Sphären: 3 Schäume*. Frankfurt: Suhrkamp.

Sloterdijk, P. (2009). *Terror from the Air.* Los Angeles, CA: Semiotext(e).

Solà-Morales, I. (1995) 'Terrain vague', in C.C. Davidson (ed.) *Anyplace*, 118–23. New York: Anyone Corporation.

UN-Habitat (2006) *The State of The World's Cities*. London: Earthscan.

United Nations (2001) *Indicators of Sustainable Development. Frameworks and Methodologies.* Report number: DESA/DSD/2001/3. New York: United Nations, Department of Economic and Social Affairs

United Nations (2007) *World Urbanization Prospects The 2007 Revision.* New York: United Nations.

United Nations (2009) *State of the World's Cities: 2008/2009: Harmonious Cities*. London: Earthscan.

United Nations Human Settlements Programme (2003) *Slums of the World: The Face of Urban Poverty in the New Millennium?* Nairobi: UN-Habitat.

Chapter 5

Diffuse transgression

Making the city in the margins of the law

Dana Vais

Introduction: Margins

Post-communist urban development has often been described as being determined by prevailing informality and widespread illegalities. This view presumed a clear divide between the formal and the informal, between law and illegality in the making of urban space. But at a closer look, it is this very divide that is questionable. Law could be transgressed without being broken, through overlaps and gaps existing in the law itself. It is often in these margins of legality that the city is made.

These margins are the kind that can be found at the very core of a system, in our case the formal system that rules over urbanism and architecture. They are edges of approximation and indetermination of the law itself, not peripheries of illegality. They concern liminality, not marginality; they have a neutral, not a negative sense. The notion of *transgression* is therefore most relevant in this context. It introduces subtler nuances and continuity in what usually seems to be a clear opposition. In Foucault's definition, transgression 'is not related to the limit as black to white, the prohibited to the lawful, the outside to the inside'; 'transgression has its entire space in the line it crosses' (Foucault 1977: 35,34). It is not the escape beyond this line that is therefore interesting about these margins, but the possibility to make use of the substantiality of the line itself. Transgression is about 'the distance that it opens at the heart of the limit' (Foucault 1977: 35). In our context, transgression 'opens a distance' inside the limit between the formal and the informal in urban development. We are not facing a radical evasion into informality, but rather a diffuse way of dealing with the formal informally.

Formal and informal

It is hardly a revelation that the legal system itself allows such approximations in general. 'Law is notoriously indeterminate and ambivalent', as legal anthropologists Monique Nuijten and Gerhard Anders remarked (2007: 14). There is 'room for manoeuvre inherent to the legal order', a 'wide margin' which is opened by 'the indeterminacy of the law and the gap between abstract legal rules and actual real life situations' (ibid.) In urban development, this 'room for manoeuvre' is often used, and the Romanian case may give us insights into this 'wide margin' of the law. Indeed, it was not the outright lawless condition that was most relevant for how Romanian cities have evolved during these last two decades, but rather the uncertain way a Western-like system of regulation has been gradually internalized. Although sheer illegalities have been an issue, it is the oscillation of the legal frame itself that turned out to be the most consequential for the making of the city: derogatory urbanism and derogation as a rule; retroactive legalization of illegal developments; duplicitous regulation of property restitution and privatization producing conflicting overlapped ownerships; privatization of urban planning itself, leading to conflicts of interest; delayed or impossible enforcement of urban regulation, and so on.

The first 'Law of Urbanism' in post-communist Romania has been enacted in 2001.[1] During the 1990s, for about a decade after the fall of the communist regime, urbanism had evolved without properly regulating new developments, in a kind of 'legal vacuum', as sociologist Iván Tosics called it (2004: 4). Informal construction activities became a significant feature of Romanian cities.

Informalization has been the main characteristic of the entire Balkan region, as urbanist Kai Vöckler remarked. It was generated by the 'unfettered neo-liberal capitalism', 'with a weak city oversight or even an outright lack of regulation' (Vöckler 2010: 186). In his opinion, the informal quality even produced a 'distinctive type of urbanization', which he called 'turbo-urbanism': like turbo engines, cities were accelerating into 'new construction booms'. In other words, informality not only resulted from, but also fuelled the most intensive post-communist urban developments.

However, in Romania the most substantial wave of urban constructions – the 'turbo' momentum of a 'boom' – didn't in fact occur during the years of predominant informality. The first wave came in around 2003–2004, most obviously after the 2001 law regulated urbanism and the architectural profession; it was also triggered by a series of land restitution laws enacted between 1997–2000.[2] A second wave, following the global real estate boom and the EU accession, came in 2007–2008. So 'construction booms' were not due to informal building and 'legal vacuum', but quite the contrary, precisely to the intensified momentum that emerged when the legal 'void' has begun to be superseded by an increasingly formal planning regulation system. In fact, the mixture between the formal and the informal in urban development was more stimulating than informality alone.

Moreover, the law itself gave its consent for the informal to pervade the formal by introducing the large possibility of derogation; this is called in Romania 'derogatory urbanism'. The very first law that regulated post-communist urbanism in 2001 specifically allowed urban regulation to be relativized: a privately promoted Urban Design Plan could easily deviate from the General Land Use Plan. The law also introduced the 'opportunity notice', which made almost any project that does not comply with regulations still be eligible for approval, if convincingly lobbied as 'opportune'. What is important to stress is that derogation became the norm in urban development; it was not only the exceptional case, but the regular practice. The habit to transgress the formal system was produced by the system itself.

Derogatory practice has been much decried in Romania, and for good reason: it impeded any coherent general visions of the city development; it created the chaos of uncontrolled city expansions; it allowed the destruction of green spaces and increased environmental problems; it stimulated the excesses of private projects and their abuse over public space; it led to an explosion of litigation which affected investment; it fed corruption, by giving public officials too much margin to negotiate. Actually, this is the idea of 'permissive planning' and it is not a Romanian thing; it is the epitome of neo-liberal urban development policies. Although any interpretations are context based and have to be relativized, very similar criticisms have been raised in Western Europe too. For instance, planner Barrie Needham (2005: 327–9) wrote about Dutch spatial planning that it may seem 'a patchwork' of 'legal inconsistencies', with too many flexibility clauses allowing building permits to be granted contrary to the land-use plan, and even large-scale deviations from the plan, seriously weakening its legal significance; also, municipalities sometimes turn the blind eye on illegal constructions. 'Dutch practice is strongly influenced by informal ways of using formal rule', Needham concludes (Needham 2005: 336). In the UK too, the notion of 'discretionary planning'[3] concerns a deliberate 'blurring' between the certainties of legal limitations and the possibility of 'unhealthy arbitrariness in the policy process', as planner Philip Booth writes (1999: 31–2). Booth shows that it is the law[4] itself that 'weakens the link between plan and development control decisions'. All these sound perfectly in tune with the Romanian context.

After Romania's EU accession in 2007, with Western assistance, attempts were made to produce a stricter legislation. In order to inform a Romanian code of urbanism, French governmental experts were invited to make a report in February 2007; this clearly condemned the practice of 'private urbanism' (Peylet *et al.*, 2007). A first try to limit derogatory urbanism was made by a governmental ordinance in 2008;[5] private urban projects were allowed no more than 20 per cent excess over the maximum limit imposed by public plans. Indeed, the margin of transgression has been precisely calculated; it is transgression's role 'to measure the excessive distance that it opens at the heart of the limit' (Foucault 1977: 35). However, it was only in 2011 that another ordinance actually ended with derogations. Making reference to a series of European documents, the act specifically aimed at 'the drastic reduction of the practices of derogatory urbanism' and condemned its consequences.[6] The ordinance came into effect in February 2012. 'Derogatory urbanism' had endured for more than a decade.

The only problem with its termination was that it didn't work. In September 2012, the new act was already contested as too restrictive. For instance, it limited the right of making local area plans (LAP) to the public administration exclusively. As local governments don't have the proper staff and resources to do that, land in insufficiently regulated areas remained simply unbuildable. The new law has been perceived as the outright top-down intervention set up against all private initiative.[7] A new law reinstating the possibility of derogations was enacted in February 2013. LAP may be again privately initiated in the interest of a parcel only. Moreover, the law granted tacit approval to all private projects submitted to the local administration that were not answered in due time. This introduced an informal kind of permit by delay, and thus the potential of clean corruption: the occult power of authorization by doing nothing. In spite of the opposition from the civil society, the law came into effect in July 2013. After only 17 months of break, 'derogatory urbanism' – the lawful transgression of urban regulation, the formal legitimation of informal practice – has been reinstated. What is it that makes this complicity between the formal and the informal so enduring?

'Lawscape'

An answer could be found in what legal theorist Andreas Philippopoulos-Mihalopoulos calls 'lawscape'. He describes the relationship between law and the city as a 'continuum' (Philippopoulos-Mihalopoulos 2007: 7); 'lawscape' is the field in which law and urban space continually make each other. It is this continuity that also explains the 'permeability between legality and illegality' (Philippopoulos-Mihalopoulos 2007: 15) in urban space. Law becomes inescapable and permeates everything. It infuses both the formal and the informal; no object is independent from its normative effect. There is an informal sense of normativity itself, which allows law to make itself invisible. 'This is the paradox', Philippopoulos-Mihalopoulos (2012: 8) writes, 'the more universal the law, the more diffused it is. The more diffused it is, the more anomic a space appears.'

Indeed, at a closer look into Romanian urban 'lawscape', even the 'legal vacuum' of the 1990s was far from being a void. A law has regulated building permits since 1991[8] and there were also other laws consequential for urbanism which were enacted during that decade, especially privatization and restitution laws. Even if it was nothing like the communist state, the new state was already there. However, there was a general sense that the state was all but absent, and its legal system as well. Law's indistinctness was increased by its frequent change. The legal context has been considered 'transitory' for a very long time in Romania. Legislation in urbanism has changed eleven times only since the 2001 law (Ivanov 2013).[9] Even if most of these changes were actually minor, the perception was one of incessant hesitation and instability of the legal frame. Law was indeed diffuse and dissimulated in the urban 'lawscape'.

Philippopoulos-Mihalopoulos remarks that by the process of diffusing and dissimulating, the force of law becomes a kind of 'smooth, anomic atmosphere' (2012: 2). It is this 'atmosphere of law' that covers the lawscape and explains law's elusiveness in it. Philippopoulos-Mihalopoulos takes this notion from philosopher Peter Sloterdijk. It was Sloterdijk's idea that bodies are best affected through their environment rather than by targeting the bodies themselves; Philippopoulos-Mihalopoulos too observes that all laws that 'categorize, determine and restrict urban space' – such as planning law, property law, environmental law, health and safety regulations etc. – target the environment by controlling its 'atmosphere', and it is precisely this 'diffusing manoeuvre' that has 'the greatest impact on the body' (2012: 8). There is only one atmosphere and it 'does not let bodies escape' (2012: 7); everything is engulfed by it. Through this diffuse indirect strategy, law becomes eventually effective.

Sloterdijk (2006) calls this 'field of efficacy' the *nomotop*; this is actually the original name for lawscape. However, unlike lawscape, the *nomotop* is centered. It is the 'insulated human groups' that each generate a field of 'valid law as an apparatus of obligatory principles, and as a coercive normative reality', in order to preserve 'social statics' (Sloterdijk 2006: 1–3). 'State and statics stem from a common source', Sloterdijk remarks (2006: 4). From buildings to institutions, 'statics has become The First Science', and this shows, in his opinion, 'the inner link between the two arts of building: the building of norms and the building of houses' (2006: 4). Indeed, architecture is in general for Sloterdijk a favourite metaphor for social structures, because architecture is 'the art of immersion',

> the original form in which the immersion of humans in artificial environments has been developed into a culturally controlled process ... a sort of basic version of immersion technology, while urbanism is the developed stage.
>
> (Sloterdijk 2011: 105)

It is the greenhouse, the most explicit type of an artificially air-conditioned interior, that Sloterdijk often refers to. The city as *polis* has something of a 'greenhouse theory', he says; it is 'in essence nothing other than a construct ruled by *nomos*', 'a very artificial way for people to live together' under shared laws (Sloterdijk 2005: 946). But in which the atmospheric *nomotop* is specifically concerned, the model of pneumatic architecture serves best. In the case of 'air structures' and 'the pneumatic cupola', Sloterdijk observes, it is precisely the 'slight excess pressure in the interior', 'the principle of stabilization ... through atmospheric tension', that keeps the structure standing. It is 'the production of the group-specific excess pressure or pulling tension that binds the group members' together', Sloterdijk concludes (2006: 4–5). Excess is constitutive for social stability.

Excess

Transgression is excess by definition: 'transgression is that which exceeds boundaries or exceeds limits', as sociologist Chris Jencks writes (2003:7). He takes from Georges Bataille the idea that transgression is not in itself subversive or a deliberate challenge to the law, but it naturally concerns 'a surplus of energy', a human need to 'consume excess' and 'create waste' (Jencks 2003: 102–3). In which urban space is concerned, architect Andrea Branzi remarked on the importance of excess, when he wrote that, in the 'weak and diffuse' city of the twenty-first century, the 'energies of society' would be indeed 'overflowing every possible designed form of containment' (Branzi 2006:24). The city as embodiment of the *nomotop* or lawscape evolves and preserves its statics through the atmosphere of law, which is 'the excess of affect that keeps bodies together', as Philippopoulos-Mihalopoulos put it (2012: 7). In other words, excess creates a stabilizing entity effect over the multiplicity that is the city.

'A singular, yet multiple folding', this is how legal theorists Anne Bottomley and Nathan Moore (2008: 573) describe the relationship between law and the city. They introduce a distinction between 'law and control', control being the continuous regulation and 'diagram of law'. Otherwise stated, there is the system of law as an entity on the one hand and the diffuse (they say 'blurred') multiple regulations on the other. This distinction is relevant, for instance, in derogatory urbanism, where a too permissive law does not actually undermine itself, but on the contrary the entire system becomes more resilient on the whole by transferring all the exceeding pressure lower, on the diffuse level of control.

Derogations open a multiplicity of inner margins at the heart of the system. In Bottomley and Moore's words, the 'folds' in the 'diagram of law' are 'characterized by a certain brittleness' (Bottomley and Moore 2008: 574). According to an interesting observation they make, what happens in these margins is regularly pushed at a maximum limit; there is a constant realignment 'upon a maximum degree'.

> This maximum degree is then mistakenly taken as a type of truth, allowing the limit to become all defining. Law then tends to play with this maximum, crossing its boundary in the names of transgression and inclusion.
>
> (Bottomley and Moore 2008 574)

For the space of the city, Branzi too observed this attraction for the extremes, when he wrote that 'spaces for play' appear as so much the more vital in a world all-defined by formal limits; these become, he says, the 'extreme margins of survival' (Branzi 2006: 37). However, what is important to stress here is not the very fact of crossing beyond the limits of law, the literal transgression, but rather the urge of keeping the maximum proximity to them. Chris Jencks writes that 'though diffuse and ill-defined, the limits, the margins' took a greater role, because 'asociality or chaos' became 'ever more vivid' when in greater immediacy to them (Jencks 2003: 4). It is the closeness to the limit, not the very act of crossing it, that is the most empowering. This close transgression can be benign, as Branzi envisions it, or malign, as Jencks implies; the principle is the same.

Illustrations for the maximizing value of the proximity with a legal limit could be found in the Romanian context. A group of residential developments built in Cluj between 2007–2011, for instance (Figure 5.1), nicknamed by the local press the 'blocks in the forest', are playing with several sorts of limits. They eat into the woodland limiting the city, which is an obvious abuse over green space; however, their relation to legality is blurry. The point is that these blocks have been built precisely during the interval in which a series of laws protecting green space was in the making. Green spaces have only been properly regulated in Romania since 2005; several successive

amendments of the law have been enacted until 2012. There was a delay before the law could work properly, for instance it took some time while the registers of green spaces, demanded by the law, were actually made. It was a delay that proved to be most fertile for developers, who promptly exploited the value that came from the certainty of a future interdiction. The fact that these blocks were built as close as possible to a legal impossibility was what made them attractive to the market: it was part of their value. The most effective transgression is indeed the one that keeps nearest to the limits of the law.

Figure 5.1
**Blocks 'in the forest',
Cluj, 2007–11**

Bottomley and Moore observe that if the law is on the whole permissive, this fact only transfers the pressure of normalization to smaller scales; 'massive denormalization is undertaken only to ensure a miniaturized, and more virulent, renormalization at a lower level', they write (2008: 574). Excess practised on lowest urban scales can be illustrated by a trick some Romanian architects devised in order to exceed the maximum floor area ratio (FAR) limit imposed by local regulations. Pressure is enforced on each plot of urban land – the parcel – to maximize its efficiency. (Figure 5.2) The maximum FAR limit allowed by local regulation is reached in a building concentrated at one side, leaving a large portion of the land unbuilt. Then the parcel is cut in two, with a minimum open space left around the new building; the unbuilt area becomes a 'new' parcel, on which the process starts again, with another construction on one side; the scheme is repeated until the ability of the plot to produce 'new' parcels is exhausted. It is a transgression process in successive small steps. Taken separately, each step observes the letter of the regulation; each new parcel, at the moment of its construction, has the new building rigorously respecting the allowed FAR to the limit, without exceeding it. However, the overall result for the initial parcel substantially exceeds it. The limits imposed by local regulation are clearly transgressed, but in a way that is not explicitly illegal. Actually, the moments of transgression do occur not by breaking the rule itself, but as successive redefinitions of the situation in which the rule applies.

These kinds of practices eventually could raise the question of corruption. The law itself, instating derogatory urbanism, with stipulations such as 'opportunity

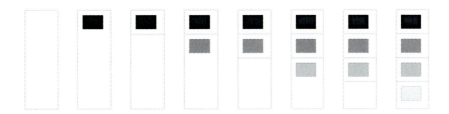

Figure 5.2
Diagram illustrating the steps by which the FAR limit of a parcel may be transgressed
Building to the maximum limit, subdivision, building on the new parcel to the maximum limit, subdivision, and so on, until the possibility of subdividing into 'new' parcels is exhausted

notices' or 'tacit approvals', actually encourages corruption. Good governance would now require local administration to come up with positive actions of additional control, not simply to abide by the law; the law itself, in itself, is not enough. As Monique Nuijten and Gerhard Anders have shown in legal theory, there is a hidden continuity between corruption and law in general; it is the secret of law that 'the possibility of its transgression or perversion is always already inscribed into the law as hidden possibility' (Nuijten and Anders 2007: 12). It does not mean corruption is invincible; it means it could be efficiently fought mostly at the lower diffuse level of control and only by active everyday practice.

Life

Eventually, what truly makes the city is not the letter of the law itself, but how it is lived out in every particular situation. Studying the making of law, Bruno Latour remarked that French administrative law is entirely jurisprudence – not code-based law but a precedent-based legal corpus entirely fabricated by judges over a long time. It is difficult to make generalizations about law and it is impossible to make absolute perfect laws. Compared to science and technology, which 'are supposed to be universal', 'law is so provincial, so stubbornly local' (Latour 2010: vi). But if law is not universal it does not mean it is not total. 'There is law whenever it is possible to mobilize a certain form of totality with regard to an individual case'. 'Law is fractal', Latour says. It works only in ways that are situation specific, but in each situation 'law is found in its entirety'. (Latour 2010: 256)

Such a system that is both imperfect and total resembles life itself. This is how Deleuze actually characterizes jurisprudence. For him, there is no abstract law that could defend universal rights; there is in fact only a multiplicity of specific legal situations. We should avoid the transcendent absolute sense of justice and always refer to jurisprudence, case by case, because it concerns 'the rights of life'; 'it is life', Deleuze says (Deleuze and Parnet 2004: 'G'). This vitalistic sense of law could give a positive progressive implication, like for instance in Branzi's 'weak and diffuse' city, which he defines as a 'self-reformist society', which produces new laws and rules every day (Branzi 2010:110) and where practices of excess are simply the symptom of a natural uncontained vital energy. But as critical theorists Braidotti, Colebrook and

Hanafin (2009: 5) remark, in reference to Deleuze's 'differential jurisprudence' precisely, this 'resurgence of vitalism can be seen as profoundly regressive' too.

Maybe the problem with the vitalistic claim is that it is a kind of logical shortcut; 'life' or 'nature' seem to say it all in a word, but do not say much. It is often said in Romania that a society deserves its corrupt legal system because, eventually, every society evolves a system of law that reflects its nature best. This is a standpoint that, as Latour puts it, 'instead of studying the practical means that form and shape society', considers 'a society that is already present, both mysterious and inexplicable, to try to explain the only thing that has the power to engender it'; in short, this is to 'take the consequence for cause' (Latour 2010: 262). Latour also remarked that there is actually no reliable 'nature' to count on anymore; any modernization should be now defined 'without referring to either the over-rapid unity of nature or the over-easy diversity of cultures' (Latour 2010: 246–7).

Legal theorist Suri Ratnapala explains that there is an evolutionary theory in jurisprudence that addresses what legal sociologist Eugen Ehrlich has called, about a century ago, the 'living law' (Ratnapala 2009: 203). This is a notion in which society and law are seen as caught together in a natural evolutionary process. Considering this theory, Ratnapala concludes that there is actually 'no contradiction between the notion of deliberate institutional design and the notion of a natural evolutionary process' (Ratnapala 2009: 290). Law is both a living evolutionary system and artificial engineering. Laws that are established 'predispose the legal order to evolve in particular directions', but 'the legal system can gather a momentum of its own after it is set on a particular course'. There may also be 'lock ins' within the system, he remarks, laws and practices that are difficult to repel, which result from the fact that urban agents naturally 'arrange their lives' after them (Ratnapala 2009: 288). In our context, for instance, derogatory urbanism is obviously such a 'lock in', with most powerful urban agents relying on it. It has been deliberately instituted by written law, but has become somehow natural too. A more rigorous system could be also explicitly established, but in order for it to work, it should be instated by small steps over a long time, so that it could become a natural practice, inscribed in the making of the city as an evolutionary process. It is the diffuseness of an act that makes it successful on the long run.

Conclusion: diffuse transgression

This chapter has shown that the notion of transgression is useful in understanding the relationship between law and the making of the city. It has argued that, in cases such as post-communist Romania, it is neither the direct application of a clear system of laws and regulations, nor the deviations from it by informalities and illegalities, that are most relevant for this relationship, but rather a grey margin within the limits of legality itself. The formal is contaminated by the informal in the making of the city. This sort of transgression is very enduring. A few theoretical concepts helped us understand why.

The notion of 'lawscape', defined by Philippopoulos-Mihalopoulos as the common realm of law and space, explains the continuity between the formal and the informal in an all-embracing field. Law becomes actually more efficient by becoming diffuse in this field; it becomes an 'atmosphere of law', which engulfs everything and lets no body escape. Sloterdijk's theory, and particularly the notion of 'nomotop', uses the analogy with architecture as 'the art of immersion' and explains the efficacy of the atmospheric action of the law: it is a system that works through excess pressure. It is this excess that assures the statics in the social structure and keeps it standing. It is also excess that brings about transgression.

When the system of law involves transgression, it actually transfers excess onto control. Bottomley and Moore observe this distinction between law and control, along with the maximizing effect on the limits of transgression. In fact, as our examples have shown, it is not the actual crossing beyond the legal limits that is the most empowering for urban agents, but rather the possibility of exploiting the maximum proximity to them. Urban agents turn the limits themselves into profitable rooms for manoeuvre, opening a multiplicity of inner margins of play. More excess pressure is dispersed on a smaller scale. Transgression spreads in the 'lawscape' and becomes all pervasive, self-stimulating and addictive.

By its diffuseness and continuous pressure at the lower level of the system of law, transgression empowers rather than challenges the system on the whole. 'Law is fractal', Latour remarks. It is always mobilized in its entirety and acts as a totality, but it is situation specific and performs in each case differently. This constant need to adjust is why the margins of the law are both inevitable and neutral. Transgression is not in itself positive or negative; it is an everyday practice that continually redefines the relationship between law and the city and gives transgression its positive or negative value. Diffuse transgression is neither an accidental event nor a transitional stage; in the long run it is how the city is made.

Notes

1   Law 350/2001
2   Laws 169/1997, 54/1998, 1/2000
3   I am grateful to the editors for bringing this notion to my attention.
4   The 1990 Town and Country Planning Act
5   Ordinance 27/2008
6   Government Emergency Ordinance 7/2011
7   Public debate, Romanian Chamber of Architects (OAR) Headquarters, Bucharest, 27 September 2012
8   Law 50/1991
9   Ord. 69/2004, Law 289/2006, Ord. 18/2007, Law 168/2007, Ord. 27/2008, Law 242/2009, Law 345/2009, Ord. 7/2011, Law 162/2011, Law 221/2011, Law 190/2013

Bibliography

Booth, P. (1999) 'Discretion in planning versus zoning', in B. Cullingworth (ed.) *British Planning. 50 Years of Urban and Regional Policy*, London: The Athlone Press, 31–44

Bottomley, A. and Moore, N. (2008) 'Blind stuttering. diagrammatic city', in *Griffith Law Review,* 17(2): 559–76

Braidotti, R., Colebrook, C., and Hanafin, P. (2009) 'Introduction', in R. Braidotti, C. Colebrook and P. Hanafin (eds) *Deleuze and Law: Forensic Future*, New York: Palgrave Macmillan, 1–5

Branzi, A. (2006) *Weak and Diffuse Modernity. The World of Projects at the Beginning of the 21st Century*, Milan: Skira

Branzi, A. (2010) 'For a post-environmentalism: seven suggestions for a new athens charter and the weak metropolis', in M. Mostafavi and G. Doherty (eds) *Ecological Urbanism*, Baden: Lars Müller Publishers, 110–11

Deleuze, G. and Parnet, C. (2004) G from 'Gauche', *L'Abécédaire de Gilles Deleuze*. 3 DVDs. Paris: Éditions Montparnasse

Foucault, M. (1977) 'A preface to transgression', in D.F. Bouchard (ed.) *Language, Counter-memory, Practice: Selected Essays and Interviews*, Ithaca, NY: Cornell University Press, 29–52

Ivanov, C. (2013) 'Parlamentul a modificat Legea Urbanismului' ['Parliament has modified the Law of Urbanism'], *hotnews.ro*, accessed 20 February 2013, http://www.hotnews.ro/stiri-administratie_locala-14268797-analiza-parlamentul-modificat-legea-urbanismului-vezi-schimbari-produs-cum-afecteaza-orasele.htm

Jencks, C. (2003) *Transgression*, London/New York: Routledge

Latour, B. (2010) *The Making of Law. An Ethnography of the Conseil d'État*, trans. M. Brilman and A. Pottage, Cambridge: Polity Press

Needham, B. (2005) 'The new Dutch Spatial Planning Act: Continuity and change in the way in which the Dutch regulate the practice of spatial planning', in *Planning, Practice & Research*, 20(3): 327–9

Nuijten, M. and Anders, G. (2007) *Corruption and the Secret of Law. A Legal Anthropological Perspective*, Aldershot / Burlington, VT: Ashgate Publishing

Peylet, R., Chapuis, J-Y., Jegouzo, Y., and Lebreton, J-P. (2007) *Raportul expertilor francezi referitor la elaborarea codului urbanismului in Romania* [*French Experts' Report on the Development of the Urbanism Code in Romania*], Paris: Ministère de Transport, de l'Equipement, du Tourisme et de la Mer, accessed November 2013, http://www.oar.org.ro/upload/2007/Raport_francez_ro.pdf

Philippopoulos-Mihalopoulos, A. (2007) 'Introduction. In the lawscape', in A. Philippopoulos-Mihalopoulos (ed.) *Law and the City*, London: Routledge-Cavendish, 1–20

Philippopoulos-Mihalopoulos, A. (2012) 'Atmospheres of law: Senses, affects, lawscapes', in *Emotion, Space and Society*, xxx: 1–10, doi:10.1016/j.emospa.2012.03.001, accessed November 2013, https://www.academia.edu/3092470/Atmospheres_of_Law_Senses_Affects_Lawscapes

Ratnapala, S. (2009) *Jurisprudence,* Cambridge: Cambridge University Press

Sloterdijk, P. (2005) 'Atmospheric politics', in B. Latour and P. Weibel (eds) *How to Make Things Public*, Karlsruhe: ZKM Center for Arts and Media, 944–51

Sloterdijk, P. (2006) 'The Nomotop: On the emergence of law in the island of humanity', in *Law and Literature*, 18(1): 1–14

Sloterdijk, P. (2011) 'Architecture as an art of immersion', trans A.-C. Engels-Schwarzpaul, *Interstices: Journal of Architecture and Related Arts*, 12: 105–9, accessed August 2013, http://interstices.ac.nz/wp-content/uploads/2011/11/INT12_Sloterdijk.pdf

Tosics, I. (2004) 'Determinants and consequences of spatial restructuring in post-socialist cities', paper presented at 'Winds of Societal Change: Remaking Post-communist Cities' Conference, University of Illinois, Urbana-Champaign, IL, 18–19 June, accessed February 2013, http://qcora.web.elte.hu/1/!!!!Orsi/Havanna_lak%F3telep/restate/Tosics.pdf

Vöckler, K. (2010) 'Turbo urbanism', in A. Serban (ed.) *studioBASAR: Evicting the Ghost: Architectures of Survival*, Bucharest: Centre for Visual Introspection, 184–95

Chapter 6

Transgression and temperance

The Newcastle Hoppings

Ella Bridgland and Stephen Walker

Corns on the feet differ from headaches and toothaches by their baseness, and they are only laughable because of an ignominy explicable by the mud in which feet are found. Since by its physical attitude the human race distances itself *as much as it can* from terrestrial mud – whereas a spasmodic laugh carries joy to its summit each time its purest flight lands man's own arrogance spread-eagle in the mud – one can imagine that a toe, always more or less damaged and humiliated, is psychologically analogous to the brutal fall of a man – in other words, to death.

Georges Bataille 1985 (p.22, emphasis in original)

The seemingly unremarkable difference between pains in the head and the feet manifest for Bataille more significant tensions between human aspirations and realities, civilization and nature. Elsewhere, he associated architecture with this 'civilizing' impulse, to the extent that 'increasingly static, increasingly dominant' forms of architecture threaten to overcome human beings by assuming the final form of earthly evolution. (Bataille, 1992: 25).[1] While Bataille's interest – in his direct address to architecture at least – was in the consequences of a direct attack on architecture, and the direct transgression of the authority of Church and State that this would represent, this chapter will instead dwell on, or in, the mud in which feet are found. Through one particularly muddy example – the 2012 Hoppings Fair that took place on the Town Moor in Newcastle upon Tyne, England – some of these alternate threats to good order, and alternate modes of transgression, that mud offers will be explored.

The annual Newcastle Hoppings Fair was established as a Temperance Festival in 1882, one of many Victorian moralizing attempts to improve social norms and promote 'good' behaviour. (Figure 6.1) From its initial situation through to the present day, the Hoppings has remained something of a straw man. Witness the fine oxymoronic notion of the Temperance Festival: established on the Town Moor, away from and in deliberate opposition to prevailing Victorian urban fears that believed fairs were sites of social depravity and transgression injurious to local inhabitants (an attitude enshrined in the Fairs Act of 1871, designed to close down existing fairs), the Hoppings provided something of a decoy, akin to the *slander of a licensed fool*, through which transgression could be controlled by promoting 'good' behaviour by actively encouraging people to act morally and not drink.[2] Meanwhile, a more thoroughgoing transgression would inevitably be exercised elsewhere: nowadays, look no further than Newcastle's infamous Bigg Market, scene of nightly debauchery of mediaeval proportions. But for all the worry about bad behaviour, the perils of drink, and so on, such instances are localized and short-lived: notwithstanding the perceived threat they could bring to 'social order', we can consider such behaviour as a minor transgression. In contrast, we want to focus on other aspects of the event; these are much less perceptible, less about human behaviour *per se*, and more about a prevailing attitude – observed with such acerbic humour by Bataille – that humans can assert lasting control over their environment, physically and conceptually.

In *The Politics and Poetics of Transgression* (1986), literary and cultural theorists Stallybrass and White note:

> In the [fair] pure and simple categories of thought find themselves perplexed and one-sided. Only hybrid notions are appropriate to such a hybrid place.
>
> (Stallybrass and White, 1986: 27)

Side-stepping the numerous examples of minor transgressions that events at the Hoppings can provide, we want to suggest that behind the scenes, action is taken to police and prevent potentially major transgressions of social and cultural norms, and that such action can only be grasped through the development of hybrid notions. In contrast to their strong advocacy for what we might call the muddy categories needed to account for the fair, Stallybrass and White name and shame a range of respected historians and theorists – Robert Malcolmson, E P Thomson, Mikhail Bakhtin – who maintain an implicit binary in their various (clean) interests in the fair. According to these clean accounts:

> [t]he fair is located on one side of a series of oppositions as 'popular', celebratory, grotesque, and its history becomes one of a transformation from 'licence' (i.e. excess) to 'licensed' (i.e. authorized), with the concomitant suppression of the 'unlicensed' fairs'.
>
> (Stallybrass and White, 1986: 34)

Acknowledging Stallybrass and White's challenge to the clean, we will explore the categorical difference between headaches and muddy feet announced by

Figure 6.1
**General scenes
from the Newcastle
Temperance Festival
or Hoppings**
Temperance Poster
(1882), various general
views, including muddy
scenes, from the 1920s
to the 1960s, and 2012

c.1920   23 June 1949   c.1960   1960   29 June 2012

29 June 2012

Bataille, approaching the Hoppings from above and below (or, roughly, before and after) as an architectural site of major transgression, examining with head and feet the very ground on which it stands and the threat this poses to human authority and control.

Indeed, the head–foot connection, emblematic of Bataille's philosophical economy, marks out the macabre axis of a lightning strike on the Hoppings site in 1911, which was reported thus in the local press:

> A tragedy occurred at the Temperance Festival at the beginning of the week. On Monday, a young man called Fielding was visiting the festival field watching the showmen erecting their stalls when a thunderstorm developed. The young man does not appear to have taken cover when a number of flashes of lightning were seen by other people present. Fielding was unfortunately struck dead by one of the bolts. A police sergeant who was on duty in the area at the time rushed to his assistance but was unable to help him.
>
> (anon. in Baron, 1984: 45)[3]

Fielding's death was subject to a coroner's enquiry, where it was mentioned 'that the deceased had a hole burnt out of the top of his cap and all the hair was burnt from his body. The soles of his boots had been ripped off.' (anon in Baron, 1984: 45) And his big toes presumably had reconnected with the mud of the Town Moor. As Bataille frequently noted, this vertical connection runs both ways, much as human beings would like it simply to ascend. Indeed, the discipline of architecture aspires to this same movement out of the mud and dirt of the earth, of bad weather, of contingency, in order to attain the lofty heights of a discipline concerned instead with unchanging, intellectual ideas and an Archimedean viewpoint over the hoi polloi. But as Fielding's tragedy reminds us, all these aspirations, and their concomitant enshrining in various social mores and architectural rules, are subject to transgression by the overwhelming forces of nature.[4]

Beneath the brief razzamatazz of the fair, the ground itself registers a different and cyclic approach to the *tabula rasa* than that associated with architecture, and it is the attitude towards this ground – indeed, more strongly, to the very surface of this ground in its 'natural', neutral state – that demonstrates a qualitatively different approach towards (preventing) transgression than the attitude towards the activities, behaviour, or even the architecture, at the fair itself. The threat of an ignominious descent into the mud reveals complex issues of ownership and stewardship, land rights, air rights and grazing rights amongst other enshrined codes governing the Moor. This threat of major transgression is felt most acutely behind the scenes by the various institutions involved, and resonates far beyond the Town Moor, touching as it does on the foundational presuppositions of Architecture (with a capital A), the Law (with a capital L, in contradistinction to the 'laws of nature' which in this case pose the threat), and the stability of the state and its ability to promote and uphold a 'good society'.

In the sections that follow we will set out these competing forces, and the nature and scope of transgression they threaten, through a number of close, muddy readings of the surface of the ground. These will progress from head to feet, from the drafting out of the architecture of the fair on paper, to the drawing out of positions on the grass of the Town Moor, to the desperate attempts to maintain the architectural order of the fair's layout in the face of bad weather, to the final acrimonious determination of responsibilities for surface damage and repair after the fair has packed up and gone.

Head/surface (The story of Albert's Kit)

Preparations for the fair begin in the head and on paper. Although many parties are involved in these preparations, particularly the allocation of sites and the overall layout of rides, stalls and attractions (as well as ancillary services such as the school for the children of travelling show families, the fair office, St. John's Ambulance, 'Swag Alley' and so on), this complexity can be focused on the figure of the fair's surveyor, whose responsibility it is to coordinate all these tasks. As a proxy for some of these key activities, this section takes the setting out kit used by Albert Austin, Surveyor to the Fair between 1988–93. (see Figure 6.2) Albert died on 23 February 2010, but such is his continuing presence around the Hoppings that it seems to make sense to refer to his activities continuing into the present.

Albert's setting-out activities could take up to three weeks, projecting the fair layout onto the surface from an overlay at 'head height'.[5] The preparation of this layout attempted to exert control and maintain architectural order through the geometrical set up of markers, paths and plots. It also acknowledges, and in parts makes explicit reference to, past positions of certain rides and the accrued showmen's rights over these sites.

There are two moments to mention in this context, where Albert's Kit helps mediate between the head and the feet: the preparation of the plan, and the preparation of the ground. There are some anomalies in the plan, the kit, and their inter-relationship, introducing some of the instabilities that can be encountered in the event more broadly.

The 'plan' of the fair is something of a synthetic document, gathering and recording different claims to authority, control, ownership, rights and so on. (Figure 6.2) The plan itself also experiences differing internal rates of change. The 'archetype' or base layer is brought out every year as if unchanging, although looking at earlier plans from early and mid-century, this basic layout has clearly shifted, now following an essentially linear arrangement parallel to the Great North Road, in contrast to the earlier kinked plan sited more centrally. The main rides have inherited 'standing' rights, but the positions of so-called 'side-stuff' (smaller rides and stalls) are re-allocated every year by ballot, in a flagrant transgression of Showmen's Guild rules by the 'Northern Syndicate', a proxy for Newcastle City Council and the Freemen's Stewards' Committee with the responsibility for organizing the Hoppings.[6]

The process of Albert setting out brings this ideal plan(e) down to earth. The timber 'rods' in his kit are (paradoxically) more enduring than the paper copy of the 'ideal' (quasi-transcendent) plan. The notes on this plan that indicate points of contact between the ideal projection and the physical world (the HP or *hinge point*, various 'post

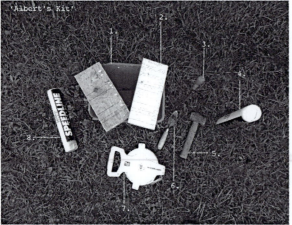

1. Red Bucket:
To store tools in, colour
makes it easily to spot in
a green field.
2. Fair Layout Plans:
Drawn on wooden boards to
ensure marking out can take
place even in bad weather.
3. Red Screw Driver:
To find first permanent
marker point buried in the
ground.
4. White Spray Paint:
To indicate the plot corners
with an 'L.'
5. Hammer:
To secure pegs.
6. Trowel:
To dig around peg.
7. Measuring Tape:
Measure out the sizes of
positions.
8. Red Spray Paint:
To easily detect the top of
the pegs.

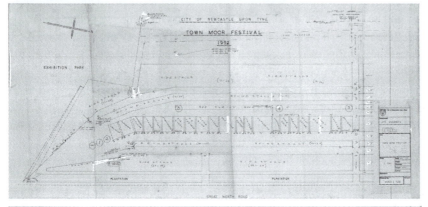

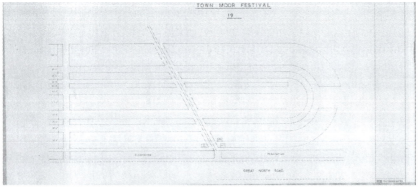

Figure 6.2
**Albert's kit, fair layout
southern section (1992)
and base layer**

holes' and fence markings illustrated in Figure 6.3) all hint at a feedback loop that mixes precision and approximation, a loop that most (setting-out) plans don't accommodate, let alone record.

Clearly, neither of these moments is 'transgressive' in any strong sense, nor associated with any deliberately transgressive motivation, yet Albert Austin's actions do transgress the expectations normally pertaining between planning and setting out. Compared to most architectural plans, the level of resolution and detail on these setting-out plans is far lower than most architects could stomach, leaving much more

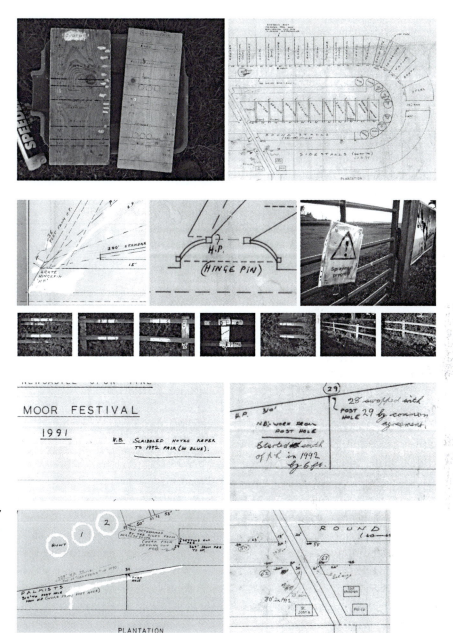

Figure 6.3
Timber setting out 'rods' from Albert's kit, details of setting out drawings and notes, the Hinge Pin (HP)
Photographs of some of the physical markers on the boundary fence marks; and over-writing on 1991 and 1992 plans.

'in the head' (of Albert, and the fair's organizers more broadly) and much more 'on the ground' (left to individual stall holders or ride-owners). Perhaps more significant is that the setting-out plan, which more than most other versions (for 'normal' buildings), is a site of ongoing construction in its own right. As some of the examples in Figure 6.3 indicate, the information recorded on these plans not only precedes the setting out of the event, but also records for use the subsequent year those observations and tips that have resulted from the setting-out process. The setting-out plan is thus not simply a preparatory drawing or stage to be passed through, but as an object becomes incorporated in the annual cyclic process of planning and staging the fair. We might say that contrary to the movement of most setting out, Albert's inscription returns upward, to the head, and endures on the setting-out plan rather than down on the ground.

Indeed for the Freemen, this is perhaps the ideal situation, and announces a tension between the event and the everyday surface of the Moor. In *Earth Moves*, Bernard Cache asserts that the identity of a site 'is always the outcome of a construction.' (1995: 15.) Although the moves that interest Cache relate more comfortably to the everyday situation of the Town Moor than to the particular event of the Hoppings, his criticisms of 'pure form' as a 'map without a plan' relate to what the Freemen inadvertently try to maintain, namely, a (setting-out) map without 'projection', without time figuring.[7] As the next section will discuss in more detail, they are charged with maintaining the surface rather than the depth of the Moor, and their actions over time suggest that the identity they are attempting to foster and maintain is one of a natural, bucolic place.[8]

Feet/depth (the story of the 'Earth Slices')

Albert's kit opens up one story of this event, where his setting-out plan and activities are designed to project control with a light but firm touch onto the surface of the Moor. Below this, the Town Moor can be understood as a site of ongoing tensions and transgressions that penetrate deep under Albert's overlaid geometry. Developing his account of identity construction, Cache talks about 'working beneath the surface of identity' (1995: 15) and the forces that bring about transformations from one identity to another on the same site. In this context, he expresses interest in *geo-graphy* as pure-surface image, in explicit opposition to *geo-logy*, an image or concern with the depth of the earth.

Over many centuries, there have been tensions between the Freemen, the City Council and residents relating to the rights over, and ownership and use of, the Town Moor. These tensions can be understood in Cache's opposition between *geo-logy* and *geo-graphy*. The City Council attempted to gain sole rights to the Town Moor by buying out the Freeman in 1773, which led to the Town Moor Act, 1774, the Act of Parliament placing the area of the Moor in the guardianship of both the City Corporation and the Freemen. This act set out the management of the Moor and the rights and ownership of the land, with the Corporation legally owning the 'subsoil and minerals' while establishing forever the right of the Freemen to the 'herbage' or grazing on the Moor. A number of acts followed, which established the governance and use of the Moor and constituted the so-called 'dual control' approach, requiring the mutual agreement of City Council and Freemen in any decisions affecting the Moor. This was reaffirmed in the most recent Town Moor Act of 1988. As Section 8. – (I) of that act states:

> The Town Moor shall be maintained as an area of open space in the
> interests of the inhabitants of the city, so that it shall continue both to

satisfy the herbage right and to afford air and exercise for the enjoyment of the public.

A sectional slice through the ground on which Albert stood reveals the layers of control that exist, invisible to the eye but felt through the base of the feet. Considering these 'Earth Slices', (recreated in Figure 6.4). it can be argued that the transgression we are discussing here does not lie on or emerge from within any one stratum, but is produced between the various physical and legal layers of strata when they come into conflict. This becomes particularly noticeable when studying attempts to restore the land to its natural 'grazing' state following damage by the annual disruption of the Hoppings. When all is well, these strata behave as a whole – the depth, surface and the air above – but as the long-disputed history of the regulated and restricted use and ownership of the Town Moor suggests, arguments are frequent and fierce, causing this apparent wholeness to delaminate. Although the Freemen have rights to herbage, they also have the responsibility for managing and maintaining the surface condition of the Moor, mediating the relationship between upper and lower zones. Material damage (actual or anticipated) to the surface has consistently threatened the fragile harmony of this legal relationship, precipitated by rain and pedestrian traffic which brings about moments of separation between the surface and depth of the Moor, and revealing all manner of instabilities where none is meant to exist.[9]

Adverse and apparently worsening weather conditions have frequently led the Freemen to intervene and attempt to repair the site, not only as a measure to restore the damage done after the fair has packed up and gone, but as an attempt to prevent the cancellation of the event whilst it is in motion. The deployment of straw and wood chips illustrated in Figure 6.5 typifies the Freemen's material response to the deteriorating conditions as the Hoppings was taking place during 2012. Heavy rain during the period leading up to and during the fair caused the site quickly to become a mud bath. Interaction between mud and feet caused this temporary straw and wood-chip surface of the Moor to mutate, while it was continually replenished to reinstate a blurring pathway between rides and side stalls to ensure the site remained in a safe and useable condition. The solid 'Forsyth Footpath' marked the only route through the fair site that provides a regular access throughout all phases of the year.[10]

So we might ask why the Stewards' Committee of the Freemen appears to become disproportionately upset when the Moor surface gets damaged. Their concern seems to lie much less with the punters who have to negotiate horrible conditions underfoot, less with the showmen whose takings suffer during bad weather, and more with the 'stain' that will be left on the Moor's surface after a muddy fair. This reveals their incapacity to exercise control over the horizontal slice of Moor that falls into their jurisdiction (a major transgression), while the event of the Hoppings that takes place in the air above recalls human capacity for temperance and (self-)control, albeit with some minor transgressions. Moreover, the contrast that the Hoppings writes large into the depth of the Moor, between temporary and permanent, restoration and prevention, natural and human intervention, hints at a number of conflicts that transgress the assumption that land below the feet is inert. We could say that in the attitude of the

Slice 1. Swag Alley

Straw Path

Wood Chips

Damaged Surface

Temporary Infrastructure

Soil: Managed by the Freemen

Land: Owned by the City Council

Slice 2. Forsyth Footpath

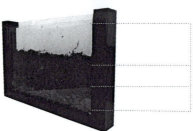

Public Rights to 'Air and Excersise'

Solid, Permanent Pathway

Substrate: Managed by the City Council

Land: Owned by the City Council

Slice 3. Damaged Walkway

Space for Growth
Freemen hold 'Herbage' Rights

Grass Seed: Planted by the Freemmen
to restore land back to original state

Damaged Earth: Traces of fun fair and
effects of adverse weather conditions

Land: Owned by the City Council

Figure 6.4
Earth slices (annotated photographs showing layers of material and ownership, and a diagram showing the outline of the Town Moor)

The land or the depth of the site is owned by the City Council. Above this, the public have rights to 'air and exercise' over the Moor. Sandwiched between these two parallel zones, the Freemen have rights to herbage, but are left with the responsibility to manage and maintain the relationship between these upper and lower zones, the land as owned and the space as it is used.

Stewards' Committee, the surface is denied its own agency, denied involvement in various other (different) economies beyond the calendric cycle of preparation and maintenance set out in the diagram in Figure 6.5.

The transformations from one identity to another that Cache notes occur at moments when the surface – the Moor's *geo-graphy* – becomes involved in and behaves according to different economies, when the various strata – or *geo-logy* – shown in the 'Earth Slices' interact in unwelcome (but wholly foreseeable) ways and construct a different (unwanted) identity. What is transgressed is the human delusion of wholeness and control: as Bataille reminds us, each time we attempt to distance ourselves from terrestrial mud, it lands us back spread-eagled.

The in between ('Pulse'; or the story of the 'golden carpets')

We'd like to finish with a third story, balanced in between head and feet, in between the contested constructions of the site and the erosion or transgressions of (dis)order, a neat muddy mess. We have already mentioned the straw and wood chips laid down by the Freemen in a Sisyphean attempt to protect the surface and keep it mud-free. Moving from the 'Earth Slices' to a more horizontal register, the distribution of this sacrificial material traces various power structures and vested interests within the layout of the fair. As the documentation of these 'golden carpets' reveal, in 2012 at least, the mud wins through. (Figure 6.5) To pick up Bataille's differentiation between 'corns on the feet' and 'headaches and toothaches', and his broader interest in mud and the formless (*informe*), it is important to emphasize that their relationship is not symmetrical or balanced. Nor is that between our first two stories.

As Rosalind Krauss has pointed out (albeit in a different context), the relationship between form and *informe* is not one of rhythm or simple complementarity (with the usual narrative that humans can push disorder into order). As she reads this situation, the promise of form is either to 'ward off the violence' of the trauma threatened by *informe*, or 'to achieve the permanence of the configuration, its imperviousness to assault.' (Krauss, 1997a: 164).

While the oppositional logic (form against *informe*, and its accompanying value system) that Krauss criticizes is nothing new, it is worth dwelling a little on the temporal aspects of this relationship, contesting the permanent 'good form' of calendric rhythm ('rhythm', according to Krauss, 'puts in place both the stability of form and the fullness of meaning' (Krauss, 1997b: 221–3)) and replacing this with what she names pulse. '"Pulse", she writes, 'turns around the … condition of shock, of "bad form," of a repetition always undergirded by the rupture of total extinction, and thus a rhythm of + and 0.' (Krauss, 1997b: 223)

To go with the 'pulse' is here to acknowledge that the shock occurrences of mud – and fair-ruining bad weather more generally – lie beyond human prediction or control, as do their consequences. There is a parallel between the expectations made in space and time, where in both instances, 'we' expect to be able to make, and execute, plans. Quixotic matter is meant to give up its own agency to static,

Figure 6.5
Golden carpets
Annual planning cycle of the Hoppings and Town Moor phasing; photographs of the mud, and showmen rolling out the golden carpet of straw, and two comparative photographic surveys showing the extensive damage in 2012, the gradual repair over the subsequent 51 weeks, and how this exceeded expectations of re-seeding and repair anticipated by the usual planning cycle.

meaningful form. But to consider the 'pulse' registered on, in or at the surface of the Moor permits acknowledgement of the strange temporalities of the matter, events and agencies that converge there. Albert's setting-out plans register a defiant rhythm to and fro the ground, a relay in an ongoing conversation that convention deems should not take place (the setting-out plan should be 'used up', it's usually a single-use drawing). Irrespective of this, the intransigent regularity of the fair's timing runs into the a-rhythmic 'pulse' of bad weather, running roughshod over the careful calendric planning and good form of the Stewards' Committee, and precipitating the delamination of *geo-logical* responsibilities.

Once through the gate, past the Hinge Pin and onto the Town Moor, human control becomes more obviously contingent and subject to 'pulse'. An extreme case, Fielding's tragedy reminds us of the need to take cover if we are to avoid becoming perfectly aligned with the overwhelming forces of nature and shock – literally, in his case – that they can bring.

Taking 2012 as one example, the mud was uncontrollable, and the effects of the damage this caused to the surface of the Town Moor lasted for many more months than the usual, rhythmic, calendric planning cycle anticipated. (Indeed, this damage is still legible on the Moor today). How fragile this surface, how quickly it delaminated, and how quickly the relationships it 'supports' untangled. Indeed, such was the fall-out from the mud of the 2012 fair that the event did not take place in 2013, and after more than 130 years of operation its future looks uncertain.

The throwing down and frequent replenishment of the 'golden carpets' is an instance of unproductive expenditure, albeit accidentally rather than in the Mauss–Bataille tradition, a futile attempt to rescue the fair from the rising levels of mud (and thereby rescue a reasonable financial return). At a comfortable remove from the desperation of these attempts, we can observe that there was something poetic about the throwing down of straw – dead grass, or grass further on in a cycle of growth, preservation and decay than that still growing on the muddy Moor – in an attempt to play nature at its own game by re-setting the surface, shocking it into another (drier) point in its usual cycle.

While the arrival of this mud announced the first moment when the surface of the Moor began to delaminate – desublimate, to stick with Krauss' terminology – the process of providing and laying the straw further exposed the tensions around the varying claims to authority and control over and within the fair. The Northern Syndicate provided most of the straw, although the availability of this material to the various stallholders did not appear to be equitable. The distribution of the 'golden carpets' within the overall thoroughfares set out so carefully by Albert Austin's heirs actually involved laying out certain paths that would lead (brave) visitors between particular attractions while by-passing others, as Figure 6.5 makes clear.

Conclusion

Damage to the surface of the Moor is the major transgression that has put the Hoppings in jeopardy on many occasions, rather than 'temperance' or its absence (whether individual or collective misdemeanours). The most significant transgression is not physical, not situated at foot or head height, but is a product of the emblematic tension between these two, enacted by the shock of the pulse legible in the effects of mud on the whole event. More broadly the 'golden carpets' are emblematic of the major transgression occurring around the surface, brought about by and written so clearly in the pulsating carpeting–muddying–re-carpeting actions of showmen and Moor. As the straw and wood chips are sublimated into the muddy surface, the conceptual conceit of the Town Moor as a continuous, stable whole desublimates. Moments of separation between surface and depth of the Town Moor reveal all manner of instabilities where none is meant to exist, they upset the assumed harmony that we take for granted in the apparently benign 'natural' space of the Moor, set out and maintained by the Freemen of the city according to foundations laid in Parliamentary legislation as 'an area of open space in the interests of the inhabitants of the city, ... to afford air and exercise for the enjoyment of the public'.

Krauss links such loss of harmony to:

> the very fragmentation of th[e] 'point' of view that prevents th[e] invisible, unlocatable gaze from being the site of coherence, meaning, unity, Gestalt, *eidos*.
>
> (Krauss, 1997c: 242)

In our case, this site would be Albert's plan, but its stability and coherence fragments from within, thanks to the internal rhythm of exchange it sets up with the surface of the Moor, and also from without due to the various acts that control interests and responsibilities under, at and above the surface, becoming manifest in the fallout over – and into – the mud. This fragmentation of coherence echoes Stallybrass and White's demand for 'hybrid notions ... appropriate to such a hybrid place.' (1986: 27). Krauss continues:

> Desire is thus not mapped here as the desire for form, and thus for sublimation (the vertical, the Gestalt, the law); desire is modeled in terms of a *transgression against form. It is the force invested in desublimation*.
>
> (Krauss, 1997c: 242–4, our emphasis)

The mud of the Hoppings illustrates very tangibly the fragility of agreements over the Town Moor, and how quickly a *transgression against form* can cause the various strata and claims to de-sublimate, resulting in the transgression of received wisdom regarding human and institutional relationships with (and our assumed control over) nature, of the age-old delusion of mastery and the image of wholeness. This gentle, major transgression is threatened simply by the making of marks on the surface.

Acknowledgements

We would like to acknowledge the support of the University of Sheffield's SURE Research Scheme for funding our project on the Hoppings, and the staff at the National Fairground Archive, particularly Ian Trowell and Angela Greenwood, for their input and support. We would also like to express our gratitude to Maureen Austin and the Showmen of the Newcastle Hoppings for their welcome in 2012.

Unless otherwise stated, images are by the authors. All other material is drawn from the collections of the National Fairground Archive (NFA) and reproduced with the permission of the University of Sheffield. Individual collections are acknowledged in the captions to the images.

Notes

1　'…an attack on architecture…is necessarily, as it were, an attack on man.' (Bataille, 1992: 26.) In another essay ('Inner Experience'), Bataille suggests that architecture's essence is the annulment of time: *'L'idéal est l'architecture, ou la sculpture, immobilisant l'harmonie, garantissant la durée de motifs dont l'essence est l'annulation du temps'* ('The ideal is architecture, or sculpture, which immobilises harmony, guaranteeing the survival of motifs whose essence is the annulment of time') (Bataille, 1973, V:70). For a detailed examination of Bataille's thinking on art, architecture, transgression and desublimation, see Walker (2004: 118–141).

2　The Fair Acts of 1822 and 1871 gave the government power to abolish unchartered fairs and to limit the hours of chartered ones, giving it direct control over these events for the first time. Alongside the introduction of this new brand of polite Temperance fair, consider also the rise of the Expo through the second half of the nineteenth century: Paul Greenhalgh's *Fair World: A History of the World's Fairs and Expositions from London to Shanghai 1851–2010* (2011), charts significant changes (and expansions) of such organised Expos during the 1870s, precisely when the travelling street fairs were being challenged through this legislation. The Temperance Movement should not be conflated with any religious movement, but in the case of the Hoppings they can be seen to share a tendency to appropriate 'pagan' festivals and (de)turn them. Just as Christmas appropriated, 'sanitized' and Christianized previous pagan new year or solstice celebrations, so the Hoppings Temperance Festival appropriated and sanitised the annual horse-racing festival or 'Race Week' that had taken place (around Midsummer's Day) on the Town Moor from 1721 until 1882, when it was moved (back) out of town to Gosforth Park.

3　Somewhat defiant of this fatal encounter with lightning, and our contemporary health and safety regime, it is interesting to note that in the early years of the Hoppings, there were competitions in philosophical essay writing and kite flying, two parallel pursuits through which human beings arguably endeavored to leave the base surface of the Earth and fly free. As Baron notes: 'During the Victorian era, many different kinds of activities were held on the Moor, including "a five shilling prize for the best essay on the philosophy of kite flying, which was then a popular pastime in the area."' (Baron, 1984: 4–5.) This quote is also uncredited.

4　These natural forces are a remarkably frequent characteristic of the Hoppings, and press reports from over a century document with startling regularity the incidents of bad weather that have disrupted these temperance festivities. Stories in the press note significant disruption caused to the Hoppings by various kinds of bad weather in 1883, 1888, 1892, 1896, 1898, 1905, 1909, 1911, 1912, 1913, 1927, 1950, 1952, 1958, 1965, 1980, 1982, 1997, 1998, 2007, 2008, and of course 2012. The lightning bolt that did for Fielding was rare indeed, but reports are run through with stories of more *horizontal* problems.

5　Svetlana Alpers (1983) has discussed what we might describe as the historical movement of such 'layers' from below to above, as their role shifts from the (passive) recording of existing nature to the (active) projecting of human design. In *Architecture and the Burdens of Linearity*, Catherine Ingraham also discusses these relationships in her first chapter, 'Dividing the land', where she notes 'the "civilizing" of America by means of the grid … whereby "civilization" becomes synonymous with "line"' (Ingraham, 1998: 7–8). Shortly following this, she notes the link between architecture and authority in terms that echo Bataille: 'The breakdown of what is proper, wherever and however it may occur, is, before anything else, a crisis of form and structure. And architecture, as a discipline and a profession, controls the propriety of form and structure at both a physical and (therefore) a metaphysical level.' (Ingraham, 1998: 10).

6　The requirement for these bodies – the Stewards' Committee (a group responsible for the business affairs of the Freemen of Newcastle upon Tyne, a charitable body) and Northern Syndicate Promotions Limited (a private limited company with share capital, now dissolved) – to span the issues of 'dual control' that pertain to the Town Moor, set out in various Town Moor Acts beginning with the 1774 Act. The events leading up to the 1774 act are discussed in a little more detail in the section 'Feet/depth'.

7　Involved in many processes, Cache's discussions tend to consider geological or generational timescales, rather than the days or weeks that provide the most obvious measure of the Hoppings.

8　Stewardship of the Town Moor, exercised on behalf of the Freemen by the Steward's Committee, demonstrates a propensity to reinforce its identity as a natural, simple space that exists for the good of all, bucolic, innocent and self-sustaining: the Town Moor as a common good. The Steward's Committee has reinforced the beneficence of this space through acts such as the expulsion of horse racing (although 'Race Week' remains in common parlance), and the incorporation of the temperance festival.

9　It is perhaps worth remarking at this point that it is thanks to these muddy conditions on the Moor that a muddy point of national law, viz a legal clarification of the definition of a fair, was cleared up. See the discussion in Dowling (1994, ¶6) of the precedent set by *'Walker v Murphy*: An assembly of roundabouts shows etc although held annually, is not a fair: *Walker v Murphy* [1914] 2 Ch 293; affirmed on appeal in [1915] 1 ch 71, the latter being a decision of the Court of Appeal.' This summarizes Acts of Parliament 1774 and 1870 which govern the freemen of the town of Newcastle upon Tyne and the Town Moor. Dowling notes (1994, ¶11.1) that 'Prior to 1882 horse races with roundabouts and shows had been held on the race ground, but in that year and thereafter they were held elsewhere. From 1882 to 1912 a temperance festival was held annually on the old race ground and various persons including Mr. Murphy had been licensed to bring roundabouts and shows to the ground. It appears that this temperance festival attracted many thousands of people. In 1912 heavy traction engines used by the defendant cut up the surface of the moor and seriously damaged the grass available for pasturing cattle. As a consequence, in 1914 the successors to the freemen who held rights of pasturage sought an injunction to prevent the defendant bringing roundabout etc. on to the moor.'

10   It is interesting to note that Forsyth Footpath, as with all the existing roads and footpaths on the Town Moor, 'remain[s] vested in the city council [and is] freed from herbage right', and that '[t]he said existing roads and footpaths shall be repaired and maintained by the city council who shall continue to be responsible for the lighting thereof'. (Town Moor Act 1998, Section 5.(1) and (2))

Bibliography

Alpers, Svetlana (1983), *The Art of Describing: Dutch Art in the Seventeenth Century*, Chicago: University of Chicago Press.

Bataille, Georges (1973), 'L'expérience intérieure', [1943] in Œuvres *complètes de G. Bataille*, Volume V, Paris: Gallimard.

Bataille, Georges (1985), 'Big Toe' [1929], in Georges Bataille, *Visions of Excess: Selected Writings, 1927–1939*, translated, edited and introduced by Allan Stoekl, Minneapolis, MN: University of Minnesota Press, 20–3.

Bataille, Georges (1992), 'Architecture', [1929] trans. Dominic Faccini, *October* #60, Spring, 25–6.

Baron, Frank (1984), *The Town Moor Hoppings*, Newbury: Lowell Barnes.

Cache, Bernard (1995), *Earth Moves: The Furnishing of Territories*, Writing Architecture Series, Cambridge, MA: MIT Press.

Dowling, Peter G. (1994), 'Charter fairs and markets: An analysis of the law undertaken on behalf of the Showmen's Guild of Great Britain', Boyes, Turner & Burrows, Solicitor to the Guild, Reading, 24 February.

Fenwick, Arthur J. (1941), 'A short history of the Newcastle upon Tyne Town Moor Temperance Festival' *Merry-Go-Round*, 1(5): 5–20.

Greenhalgh, Paul (2011), *Fair World: A History of the World's Fairs and Expositions from London to Shanghai 1851–2010*, London: Papadakis Publisher.

Ingraham, Catherine (1998), *Architecture and the Burdens of Linearity*, New Haven, CT: Yale University Press.

Krauss, Rosalind (1997a), 'Pulse', in Yve-Alain Bois and Rosalind Krauss, *Formless: A User's Guide*, New York: Zone Books, New York, 161–5.

Krauss, Rosalind (1997b), 'Yo-yo', in Yve-Alain Bois and Rosalind Krauss, *Formless: A User's Guide*, New York: Zone Books, New York, 219–23.

Krauss, Rosalind (1997c), 'The destiny of the *informe*', in Yve-Alain Bois and Rosalind Krauss, *Formless: A User's Guide*, New York: Zone Books, 235–52.

Stallybrass, Paul and White, Allon (1986), *The Politics and Poetics of Transgression*, London: Methuen.

Stewards' Committee of the Freemen of Newcastle upon Tyne, (1962), *A Short Account of the Rights of the Freemen of Newcastle-upon-Tyne in the Town Moor*, [1948], Newcastle upon Tyne: Freemen of Newcastle upon Tyne.

Walker, R. F. (1997), *The Institutions and History of the Freemen of Newcastle upon Tyne*, Newcastle upon Tyne: Stewards' Committee, Freemen of Newcastle upon Tyne.

Walker, Stephen (2004), 'Sacrificing architecture? Gordon Matta-Clark's building dissections', in Andrew Ballantyne (ed.) *Architectures: Modernism and After*, London: Blackwell, 118–41.

Intervention 3

Art/architecture practice

Didier Faustino

The following text is an edited fragment of the keynote presentation delivered by Didier Faustino at the AHRA conference on Transgression, 22 November 2013, at the Arnolfini, Bristol, UK.

I began work by forming, in 2001, an office in Paris – the Bureau des Mésarchitectures. My practice is partly an *homage* to Gordon Matta-Clark, for me one of the most honourable architects of the twentieth century, while the name is partly sourced from a plumber working on one of my very early projects who commented about the mis-architecture. I don't know if he was joking, but I took it really seriously and that concept, a mis-architecture, has informed our practice for nearly 15 years. I cannot be sure if we operate transgressively, but we are certainly digressive. I prefer not to qualify our office, or the people we work with, as architects, professionals, artists and so on – I'd rather consider ourselves as anarchist amateurs working obsessively on one particular topic: the nature of space, and asking 'what can be space today?'

The word 'fragility' has long been an important consideration within my work; indeed, it has been a source of inspiration for me since writing my diploma statement. Part of this fragility is found in the relationship with a client; there is always some doubt within this relationship; you can never know how, or when, the project will really end. And when thinking about space and architecture, there can also be a fragility in its resolution and practice. Even a minimal intervention, or renewal of a territory, can encourage a new way of looking at a space. I would also pose this very simple concept: there is no good or bad architecture, no good or bad clients, no good or bad situations –

Figure I3.1
My First House, 1996

there is only architecture. Creating architecture can be considered as embarking on an adventure; an adventure can be positive or negative, but it is always an experiment. You never know how it will end, and whether it finishes well or not simply depends.

One thing I'm sure of is that the paradigm of architecture has changed dramatically over the last century, so we need to adapt our practice and to explore the new situation. Peter Sloterdijk described how architecture ought not be the construction of islands; we must invert that sensibility. Architecture, says Sloterdijk, ought not be the practice of placing buildings in the environment but to place environments inside buildings.

One of my key references is George A. Romero's 1978 zombie film *Dawn of the Dead*. The first scene of the movie shows a television studio where an angry debate is being broadcast concerning the necessity of killing zombies. It is a very spatial discussion, and focuses on the moment, the situation, in which killing is morally, practically, ethically correct; while zombies are people who are 'getting killed and then getting up and killing' they are also family members. Thus there is this hesitation and a sense of action which swings one way and then the other. There is a very real ambiguity being tested.

If we are to consider transgression, the only way to arrive at a genuine transgression is not alone but with an accomplice; mostly this accomplice will be a client. That's why I like private clients; with a private client, where there is direct

Figure I3.2
**Revolution(s), 2004
Couvent des Cordeliers,
Paris**

contact, it's possible to explore and travel far from the starting point. My first client was a family in Portugal who commissioned me to create a cheap summer house – a house to last for just one summer. The reality is that six months after completion this first house of mine disappeared. There was a kind of 'brutal fragility' to this event, to quote a student of mine. I love this phrase. There is a transience to our work.

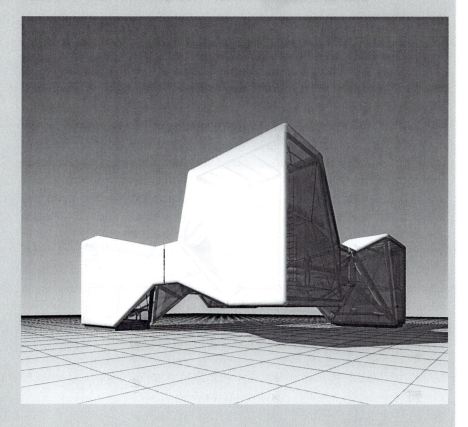

Figure I3.3
Porcelain bunker, 2006

Figure 13.4
**Les liaisons dangereuses,
2009**

Our 2004 work to create a temporary lecture hall for the Musée d'arte Moderne de la Ville de Paris began with the idea of fragility, focused on the creation of a double-inverted vortex, a kind of spiral, fabricated from the most ambiguous material we could find – the survival blanket. There is an ambiguity, a double meaning, to this material in that it was developed by NASA with DuPont as a reflective and protective element; it is a super-fragile, lightweight material used in the most dangerous and volatile conditions. The material can be described as a membrane, existing as a tension between states. It was, we felt, an ideal choice for communicating the idea of temporality, of a fragile intervention within a historic space. Simply by moving, the occupant could threaten to plunge the structure into a state of instability.

What might be the limits, or at least the consequences, of exploring transience, fragility, tension? One might imagine a porcelain bunker. I have proposed a hypothetical house for a couple who are not officially lovers, but who asked me to design a structure for the hypothetical possibility of them being together. The result was a proposal for a huge netted structure where the couple could, plausibly, make love anywhere. It is a huge bed of a house, a terrain of pleasure. There is of course a zone for bathing, and a small element reserved for cooking food (which one could eat beneath the house). The overall idea was to create this almost ephemeral structure from porcelain which embodies, like love, the condition of fragility.

I have had the good fortune to have been selected by many interesting clients, who engage an architect because they desire to be pushed far. What emerges is not always permitted to be realised, however. Our concept for a nightclub deliberately played with ideas of public/private, intimacy and desire, the trajectories of the body; however, the Mayor of Lyon refused the project. Occasionally we need to reconsider meeting places, to reimagine how we can exchange ideas, to question where and how power is exercised. Sometimes we need to consider inverting things to slow us down.

In 1960 Yves Klein produced an image of himself floating serenely in the air, *Le saut dans la vide (Leap into the Void)*. There is both an absurdity and brutal reality within such a jump, but it is one we must entertain.

Part III

Place

Chapter 7

Transgressing origins

Dialogical narratives in contemporary Japanese architecture

Robert Brown

At issue is the performative nature of differential identities ... negotiation of those spaces that are continually, contingentally, 'opening out', remaking the boundaries.

(Bhabha 1994: 313)

The activity of a character in a novel is always ideologically demarcated; he lives and acts in an ideological world of his own [and not in the unitary world of the epic], he has his own perceptions of the world that is incarnated in his action and in his discourse.

(Bakhtin 1981: 335)

Introduction

External and internal readings of contemporary Japanese architecture have generally situated it within overarching narratives, notably in some form of dialectic, which have often tended to focus on (though not been limited to) dualisms of traditional/modern (and/or Japanese/Western).[1] Intrinsic to these interpretations is a positioning of Japan's traditional architecture as a reified legacy underpinning the present day, whether in opposition to or in negotiation with Western/modern influences. It is a litany that incorporates, in particular here, a special relationship proclaimed for Japan between its architecture and nature, in which buildings are conceived of as an integral part of nature, and nature as intrinsic to the idea and actuality of building. This conception is underpinned by the assertion of a special affinity between its people and nature as a unique Japanese value.

These totalizing views of Japan, and narratives of Japanese-ness have in recent years however been exposed through interrogation as constructions that continue even today to structure conceptions of Japan (Dale 1986; Ivy 1995; Tanaka 1993). Unmasked, notably here, has been the very explicit appropriation of elitist values grounded in a particular aesthetic cultivation of nature, and their manipulated projection as a shared, and distinctly national trait (Goto-Jones 2009).

The premise of this chapter is not, however, to rewrite Japanese (architectural) history, though inevitably the inquiry here will raise questions of prevailing, and reductive, analysis of this history. Rather, my aim is to consider the role of the individual in transgressing the boundaries of projected origins, and how this might expand our understanding of both cultural identity and production. Drawing in part on Homi Bhabha, this perspective acknowledges that cultural identity is not driven only by authorized histories, but equally (if not more so) by a contingency of the everyday, and that cultural identity is in a continual process of (re)construction (Bhabha 1994). This view is expanded in Mikhail Bakhtin's possibility for the individual to articulate a sense of self in the context of overarching narratives (Bakhtin 1981).

To illustrate this argument I will consider here one contemporary Japanese architect, Taira Nishizawa. His work is neither limited by a lens founded in canonized views of Japanese architecture and nature, nor in a dialectic of the universal/modern and Japan-ness/traditional; rather, discussion with Nishizawa reveals that a more individual narrative of cultural (and personal) identity is being authored. This inquiry reveals more broadly the role of the individual in writing his/her own historicity.

Exposing grand narratives

Accounts of contemporary Japanese architecture, including those generated both externally and internally, have tended to position it within discussions of totalizing perspectives; these have most frequently been rendered as some form of dialectic, in which two traits are placed in some form of duality, whether in opposition or as generative of some grand hybrid. Though these dialectics have typically focused on a dualism of traditional/modern (and/or Japanese/Western), they equally extend to include the framing of further dichotomies such as chaos/order, heavy/light, minimalist/exaggerated, or substance/ephemeral.[2]

Intrinsic to these interpretations is a positioning of Japan's traditional architecture as a reified legacy underpinning the present day. Evidence of this is found in numerous sources: 'Extensive knowledge of the past provides the origins of present. The power of this ever-present history forms the basis of all contemporary values' (Fanelsa 2008: 6); 'For the Westerner visiting Japan … the most profound lessons in architecture lay, of course, in its glorious architectural heritage … My reaction to any new work in Japan is inevitably conditioned by these exemplars from the past' (Dixon

Figure 7.1
**Water basin
at Kennin-Ji
(Temple), Kyoto,
Japan – an
essentialized
image of
Japanese craft
and tradition**

1990: 10); 'The Japanese creative process is connected to deeply embedded traditions and philosophies' (Brownell 2011: 11).

A key aspect of the litany on Japanese tradition is a valorization of nature as a quintessential Japanese value; as Jiro Harada points out in his 1936 text *The Lesson of Japanese Architecture*, 'the love of nature [is] so strong in the Japanese' (Harada 1954 [1936]: 46), while more recently Schittich has referred to a 'love of all things natural' (Schittich 2002: 9). This acclaimed affinity for nature, it is argued, is echoed in the relationship of Japan's traditional architecture, which has continually been described as being informed by, and spatially and formally representing, the interrelationship between man and nature.[3] Botond Bognar writes that 'Japanese culture evolved from and is deeply rooted in the intense, uniquely intimate relationship of the Japanese to nature' (Bognar 1985: 23); while Gideon Golany notes that 'the ultimate goal is to achieve harmony between the two (human conduct and the environment) and create a pleasing ambiance' (Golany 1998: xxxiii). It is a sensibility that continues to be cited as having resonance in Japan's contemporary cultural identity; as Peter Kirby notes, 'Japan resonates with the belief that the singular characteristics of Japanese culture derive from the particularities of Japanese nature' (Kirby 2011: 73).

The casting of Japan which underpins these totalizing comments has, however, in recent years been challenged. Western conceptions (i.e., misreadings) of Japan can be recognized as having been formulated through a Western lens, with the perceived slipping all too easily into *a priori* frameworks of knowledge and understanding. What is too often analysed and interpreted is consciously, or unconsciously, selected to fit that pre-existing worldview. Concurrently, examination of Japanese self-conceptions of Japan reveal the construction of authorized frameworks of knowledge and understanding; i.e., authorized histories have been crafted to fit a culturally and politically acceptable world view.

Examining the latter point further, critical examination has uncovered the politicized and academic construction of Japanese identity (*Nihonjinron*, i.e., discourse on Japanese-ness), a modernizing agenda reactive to the external gaze and the infiltration of Western culture, as well as nationalistic forces which have sought to locate and define an authentic origin (*moto no tokoro*) (Ivy 1995). This forging of national identity first commenced in the years immediately following the Meiji Restoration in the middle of the nineteenth century, at a time when the Japanese nation's cultural, economic and political autonomy was under threat from external, colonizing forces. In opposition, the fledging Japanese government acted to articulate and propagate a shared sense of Japanese identity amongst what had previously been a disparate population. To do so, they specifically appropriated those aspects of Japanese culture that they felt most personified the image of Japan they would like to enculture in the nation, and simultaneously project to the outside world (Dale 1986; Ivy 1995; Tanaka 1993; Vlastos 1998); in effect, they selected aesthetic and moral values aligned with the ideal of the samurai elite (Goto-Jones 2009). This very purposeful selection reflects David Parkin's view that, 'just as memories of the past as an index of current belonging are likely to be selective, so uses of the past can indicate ideal future choices' (Parkin 1998: ix–xiv). The post-Meiji Restoration rulers' identification of the samurai as a cultural model is also a very political one; for a newly formed government seeking to engender a sense of loyalty to itself, the samurai's reputation for unflinching loyalty to their political masters constituted an ideal choice for the future from Japan's past.

The primary intention here is not to suggest that there is not some degree of veracity to these accounts of Japanese traditions, but rather that those that have been inherited are a selective interpretation of Japan's past, and that Japan's autogenic culture is a self-fiction. Unmasked, for example, have been the Chinese and Korean roots in Japan's past. To demonstrate, Ise Shrine has long been canonized, and perceived, both internally and externally, as the spiritual home of the Japanese people. This notional primitive hut has been said to concretize 'the primordial essence of the Japanese people' (Tange and Kawazoe 1965: 18–19). Yet so prevalent have been the influence of Chinese and Korean roots that even Ise Shrine bears the imprint of both, as well as of ongoing manipulations of its supposed authentic form owing to political agendas and responses to prevailing aesthetic sensibilities of the day (Isozaki 2006).

Conventional understanding of the special affinity with nature attributed to the Japanese people would seem far removed from this discussion. Yet interrogation reveals nature's place in the canonization of Japanese-ness as artificially generated and maintained. As John Clammer notes in discussing Japanese culture and nature, 'the constitution of society and the constitution of nature go hand-in-hand' (Clammer 1995: 80).

Coming from agrarian origins, the development of a relationship with nature is no surprise; the same however can be said of many agrarian-founded cultures. Moreover, while grounded in values of Shintoism, nature is neither loved nor worshipped; rather it is held in a sense of awe owing to both its beauty and destructive capability, and equally respected in that nature teaches us everything is impermanent; i.e. things change. Within this frame of reference, a sensibility towards nature was developed in which nature was cultivated to have the appearance of naturalness.[4] What is typically seen as having been inherited from a common tradition within Japanese culture is now more accurately understood as having being grounded in elite society. As Kenzo Tange notes,

> we hold a rather special view of the tradition that underlies Japanese architecture and gardens, particularly of the formalized tradition that was originally inspired by the upper levels of society.
>
> (Tange 1972: 7)

This elitist aesthetic was subsequently embedded through *Ni-hon-jin-ron* within the authorized account of Japanese culture, first notably in the geographer and journalist Shiga Shigetaka's seminal *Nihon Fukeiron* (*Japanese Landscape*) produced in 1894; this later found more philosophical expression in the historian and philosopher Tetsuro Watsuji's influential *Fudo* first published in 1935 (Dale 1986). Shigetaka's text sought to counter external forces by celebrating what he perceived as the distinctiveness of the Japanese landscape and, in parallel, its climate, and how these had helped to foster an equally distinctive relationship between the Japanese people and nature; Shigetaka's idealization was then further extended by Watsuji, who articulated a particular relationship between Japanese climate and culture, the latter as represented notably by what he saw as the traditional house (i.e., the houses of its historical elite) and the co-joined cultivated gardens.

This construction of nature was later reflected by nature's deconstruction (Brecher 2000; Callicott and Ames 1989; Kirby 2011; Tanaka 1993). Integral to this erosion was geological research carried out by Western scientists whose work helped to demystify received conceptions of mythical origins, to be replaced by an understanding of the world as part of a natural phenomenon (Tanaka 1993). This coincided with assimilation of Western conceptions of nature which philosophically delineated nature as *other*, in contrast to indigenous language which articulates that *everything* is nature (Brecher 2000). 'The separation of nature from culture destabilized such inherent understandings that had organized society and raised the possibility that the texts and knowledge that had been accepted as natural or originary are cultural, that is, created' (Tanaka 1993: 64).

Still later, nature was reconstructed through intertwined economic–political initiatives to re-emplace narratives of Japan's origins. One of the primary examples of

Figure 7.2
**Tree and rock
garden at Kennin-
Ji (Temple),
Kyoto, Japan
– the cultivated
garden as nature**

this is the *furusato* movement. Literally translated as 'hometown', *furusato* is identified with government-supported agendas throughout the twentieth century to both identify the home Japan's native culture, and to reconnect urban Japan with its traditional roots in a rural, agrarian past (and in so doing revitalize an economically and socially declining countryside). This celebration of a return home was prompted through the designation of villages that urbanites might visit and so again return to their spiritual origin. Parallel to this was 'Discover Japan', a national advertising campaign run by Japan National Railway during the 1970s (Hendry 2003; Robertson 1998). Marilyn Ivy has examined the latter in particular, noting that 'the campaign inundated Japanese with hundreds of condensed images of authentic Japan, generically imagined and presented' (Ivy 1995: 35). Ivy continues, observing that 'Discover Japan stressed the interaction of the traveller with nature (*shizen*) and tradition; by touching (*fureau*) nature and tradition, Japanese would discover themselves as Japanese' (Ivy 1995: 43). In essence, it 'evoked the possibility of a return to native origins and ethnically true selves…[and Japan] (re)discovering its authenticity by moving through originary landscapes' (Ivy 1995: 41).

The place of nature within Japanese identity has been shown to have been subject to more fundamental construction. A prime example is the assertion that the

Japanese people's affinity is directly attributable to Japan's climate, the argument being that Japan's benevolent (though changeable) climate and abundant resources predispose existence in harmony with nature (Kirby 2011). This argument extends from Shigetaka in the late 1800s through Watsuji in the 1930s and continues to be echoed today. Yet as Peter Dale notes:

> such works drew inspiration from that vein of Western writing, from Montesquieu to Herder, which related the diversity of societies and cultures to geographical factors, and redeployed [it] on the West–Japan axis.
>
> (Dale 1986: 41–2)

In a similar sense we know that Watsuji's *Fudo* was both inspired by and written as a nationally-motivated response to Heidegger's more 'European' texts. 'This rendering of "Japanese nature" has thrived within the quasi-scholarly genre of conservative, essentialist Japanese writing ... and has influenced many in a country prone to collective introspection' (Kirby 2011: 73).

This archaeology of Japan's cultural origins should come as no surprise; postmodern (and postcolonial) discourse has revealed various accounts of authentic origin as constructions (Anderson 2006; Hobsbawn 1983). On these concepts I will not long dwell; external categorization imposing cultural identity has long since been critiqued (Brown and Maudlin 2012), while the intentional fabrication of culture and authentic origins has been well exposed (Anderson 2006; Hobsbawn 1983). The former arises from a tendency of external agents to impose totalizing readings. They reflect an apparent need to define and normalize an understanding of the found condition. In effect, the external agent sees what he/she want to see, fulfilling his/her pre-existing conceptions, with too little consideration given to the specific aspirations, concerns or practices of those in this context.

Totalized readings of culture are not, however, limited to external projections; indeed, equally exposed has been the very purposeful fabrication of authentic origins from the internal condition. Eric Hobsbawn has articulated such acts as 'invented tradition', by which he means 'a set of practices which seek to ... [imply] continuity with the past' (Hobsbawn, 1983: 1). Michel Foucault suggests that these links to the past are typically positioned as part of a chronological, sequential development, even when this origin has no claim in reality (Foucault 2002).

Central to this analysis is that depictions of cultural origins are commonly accorded a sense of authority. Stories of origin reify a totalizing history, bringing fragmentary accounts of events and tales of shared experience together into a grand narrative. This grand narrative is assumed to be true and absolute (Said 1985), and so accorded a power over people's lives. It is in this convergence of claims of origin with power that the act of fabrication of origins is more fully revealed.

Examination of culture reveals that any claim to an authentic cultural origin is not ideologically neutral; rather, it is motivated by economic, political and/or social agendas. Recalling Bernd Happauf's interrogation of *heimat* as a desired place of belonging (Happauf 2005), when examined more thoroughly what is exposed is that what is often portrayed as the absolute, essential attributes of a culture have instead been fabricated by those with vested interests in that cultural reading's assimilation both internally and externally. As posited by Hobsbawn, acts of cultural construction are implemented by those seeking to establish or legitimize institutions and their position of authority (Hobsbawn 1983). 'Once "there", they can serve as formal models to be imitated, and, where expedient, consciously exploited in a Machiavellian spirit" (Anderson 2006: 45).

Perhaps most distinctive in this regard have been the efforts of governments to appropriate and restructure narratives of origin in order to foster and reinforce a sense of national identity. Bhabha has noted how nationalists have 'sought authority in the authenticity of origins' (Bhabha 1994: 171), while Timothy Brennan adds that 'the evocation of deep, sacred origins ... becomes a contemporary, practical means of *creating* a people' (Brennan 1990: 50). While seemingly well-intentioned, we know from interrogation of history that accompanying such narratives have been acts of coercion, exploitation and exclusion; one of the more notable, and certainly disturbing examples of this is illustrated in returning to Happauf's critique of *heimat* (Happauf 2005).

The intention here is not to redraft Japanese architectural history. While the narratives that have tended to be projected, whether from the external or internal vantage point, represent some form of construction, running through them is some element of truth and awareness that they are underpinned by very real cultural, economic and political motivations. My aim in the preceding pages has rather been to call into question the overarching veracity of such narratives, and to lead into a parallel inquiry on the absence of the individual in such homologies. Equally, my intention is examine the capacity for the individual to transgress the boundaries of projected origins and author their own historicity.

The case for the individual's writing of cultural identity

In place of polarized identities, Bhabha argues for an ambiguous in-between. In this space grand narratives of origins are replaced by re-inscription (Bhabha 1994). My aim here is to extend this premise of re-inscription of cultural identity to the individual.

The tendency in considerations of culture, as Seyla Benhabib reminds us, is to think of its members as an abstract, generalized entity (Benhabib 1992). It is a point further articulated by Dell Upton, who suggests cultural interpretations:

> often conflate ... personal and cultural identity ... [reducing the individual] to a common body of beliefs and practices – to a cultural artifact, that is.
>
> (Upton 2001, p. 302)

Lost in this framing is the place of the individual as a unique, autonomous person with that culture, or as Benhabib would phrase a 'concrete individual' (Benhabib 1992). Equally negated is the capacity of the individual to pursue a personal dialogue within the context of wider cultural narratives.

In place of citing individuals within totalizing narratives, I posit that cultural identity is not driven only by approved histories, but equally (if not more so) by our individual actions in the everyday, and that our identities are continually under construction. This argument is not without foundation. Anthony Giddens asserts the individual is not a passive entity, with identity solely determined by external forces (Giddens 1991). Bhabha further attests people are not simply part of some body politic, undifferentiated subjects within a historicized and politicized line of discourse (Bhabha 1994; Pechey 1989; Urry 2002). We are more than simply set pieces within authorized histories, but as Foucault reasons we have our own historicity; an individual, unique experience in relation to wider society (Foucault 2002). Edward Said further argues that as individuals we have the capacity for change, even to redefine our beginnings (Said 1985). It is an argument that is moreover grounded in an acknowledgement of advances through constructs of the everyday, and shifts in anthropology/sociology towards the individual's subjective, personal narrative of their experience (Graburn 2001). As Clifford Geertz offers:

> We must, in short, descend into detail, past the misleading tags, past the metaphysical types, past the empty similarities to grasp firmly the essential character of not only the various cultures but the various sorts of individuals within each culture, if we wish to encounter humanity face to face.
>
> (Geertz 1973: 53)

This is not, however, an argument for individualism. I suggest neither a retreat into claims of self-authenticity as Charles Taylor warns against (Taylor 1991), nor towards monologue as Kojin Karatani cautions (Karatani 1995). Nor should we slip into a dualistic opposition of the individual and the collective (Kondo 1990; Ricœur 2004), a dichotomy well embedded in Western philosophical tradition. What is needed is a discourse recognizing we are both part of a larger order that can make claims on us (Taylor 1991) and that simultaneously as individuals we can make claims on wider culture.

Moreover, this world of our own making is not achieved independently; rather it is constructed through dialogical interaction with others, and that through this dialogical action we continually transgress, i.e., negotiate and remake, the boundaries of our identities. The individual is not mutually exclusive of any shared understandings of culture; the former operates in parallel with the latter. Yet at the same time the latter does not delimit the former:

> Codes of established narratives in various cultures define our capacities to tell our individual stories … nonetheless, just as the grammatical rules of a language, once acquired, do not exhaust our capacity to build an infinite number of well-formed sentences in a language, so socialization and acculturation do not determine an individual's life story or his or her capacity to initiate new actions and new sentences in conversation.
>
> (Benhabib 2002: 15)

Concurrently, 'we become aware of who we are by learning to become conversation partners in these narratives' (Ibid). This proposition recognizes that our cultural and personal identities are not fixed, but rather are constructed through our own individual choices and actions, and equally through interaction with others.

In this context I turn to Bakhtin's construct of dialogism, and the individual's possibility to articulate a sense of self in the context of overarching narratives (Bakhtin 1981). Bakhtin's conception of dialogue is not, however, located in the trappings of a dialectical relationship; i.e., a juxtaposition of opposites, nor a hybridization resolving supposed polarities. In discussing Bakhtin's work, Katerina Clark and Michael Holquist outline dialogue as expanding to a relational both/and. It is a discourse playing off a link between things, both those present and latent; concurrently, there is no absolute meaning but rather multiple meanings that can be held simultaneously (Clark and Holquist 1984).

Inherent in such an intention is an evocation of Kantian ethics' consideration of the other (Bakhtin 1993). Both founded on, and opened up by dialogue, is recognition of that outside ourselves. Revealed in this liminal space are multiple possibilities whose simultaneous presences do not negate the other, but rather whose overlaps and divergences offer opportunity for understanding, and sometimes (re)making meaning in a continual forging of one's own self-identity, and with it cultural identity.

> It is in the emergence of the interstices – the overlap and displacement of domains of difference – that the intersubjective and collective experiences of nationess, community interest, or cultural value are negotiated.
>
> (Bhabha 1994: 2)

Simultaneously, in grounding his discussion in language, Bakhtin notes that:

> Language, for the individual consciousness, lies on the borderline between oneself and the other. The word in language is half someone else's. It becomes 'one's own' only when the speaker populates it with his own intentions, his own accent, when he appropriates the word, adapting it to his own semantic and expressive intention.
>
> (Bakhtin 1993: 293)

Intrinsic to this discussion is an understanding that the playing out of this dialogue does not only happen on some grand stage, but rather is more often embedded in everyday experience. This is echoed in de Certeau's observation that 'each individual is a locus in which incoherent (and often contradictory) plurality of such relational determinations interact' (de Certeau 1984: xi).

Seemingly at odds with the sense of conformity central to stereotypes of the Japanese people (Kuwayama 1992), dialogism resonates with a Japanese sense of crafting oneself in interaction with the communal. As Dorrine Kondo submits, individuals are part of not totalizing but rather multiple relationships, rendering the boundaries of their identity far more flexible than our Western preconceptions delimit (Kondo 1990). While such an attribute is arguably stronger today with Japan's 'New Generation' (i.e., those who came to maturity during the Bubble Economy) (Hendry 2003), the roots of the conception of Japanese social relations focusing on 'we' rather than 'I' (i.e., a Western theory of individualism), lie yet again in *Ni-hon-jin-ron*. As Dale identifies:

while intent on projecting an image of Japan's national uniqueness abroad, the [those advancing the constructs of] *nihon-jinron* vigorously deny the very possibility of individual, uniquely personal identity within Japan itself.

(Dale 1986: 22)

Nishizawa and Sun-Pu Church

The selection of the contemporary scene in Japan as the site to explore this proposition is not yet another case of Western (Orientalist) fascination with Japan; rather it recognizes that present-day Japan provides a useful context precisely because of the totalizing projections, and myths of origins, made upon it. Considered here is one architect, Taira Nishizawa, from Japan's 'New Generation'; i.e., those who came of age (architecturally) during the 1980s' bubble economy. Growing out of discussions with Nishizawa, what emerges is not an essentialized figure of Japanese culture, but an individual articulating his own sense of self.

Taira Nishizawa's Sun-Pu Church in Shizuoka, Japan is at first glance nondescript; situated in a dense urban context immediately adjacent to a road and a railway line, the church is composed of two smallish and linked volumes. The smaller of the two volumes is a two-storey block with a pitched roof housing the community hall and pastor's facilities, while the larger is a cube three storeys in height with only a single entry at the corner breaking up the timber cladding of the facade. Despite its deceptive outward appearance, it is upon arriving in the main church hall housed within the timber cube that Nishizawa's handiwork is really revealed.

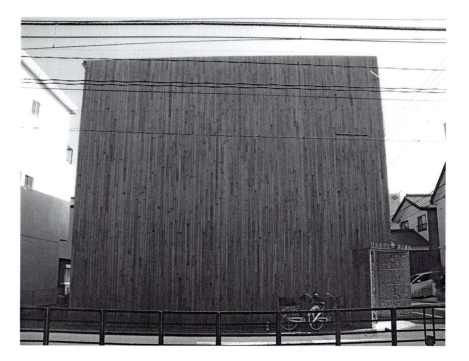

Figure 7.3
Exterior of Sun-Pu Church, Shizuoka, Japan – a simple cube in a fragmented urban context

Figure 7.4
**Interior of Sun-Pu
Church, Shizuoka,
Japan – described
as being like light
in the forest.**

Upon entering this space the eye is drawn upwards along the variegated timber lining which stands proud of the interior walls; this lining increasingly dissipates, becoming almost veil-like, as it rises to a similarly veil-like timber ceiling lining suspended below the roof. This canopy diffuses sunlight penetrating from roof-lights above, while this light simultaneously dematerializes the lace-like timber canopy it filters through, and concurrently the walls below upon which this light falls.

While the design of this space has met with acclaim both nationally and internationally, what is of interest to my discussion here is how this space has been interpreted. Fairly typical is the brief description of the church noted in the *JA Yearbook 2008*, which states, 'light penetrates through openings [in] the pine roof like sunlight filtering through a forest canopy' (Yoshida, 56). This statement immediately situates Sun-Pu Church in the context of essentialized projections of the Japanese people, and its architecture, as being rooted in a unique relationship with nature. Seen through this lens there are three distinct aspects to note.

First, the analogy 'like sunlight filtering through a forest canopy' makes a direct association with nature; i.e., it places this space as if (in) nature itself. At Sun-Pu nature is not, however, present through normalized images or symbolic representations of Japanese gardens as nature, e.g., vegetation, water, or rock.

Rather, and more abstractly, nature is present as sunlight. The sunlight penetrates into the church, interacting with its physical form, breaking down the artificial barrier between inside (man-made) and outside (nature). At Sun-Pu sunlight acts much in the same way that space is seen to act in a traditional Buddhist temple; there is no clear distinction between inside and outside space, but rather, owing to the multi-layered envelope found at the notional boundary of the building, interior and exterior overlap. In this sense the sunlight as space is perceptually and experientially both inside and outside simultaneously; in this ambiguity sunlight as space is equally suggestive of the ambiguity of nature itself.

Second, one can sense in the phrase 'light penetrates through openings' reference to a valuing in Japanese culture of the impermanence of things in nature. The dissipation of the light made tangible by the timber filigree of the canopy and the walls, and the simultaneous dissipation of the canopy and wall's physicality by the light itself, renders each seemingly less permanent and as something more fleeting. Across the day and the seasons, both the apparent physical presence of light and perceived materiality of the built surfaces are in a state of flux, from the tangible to the intangible, from present to absent, from substance to the ephemeral.

Third, the setting the author describes with the phrase 'sunlight filtering through a forest canopy' calls to mind some primal space in the forest, a space whose quintessential qualities might reconnect us with nature, and with it God. This archetype has resonance in Japan, and in particular with associations of Shinto practice of going into nature, notably to spaces seen as having some essential quality of nature and so emplaced with the presence of a *kami* (god). To such a place one goes to purify and thus refresh oneself, typically spiritually, though this purification may equally be about cleansing oneself emotionally and mentally, if not also physically. The author's evocation of a primal space suggests that in entering the church one has returned to nature, and found a space of sanctuary in which to purify oneself.

Each of the above in themselves, as well as collectively, would seem to reinforce a sense of a harmonious connection with nature, and of a contemporary Japanese architecture working with traditional values through a modern re-interpretation. Nishizawa's intentions, however, defy such readings. However much the interpretations noted above may resonate both with what we have read and heard about the dialectics of the traditional and modern in Japan, and a special relationship with nature in Japanese culture, Nishizawa's use of light, and its interplay with the physicality of church, emerges from a far different motivation.[5]

Nishizawa's interest in light is not founded in some harmonic, benevolent interplay between nature and the spatial form of the building. Rather, he sees the relationship between nature and the man-made as part of a struggle. Reflecting the reverence and fear with which nature is simultaneously held, Nishizawa believes that architecture has always had to compete with nature, and that it is architecture's only true rival. Here nature is not something to be eliminated, but neither is building somehow subservient to nature. He believes that man cannot survive in nature without the man-made, but simultaneously that man has moved away from nature and that this is equally not viable. Rather, he believes a balance must be found between the

Figure 7.5
**Interior detail of
Sun-Pu Church,
Shizuoka, Japan
– architecture
and nature in
competition**

two that places both on the same level in a dialogical relationship, in which neither is
negated or diminished but in which the other is equally recognized.

This dialogue, if not a sense of competition, between the man-made and
natural, informs not only his general attitude, but equally his research on nature
which informs his praxis (Nishizawa 2008). For Sun-Pu, Nishizawa's research focused
on light, and on controlling that light. This extended from studies of a rigor and
methodology reflecting his formal architectural education, his interest is underpinned
by a worldview informed by the particular circumstances of his own life (a childhood
illness resulting in over-sensitivity of his skin to sunlight) and his own philosophical
(and here at Sun-Pu, his own Christian) beliefs (Brown and Terazono 2010).

Similarly, Nishizawa rejects propositions of 'going back to nature', or of
some theoretically driven return to the primitive. While acknowledging value in the
latter's attitude, he feels that the primitive is a discussion that has always made more
sense in the West. Moreover, he feels that such a return is only warranted when
there is appropriate context for such a return; an evocation of some primitive form
does not make sense when projected out of its context – e.g., in an urban, developed
setting – and will only be present as a contrivance. At Sun-Pu Church spiritual space
is not manifested in some literal or figurative evocation of nature; Sun-Pu's sense

of sanctuary emerges from the sense of ease felt in being in a sensitively crafted environment; Nishizawa's architecture acts to control and keep at bay the outside world, be it nature's light or man-made chaos.

Discussion with Nishizawa reveals that another story of identity is being authored, one of his own writing. Exploring Nishizawa's intentions further, he doesn't delimit himself to any sense of Japanese-ness that might be projected onto him. Aware of traditions reaching back in time, an explicit return is not what motivates him. Nor does any dialectical reconciliation with modernity through a merging of the traditional and the modern, most particularly as some conscious, critical reinterpretation of the traditional akin to Liane Lefaivre and Alexander Tzonis's act of defamiliarization. He is critical of both longstanding notions of tradition and more recent traditions of Modernism; neither, he feels, are able to address contemporary demands.

At Sun-Pu Church nature is not, however, manifested in some literal or figurative representation. While he is well aware of such approaches, just as he is aware of Japanese architecture's historic legacy, Sun-Pu reflects Nishizawa's own personal sensibility toward nature, light and space as informed by his own experience. His engagement with nature is founded in an understanding of it as intrinsic to architecture, and that architecture must be further developed in parallel with our growing understanding of nature. His work grows out of his own worldview, in dialogue with (though not delimited nor hybridized by) an awareness of his own cultural context.

Conclusion

What unfolds from this enquiry into Nishizawa's work is a more carefully delineated comprehension of the individual in writing their own identity, in conjunction/disjunction with broader public histories. Bound neither by negotiating the traditional and modern or other constructed totalizing histories, nor by rejecting them all together, he understands his personal and cultural identity as emerging from a space of his own making in dialogue with wider cultural narratives.

Nishizawa stands alone – an individual articulating his own sense of the world. Yet his is equally a shared discussion, as he is not alone in this act. To fix Japan, its people and architecture into any bounded domain, including binaries of traditional (Japanese) and modern (Western), only limits our understanding. Equally, to site individuals within set boundaries predetermined by cultural fabrications and projections only neuters the potential of the individual. We need to understand self as formed through a multiplicity of sensibilities that may converge and diverge.

What I delineate is a comprehension of the individual in writing themselves, in conjunction/disjunction with broader public histories. Bound not by imposed totalizing histories, nor by rejecting any truths within them, individuals (re)trace their personal and cultural identity within a space of their own making in dialogue with these wider narratives.

Identities are never unified ... never singular but multiply across different, often intersecting and antagonistic discourses, practices and positions. They are subject to transformation ... Though they seem to invoke an origin in a historical past with which they continue to correspond, actually identities are always questions of using the resources of history, language and culture in a process of becoming rather than being: not 'who we are' or 'where we came from', so much as what we might become.

(Hall 1996: 4)

Acknowledgements

The author would like to thank the following: Taira Nishizawa, for an ongoing dialogue about his praxis; Plymouth University for supporting an extended visit to Japan; and my partner Toshiko Terazono, for her assistance in helping me navigate Japan.

Notes

1   The term 'Western' is introduced here with caution; such terminology has historically been utilized as a cultural point of self-reference to distinguish the 'other', that is, that which one is not. Any uncritical use overlooks how such terms have been manipulated by both East and West to serve cultural, economic and political ideologies, and the intrinsic nature of culture not as fixed entities but rather as transient, shifting and fluctuating. See: Brown 2011; Brown and Maudlin 2012. The use of the term 'Western' here draws upon various discourse which has critiqued the West for its positioning of the 'other'.
2   See for example: Brownell 2011; Dixon 1990; Golany 1998; Fanelsa 2008; Isozaki 1985; Isozaki 1996; Jodidio 1997; Meyhofer 1994; Schittich 2002; Suzuki 2000.
3   As a negative proof of this framing, celebrated Japanese architect Tadao Ando has called attention to the disappearance of 'a feature that was formerly most characteristic of Japanese residential architecture; intimate connection with nature and openness to the natural world', cited in Frampton 1983: 158.
4   See for example: Cabañas 1997; Kalland and Asquith 1997; Martinez 2005.
5   The discussion which follows, unless otherwise noted, draws on three primary sources: Nishizawa 2006; Nishizawa 2008; Brown and Terazono 2010.

Bibliography

Anderson, B. (2006) *Imagined Communities,* London: Verso.
Bakhtin, M. (1981) *The Dialogic Imagination*, trans C. Emerson and M. Holquist, Austin, TX: University of Texas Press.
Bakhtin, M. (1993) *Toward a Philosophy of the Act*, Austin, TX: University of Texas Press.
Benhabib, S. (1992) *Situating the Self*, Cambridge: Polity Press.
Benhabib, S. (2002) *The Claims of Culture: Equality and Diversity in the Global Era*, Princeton, NJ: Princeton University Press.
Bhabha, H. K. (1994) *The Location of Culture*, Abingdon: Taylor & Francis.
Bognar, B. (1985) *Contemporary Japanese Architecture*, New York: Van Nostrand Reinhold.
Brecher, W. P. (2000) *An Investigation of Japan's Relationship to Nature and Environment*, Lewiston, NY: Edwin Mellen Press.
Brennan, T. (1990) 'The national longing for form', in H. K. Bhabha (ed.) *Nation and Narration*, Abingdon: Routledge.

Brown, R. (2011) 'The elusiveness of culture', in P. Beacock, G. Makstutitis and R. Mull (eds) *Engaging in Architectural Education*, London: London Metropolitan University Press.

Brown, R. and Maudlin, D. (2012) 'Concepts of vernacular architecture', in C.G. Crysler, S. Cairns and H. Heynen (eds) *The SAGE Handbook of Architectural Theory*, London: Sage.

Brown, R. and Terazono, T. (2010) Interview with Taira Nishizawa. Tokyo, Japan, 6 September.

Brownell, B. (2011) *Matter in the Floating World*, New York: Princeton Architectural Press.

Cabañas, P. (1997) 'Bijinga and nature: a single beauty', in P. Asquith and A. Kalland (eds) *Japanese Images of Nature: Cultural Perspectives*, London: Routledge.

Callicott, J. Baird and Ames, R. (1989) 'Introduction', in J. Baird Callicott and R. Ames (eds) *Nature in Asian Traditions of Thought*, Albany, NY: State University of New York Press.

Clammer, J. (1995) *Difference and Modernity: Social Theory and Contemporary Japanese Society*, London: Kegan Paul International.

Clark, K. and Holquist, M. (1984) *Mikhail Bakhtin*, Cambridge, MA: Harvard University Press.

Dale, P. (1986) *The Myth of Japanese Uniqueness*, London: Routledge.

de Certeau, M. (1984) *The Practice of Everyday Life*, Berkeley, CA: University of California Press.

Dixon, J. Morris (1990) 'Introduction: Japanese avant-garde architects', in B. Bognar (ed.) *The New Japanese Architecture*, New York: Rizzoli.

Fanelsa, S. (2008) 'Do we know Japan?', in Y. Edagawa (ed.) *Japanese Identities: Architecture Between Aesthetics and Nature*, Berlin: Jovis Verlag.

Foucault, M. (2002 [1970]) *The Order of Things,* London: Routledge.

Frampton, K. (1983) 'Prospects for a critical regionalism', *Perspecta: The Yale Architectural Journal*, 20, 147–62.

Geertz, C. (1973) *The Interpretation of Cultures*, London: Fontana Press.

Giddens, A. (1991) *Modernity and Self-Identity: Self and Society in the Late Modern Age*, Cambridge: Polity Press.

Golany, G. (1998) 'Japanese urban environment', in G. Golany, K. Hanake and O. Koide (eds) *Japanese Urban Environment*, New York: Pergamon.

Goto-Jones, C. (2009) *Modern Japan: A Very Short Introduction,* Oxford: Oxford University Press.

Graburn, G. (2001) 'Learning to consume: what is heritage and when is it traditional?', in N. AlSayyad (ed.) *Consuming Tradition, Manufacturing Heritage: Global Norms and Urban Forms in the Age of Tourism*, London: Routledge.

Hall, S. (1996) 'Introduction: who needs identity?', in S. Hall and P. du Gay (eds) *Questions of Cultural Identity*, London: Sage.

Happuaf, B. (2005) 'Spaces of the vernacular: Ernst Block's philosophy of hope and the German hometown', in M. Umback and B. Happauf (eds) *Vernacular Modernism,* Palo Alto, CA: Stanford University Press.

Harada, J. (1954 [1936]) *The Lesson of Japanese Architecture*, London: Studio.

Hendry, J. (2003 [1987]) *Understanding Japanese Society*, 3rd edn, London: Routledge Curzon.

Hobsbawn, E. (1983) 'Introduction: inventing traditions', in E. Hobsbawn and T. Ranger (eds) *The Invention of Tradition*, Cambridge: Cambridge University Press.

Isozaki, A (1985) 'Foreword', in B. Bognar (ed.) *Contemporary Japanese Architecture: Its Development and Challenge*, New York: Van Nostrand Reinhold.

Isozaki, A. (1996) *The Island Nation Aesthetic*, London: Academy Editions Polemics.

Isozaki, A. (2006) *Japan-ness in Architecture,* Cambridge: The MIT Press.

Ivy, M. (1995) *Discourses of the Vanishing: Modernity, Phantasm, Japan*, Chicago, IL: University of Chicago Press.

Jodidio, P (1997) 'The sun also rises: Japanese architects in the 1990s', in P. Jodidio, (ed.) *Contemporary Japanese Architects* Volume 2, Cologne: Taschen.

Kalland, A. and Asquith, P. (1997) 'Japanese Perceptions of Nature: Ideals and Illusions', in P. Asquith and A. Kalland (eds) *Japanese Images of Nature: Cultural Perspectives*, London: Routledge.

Karatani, K. (1995) *Architecture as Metaphor*, trans. S. Kohso, Cambridge, MA: MIT Press.

Kirby, P. (2011) *Troubled Natures: Waste, Environment, Japan*, Honolulu, HI: University of Hawai'i Press.

Kondo, D. (1990) *Crafting Selves: Power, Gender and Discourses of Identity in a Japanese Workplace*, Chicago, IL: University of Chicago Press.

Kuwayama, T. (1992) 'Self in Japanese culture', in N. Rosenberger (ed.) *Japanese Sense of Self*, Cambridge: Cambridge University Press.

Martinez, D. P. (2005) 'On the "nature" of Japanese culture, or, is there a Japanese sense of nature?', in J. Robertson (ed.) *A Companion to the Anthropology of Japan*, Malden, MA: Blackwell.

Meyhofer, D. (1994) 'The Japanese miracle: from a Western viewpoint', in D. Meyhofer (ed.) *Contemporary Japanese Architects*, Cologne: Taschen.

Nishizawa, T. (2006) 'Bodies and activities', *AA Files*, 54, 15–22.

Nishizawa, T. (2008) 'Research on the natural world', *Japan Architecture*, 71, Autumn, 12–19.

Parkin, D. (1998) 'Foreword', in N. Lovell (ed.) *Locality and Belonging*, London: Routledge.

Pechey, G. (1989) 'On the borders of Bakhtin: dialogisation, decolonization', in K. Hirschkop and D. Shepherd (eds) *Bakhtin and Cultural Theory*, Manchester: Manchester University Press.

Ricœur, P. (2004) *Memory, History, Forgetting*, Chicago, IL: University of Chicago Press.

Robertson, J. (1998) 'It takes a village: internationalization and nostalgia in postwar Japan', in S. Vlastos (ed.) *Mirror of Modernity: Invented Traditions in Modern Japan*, Berkeley, CA: University of California Press.

Said, E. (1985 [1975]) *Beginnings: Intention and Method*, London: Granta Books.

Schittich, C. (2002) 'Japan: a land of contradictions', in C. Schittich (ed.) *Japan: Architecture, Constructions, Ambiances*, Basel: Birkhauser.

Suzuki, H. (2000) 'Nature, material, and substance', *Japan Architect*, 38, Summer, 10.

Tanaka, S. (1993) *Japan's Orient: Rendering Pasts into History*, Berkeley, CA: University of California Press.

Tange, K. (1972) *Katsura: Tradition and Creation in Japanese Architecture*, New Haven, CT: Yale University Press.

Tange, K. and Kawazoe, N. (1965) *Ise, Prototype of Japanese Architecture*, Cambridge, MA: MIT Press.

Taylor, C. (1991) *The Ethics of Authenticity*, Cambridge, MA: Harvard University Press.

Upton, D. (2001) 'Authentic anxieties', in N. AlSayyad (ed.) *Consuming Tradition, Manufacturing Heritage: Global Norms and Urban Forms in the Age of Tourism*, London: Routledge.

Urry, J. (2002 [1990]) *The Tourist Gaze*, 2nd edn, London: Sage.

Vlastos, S. (1998) 'Tradition: past/present culture and modern Japanese history', in S. Vlastos (ed.) *Mirror of Modernity: Invented Traditions of Modern Japan*, Berkeley, CA: University of California Press.

Yoshida, N. (2008) *Japan Architect 72. Yearbook 72 – The Japanese Scene in Japan 2008*, Japan: Japan Architect.

Chapter 8

Rupturing the surface of the known

Phoebe Crisman

The concept of transgression, to go beyond established limits, has re-emerged in architectural discourse as a powerful way to produce architectural knowledge and new forms of practice.[1] Processes that destabilize accepted social, political, and spatial boundaries may also benefit architectural pedagogy and programs. This volume is an appropriate venue to consider the value of transgression for architectural education, while bearing in mind that each temporal, geographic, and institutional context establishes specific limits. This chapter examines how an international traveling studio and the author's associated trans-disciplinary research intentionally disrupted established conventions that limited where, what, and how an architecture studio could be taught at an architecture school in the US. These accepted conventions included: the necessity of a fixed studio space with *cutting-edge* computing equipment; a lack of appreciation for the architectural importance of cultural difference, non-Western history, local materials and methods of making, and sustainability broadly conceived; a focus on the disembodied acquisition and digital mapping of quantitative data; and the privileging of parametricism as a process and a style disengaged from the everyday realities of people and place.[2] Instead, the traveling studio had an alternative agenda that sought to help students understand architecture as part of a larger cultural context and to construct knowledge through exploration. Questions of how limits on location, content, and design methodology are established, by whom, and to what end are essential considerations for studio instructors operating in the perceived margins. Such transgressive studio actions distant from the location of institutional control can potentially disrupt the center through student agency upon their return. Changed values, broader perceptions, and *foreign* ways of designing can infiltrate and unsettle the given.

In this chapter I examine how students studying architecture abroad are compelled to question their own assumptions and challenge the limits and limitations of the accepted studio pedagogy. This happened in two distinct ways: by experiencing and studying spaces of difference, and by creating speculative proposals for an unfamiliar culture, climate, and place. The examples discussed come from the *India Initiative,* a traveling studio and interdisciplinary research platform at the University of Virginia. By transgressing expectations about the location of bodies in the space of architectural education, this studio broke free of the normative spatial and curricular regimes of control. A peripatetic group of architecture students and instructors traveled for six weeks with the purpose of experiencing and understanding sustainable practices in the ancient villages and emerging megacities of India.[3] By moving through a *foreign* space where one's identity is challenged, for instance, by differences in acceptable physical proximity and the use of public space, participants achieved a bodily understanding of Henri Lefebvre's argument that space is socially produced. Examining the relationship between cultural identity and architecture became essential. Several theoretical concepts informed the India studio pedagogy, including the educational value of spatial dislocation; experiential learning that engages the bodily senses; drawing as reflection; and constructed knowledge and other ways of knowing. The *India Initiative* builds on several years of my pedagogical experimentation structuring design research studios to explore design agency in challenging places and with underserved populations. Working with local communities, my students designed buildings and urban interventions to revitalize contaminated and underutilized waterfront industrial sites in the US. By critically engaging social and ethical considerations in difficult *real world* places, those studios provided students with hands-on experiences of agency through live projects.[4]

Recently this intertwined research and teaching agenda has extended to global sustainability challenges and opportunities on the Indian subcontinent, where a complex mix of religions, ethnicities, languages, geographies, arts, and architecture produces hybrid and rapidly transforming cultural conditions. As the world's most populous democracy, the Republic of India is experiencing massive rural to urban migration, increasing economic disparity, and dramatic population growth. Widespread environmental degradation and natural resource depletion plague the country. Yet there is much to be learned from a close study of the culture and sustainable practices that have emerged from a combination of necessity and ingenuity in traditional rural settlements, globalized urban conurbations, and roadside conditions in between. For instance, we studied how the natural cooling systems of the medieval settlement of Udaipur keep residents comfortable in the scorching summers, and how the exquisite fountains and water channels found throughout the arid states of Rajasthan and Gujarat use intelligent evaporative cooling strategies to create pleasant courtyard microclimates. We examined how such strategies have been reinterpreted in the contemporary work of Rahul Mehrotra, Arun Rewal, and Studio Mumbai. These are just a few examples of synthesized sustainable strategies for infrastructure, landscapes and buildings that the India studios sought to understand in a deep and synthetic way. It was important that students not only read about these sustainable design approaches, but that they were directly engaged while learning to document their experiences through drawing and writing in their sketchbooks.

These traveling studios were conceived as a series structured by the five Hindu elements or *panchabhuta,* water, fire, earth, air, and void, which were examined within the specificity of distinct cultures and individual bodily experience. During the first year we studied water as a spatial generator of highly particular forms of infrastructure and architecture that support the occupancy of water itself, and those that use it. We examined the formal, material, and cultural significance of enduring and contemporary water architecture in India, while proposing new design strategies. In 2013 we focused on fire—the most sacred of the five physical forces according to Vedic philosophy. Fire represents light, heat, and energy manifest in architecture through spatial configurations, symbolism, materials, shade and shadow, and apertures that regulate light and heat. Prior to each summer studio, students explored historic and contemporary texts, films, art, and architecture in a seminar enriched by guest lecturers from the faculties of religious studies, art history, politics, literature, and linguistics. Students also developed proposals to guide their independent summer research. During six weeks of intense summer travel and immersive learning, they participated in the larger studio investigation and pursued their own independent research that enriched the collective endeavor. During the 2012 studio that focused on water as a spatial generator, for example, students independently investigated how to create microclimates with evaporative cooling, ways of combining a point-source public water supply with other public amenities, and the symbolism of water in India. In this way, both the individual and the collective research were furthered by reciprocal exchange and critique. This format differs from most *home-based* studios, where students are either enrolled in a studio with a prescribed focus defined by the instructor, or left to develop their own thesis or independent research with limited group interaction and instructor guidance. By combining the benefits of both models, a synergy developed between them. Students also maintained journals during the program and reflected on their experiences six months after our return. Their unedited writings are quoted throughout this essay.[5] The theoretical concepts that structure this pedagogical experiment and the essay itself are largely drawn from the direct observations of the students themselves.

Dislocation

Scholars from many disciplines have posed the question: why do we travel? In his book *Bewildered Travel: The Sacred Quest for Confusion,* theology professor Frederick Ruf argues that we often travel to unlearn, to challenge and rupture the surface of the known and expected. He examines the powerful inspiration and subject matter that travel provides for writers and artists. Although not specifically referenced, one may draw parallels with the significant role of travel for architects both past and present. From the obligatory Grand Tour in the seventeenth and eighteenth centuries, to the twentieth-century fascination with independent international travel as exemplified by Le Corbusier, Kahn or Venturi, both architects and architecture have been shaped by travel

Figure 8.1
**Harsh Jain and
Kathleen Lavelle
drawing at
Adalaj stepwell,
2012**

to unfamiliar places.[6] Architects have written numerous books about how travel has affected their worldview, their ways of representing what they experience and imagine, and the architectural designs that they produce.[7] For instance, young Le Corbusier's 1911 travel journal, later published as *Journey to the East,* provides insight into the personal and architectural transformations that occurred while he was spatially dislocated and personally disoriented in foreign lands. Ruf discusses this human craving for disorientation and recounts poet Mary Oliver's use of disruptions and difficult memories obtained while traveling to remind her 'you can creep out of your own life and become someone else' (Ruf 2007: 16).[8] Georges Van Den Abbeele, a scholar of European philosophical literature, has studied the potentially liberating force of travel in the writings of Montaigne, Descartes, Montesquieu, and Rousseau. His resulting formulation of travel as a metaphor is relevant to this discussion of architectural design and pedagogy.

> When one thinks of travel, one most often thinks of the interest and excitement that comes from seeing exotic places and cultures. Likewise, the application of the metaphor of travel to thought conjures up the image of an innovative mind that explores new ways of looking at things or which opens up new horizons. That mind is a critical one to the extent that its moving beyond a given set

Figure 8.2
**Rebecca Hora
and Phoebe
Harris drawing
at the Sri
Aurobindo
Ashram, 2012**

of preconceptions or values also undermines those assumptions. Indeed, to call an existing order (whether epistemological, aesthetic, or political) into question by placing oneself 'outside' that order, by taking a 'critical distance' from it, is implicitly to invoke the metaphor of travel.

(Van Den Abbeele 1992: xiii)

If dislocation challenges our thinking and our very being, how is architectural knowledge and self-knowledge constructed through spatial dislocation and travel? This research question generated a pedagogy and physical structure to create a dynamic relationship between body and space in the studio. Operating within a diverse range of urban and rural locations, students employed a comparative method that values the spatial act of travel. Prior to the India Studio, student Catharine Killien had participated in a twelve-week study abroad program in Rome that she described as 'much like a typical architecture studio that I would have back home. The design I developed for that [Rome] studio did not necessarily have anything to do with the Roman context or the peculiarities of that site. I had relied on design strategies and representation technique strategies I already knew'. Although Campo de' Fiori was just outside the door, the studio pedagogy and physical arrangement in a building

Figure 8.3
Section sketches,
Whitney Newton,
2012

owned by the university replicated their regular studios in the US. By comparing these two study abroad experiences, she observed that her ways of thinking and making had changed as well.

> In some sense, spatial dislocation isn't just about physically being somewhere outside of the familiar; it's a complete breaking of the way you typically do things. You give up your schedule and daily routine and the way you typically do work. You find new ways to represent new experiences, and can't rely on techniques and design strategies you typically rely on in the past.
>
> (Catharine Killien)

Other students lucidly reflected on how different it was to study architecture in an unfamiliar place and they frequently commented on how this immersive experience generated a heightened awareness of all the bodily senses. For instance, Sarah Buchholz described her India Studio experience this way.

> Instead of just researching sites from books and using computer tools to analyze spaces, the India studio gave me a firsthand experience of the site, culture, people, and traditions. It allowed to me to observe how people use

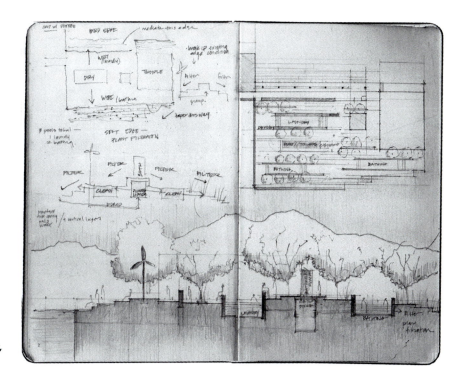

Figure 8.4
Sketchbook study for
public bath and laundry,
Catharine Killien, 2012

spaces and how architecture influences daily routines and rituals. Being in such a foreign place also affected my way of learning as I suddenly became much more aware of the types of spaces I was in and how architecture has such a huge effect on all senses. The intense summer heat combined with a variety of smells and sounds changed the way I think about spaces and environments and how they are created.

(Sarah Buchholz)

Could the advantages that the students had observed in their traveling studio experience enrich a typical *non-traveling* architecture studio at home: engaging in embodied and abstract ways of knowing, examining the crucial connections between space and use, studying relationships between culture, place and dwelling, and experiencing the powerful synergy between the bodily senses and how we understand architecture. Their observations led me to compare my teaching experience with what other instructors had discovered in their own traveling studio teaching, but a thorough literature review produced only a few publications. The edited volume *Travel, Space, Architecture* examines 'how conditions of physical and metaphorical dislocation affect spatio-architectural practices, and how these conditions redefine the parallel notions of place, culture and identity' (Traganou 2009: 2). This dislocation may be the result of travel, immigration or other types of forced and self-initiated movement in space. The author argues that 'the lens of travel can move architecture theory and practice beyond the centrality of static, place-bound principles into an understanding of more open-ended networks of relationships (of subjects and sites)' (Traganou 2009: 3). This

Figure 8.5
**Sectional intervention
on the Sabarmati River
embankment, Rebecca
Hora, 2012**

is a powerful argument for travel as an essential element of architectural education in an increasingly globalized world. While scholars in philosophy, geography, literature, and religious studies have carefully examined the role of travel within their disciplines, architecture lags behind. Though the architecture discipline is infatuated with mapping the global flows of people, goods and capital, this data fixation rarely goes beyond the quantitative to the theoretical.

Embodiment

When experiencing spatial dislocation our senses are heightened as we see, hear, smell, touch, and taste unfamiliar things. Travel stimulates us with places, people, and images that generate new ideas and ways of working. The students were particularly thoughtful about how the relationship between body and space affected their work. Nicholas Knodt observed that the 'spectacularly layered Indian cities and villages present juxtapositions between a variety of cultural, historical and architectural influences. Only through on-site drawing, mapping, recording and observation were we able to fully analyze these incredible relationships'. This statement is particularly compelling given the common production of drawings populated with image fragments that have been copied online. Vegetation, human figures, and a vast array of objects supporting human occupation find their way into architectural drawings produced by these students in studios *at home*. In the essay 'Beyond Cut-and-Paste: The Promise of Collage in Contemporary Design', artist Sanda Iliescu examines the significant problems inherent in image sampling.

Figure 8.6
**Delhi Rainwater
collection and bathing
pavilion, Sarah
Buchholz, 2012**

The uniformly digital and purely visual nature of these fragments can create a homogenized smoothness that robs such collages of the potential for double readings and multiple frames of reference. At their least successful, digital montages are strangely disembodied and weightless, suggesting placeless, amnesiac designs. The origins of fragments are suppressed, as are the particularities of place: sounds, scents, and the textures of physical materials.

(Iliescu 2008: 60)

Instead of this mediated experience, the students were fully immersed in the complex cultural, formal, and spatial Indian context as they designed. Sensory engagement and experiential learning predominated over the abstract analysis that occupies so much time in studio at home. As noted by architecture professor Kay Bea Jones in her essay 'Unpacking the Suitcase: Travel as Process and Paradigm in Constructing Architectural Knowledge', objectification and production are the primary focus of many architecture schools while 'experiential means of learning are underdeveloped' (Jones 2001: 128). While many students travel internationally in organized architecture studios, few professors have adequately theorized their educational value. Active learning and 'site-based travel pedagogy' are essential to the *India Initiative* approach, which concurs with the claim that 'by observing primary sites, architects can use original insights built on past knowledge to inform critical new thinking' (Jones 2001: 146). Traveling abroad to fully engage buildings and places is more crucial than ever for architecture students, as they are bombarded by slick digital images of global architecture rarely shown in its broader context. This situation is clear

Figure 8.7
Zach Carter drawing at
Adalaj stepwell, 2013

in student journals. For instance, Liz Kneller reflected at length on how her newfound way of understanding spaces through her body and how that embodiment directly informed her subsequent work.

> While in India, my most profound experiences were those that engaged all five of my senses, particularly that of touch. While I was previously interested in sustainability, I never knew how to incorporate that notion into my own work, and found that the focus of my studio projects was too often based solely on aesthetic concerns. In India, climate extremes require material, spatial, and geometric knowledge to create comfortable environments without the extensive equipment of typical modern mechanical systems. I was particularly struck by the wind tower at Fatehpur Sikri, the *jharokhas* of Udaipur, and Le Corbusier's *brise soleil* on the Millowner's Association. The firsthand experience of a cool breeze or shaded alcove in the midst of a hot Indian summer convinced me to rediscover the importance of designing explicitly for place. This led to a semester of research into how to design a building in my own climate that rejects energy consuming modern mechanical systems for passive systems that use less energy while providing greater thermal comfort to inhabitants through appropriate fluctuations in interior conditions.
>
> (Liz Kneller)

Figure 8.8
**Michael Goddard and Amelia
Einbender-Lieber drawing in
Udaipur, 2012**

The embodied knowledge discovered in a 'shaded alcove in the midst of a hot Indian summer' is quite different than the systematic knowledge acquired through abstract analysis, quantification, and mapping. Rather than study buildings as isolated artifacts, the students learned to understand architecture as part of a larger cultural context and construct knowledge through exploration.

Slowness and self-reflection

Taking time to fully experience a place cultivates our ability for careful observation and interpretation. All the students commented on the importance of in situ drawing. When asked what was your favorite design project and why, student Rebecca Hora replied:

> Each city introduced a new and exciting milieu to draw from and build on. Rather than one specific project, it was the overall process and culmination of sketches that most intrigued me. Designing from only my sketchbook and found materials meant expanding beyond superficial solutions and examining more contextual and site-specific considerations.
>
> (Rebecca Hora)

While drawing to discover, students learned about the intensity and slowness of the design process as well. Along with Le Corbusier's seminal monograph *Creation is a Patient Search,* others outside the discipline, such as sociologist Richard Sennett in *The Craftsman* or media theorist Steven Johnson in *Where Good Ideas Come From,* have examined the importance of the slow and sometimes circuitous path of creativity. Through the concept of slowness and the possibilities for reflection that it provides, writer Rebecca Solnit critiques the focus on efficiency, convenience, profitability, and security that pervades our culture. '…slowness is an act of resistance, not because slowness is a good in itself but because of all that it makes room for, the things that don't get measured and can't be bought' (Solnit 2007). This way of working and understanding the world embraces the differences between the normative classroom or studio and what can and must happen differently abroad and in the field. Traveling and learning in sites unknown frees students to experience, to understand and then to make. Six months after our return, I asked students to write about their learning experience in India. They reflected on the importance of their sketchbook practice, how their understanding of studio changed, and how they were able to learn in different ways upon their return. 'You tend to remember a place far more if you draw it than if you photograph it. Drawing makes you slow down and truly see and experience the space you are trying to record. I remember making every drawing from India—I certainly don't remember every photograph' (Catharine Killien). Though we had not read theories of cognition and the visual arts, the value of careful observation and drawing as a way of knowing was a common theme in their writing. Phoebe Harris described how her conception of architecture and *studio itself* changed because of her experience in India.

> Learning about architecture in India expanded the definition of my education. It meant that studio was not only a place where everyone has their headphones in and are building perfect 3D models in Rhino. But rather studio, and learning about architecture, is everywhere. Anywhere can be a place of learning and you don't need a desk and fancy tools to create inspired designs.
>
> (Phoebe Harris)

The role of sketchbooks—as a contemplative process and a means of thinking through drawing—has become central to the students' architectural design process. Student reflections on the knowledge gained and their transformed ways of seeing, drawing, and designing reveal the importance of the self, subjectivity, and the social. Each student also articulated important connections between body, mind and space. A common theme was the bodily disconnect often experienced at the computer when working while facing only the flat surface of the computer screen. Christopher Barker wrote about education in a particularly direct way.

> Even though I've spent nearly my entire waking life inside of them, I don't believe the key to learning lies in classrooms. My most memorable and breakthrough academic experiences have been on the road. I believe that

the best way to learn is to push us outside of our comfort zones ... In architecture school (and I've attended three of them by now) we're forced to sit in a chair indoors and go through the motions in front of a computer for hours on end. We can't help but get stuck and churn out projects that go nowhere. The India studio is a catalyst, and it was the best thing that's ever happened to me.

(Christopher Barker)

As an educator who teaches in studio, seminar, and large lecture settings, these shockingly honest observations support my concerns about directed knowledge and the increasing bodily disconnect in architectural education, and my attempts to develop more beneficial ways of teaching.

Constructed knowledge

Constructed knowledge, discovered through exploration or inferred from constructs, is essential in this 'disrupted' context.[9] Without immediate access to Wikipedia on their hand-held electronic devices, the process of knowing during the India studio became more embodied, patient, and deliberate. Though we did have limited access to online resources and printed publications, the default desire to 'google' everything was subverted. Jones' compelling argument for an epistemology of constructed knowledge as it relates to travel and teaching is relevant here.

If we accept that constructed knowledge offers an important alternative approach that is uniquely characterized by intuition, cross-disciplinary preferences, collaboration, ambiguity, integration, personal and social values, and historic contingencies, we can then consider observation of everyday life within the agency of travel.

(Jones 2001: 153)

Because of their traveling studio experience, several students noted changes in how they constructed knowledge and their design process. Amidst increasing quantitative analysis in architecture schools, the students acknowledged a new appreciation for their own perceptions and improved abilities to synthesize rather than merely analyze. Sarah Buchholz' reflection on her transformed design process is an example of these tendencies.

One of the most prominent ways that India affected my design thinking was through attention to detail, specifically materiality, apertures, and awareness of local context and climate. I had never before realized how subtle changes in materiality can change the feelings of spaces. In Chandigarh, the concrete space below the Open Hand Monument was one of the most exposed and hottest spaces I've experienced, while in Golconde every small aperture was well thought out to provide ventilation. In Udaipur, the sudden change in materials and openness along the water's edge created a space vastly different to the chaotic, crowded city streets. Overall, my method of designing now has changed in that instead of relying on computer programs and preconceived ideas about sites, I tend to sketch and work more with my hands to force me to think more about materials and context, and my designs are constantly adapting as a result of personal experiences, senses, and emotions, rather than being fixed and inflexible.

(Sarah Buchholz)

Agency

The India Studio was designed to transgress the normative architecture studio pedagogical structure, content, and spatial location in order to activate student learning. Grounded in concepts of embodiment, spatial dislocation, and constructed knowledge, in combination with Paulo Freire's theory of critical pedagogy, the India Studio seeks to educate agents of change who understand the inextricable connection between body and space, and the social and the environmental, as crucial considerations of architecture.[10] Each student reflection, sketch, and design proposal contributes to a fuller understanding of how student learning was transformed in that context and beyond.

Half a year after studying with the India Initiative I am still being challenged by lessons learned throughout our travels. The process of confronting preconceptions about culture and the built environment through the lens of India has enriched my design thinking, effectively adding complexity to my understanding about how life is lived through architecture.

(Nicholas Knodt)

By providing the opportunity for architecture students to question their own identity, ways of knowing, and design processes within unfamiliar cultures and places, their projects were quite different than they would have been in the studio back home. The students were less convinced of the correctness of their assumptions. Their designs were more conceptually complex and holistically conceived within the social and political conditions of this foreign place. As they constructed their own embodied understanding of the richness of difference and hybridity in these unknown spaces, their preconceptions fell away and new insights emerged.

Each institution, situated within its time and place, establishes its own particular and ever-shifting limits, yet transgression can be a powerful social process within the architectural discipline and academy. Specific acts of transgression, such as disrupting the given studio pedagogy by initiating an international traveling studio with an unconventional location and focus, challenge the boundaries set out by specific architecture programs. By structuring a nomadic studio exploration around dislocation, a heightened sensory awareness, drawing as reflection and self-reflection, and knowledge constructed through personal experience, students began to think beyond form and understand inextricable connections between bodies and physical, social, and political environments. They move beyond the strict limits of the architectural discipline, and beyond current expectations that are largely shaped by digital technologies and globally replicated forms and practices that tend to reduce and flatten difference. They question the tyranny of the eye and the slick, digitally manipulated image. They even question the cult of the new, the fast, and the young. What emerges is a trans-disciplinary understanding of architecture's agency in the world.

Notes

1   A recent issue of *Architectural Design* journal, 'The Architecture of Transgression', assembled a representative range of projects that destabilized accepted social, political and spatial boundaries.
2   Many architects and university architecture programs insist that parametricism is the inevitable and only relevant design method (and style) in a globalized, post-Fordist culture. Humans and their everyday needs, along with culture, history and natural resource conservation (from a deep sustainability standpoint) are typically missing from these technocratic discussions. For instance, in Patrik Schumacher's essay, 'Parametricism as Style: Parametricist Manifesto' (2008), the words (and concepts) *human, person, people* or other reference to architecture's inhabitants are absent. His recent essay 'Transgression Innovation Politics', published as a counterpoint in *The Architecture of Transgression* (2013), recycles his manifesto argument to dismiss the political and social agency of architecture.
3   The India Summer Studios and associated India Research Seminars referenced in this chapter were offered in 2012 and 2013. The courses were co-taught by University of Virginia Architecture Professors Phoebe Crisman and Peter Waldman.
4   See the two essays listed in the bibliography for more on the author's research on agency in the architecture studio.
5   All the student quotes contained in the essay were sent to the author by student participants from the 2012 India studio. On February 20, 2013, six months after our return from a six-week sojourn in India, I contacted all fourteen students with the request: 'I'm writing two essays about the India studio pedagogy and I'd like to include student reflections on how that experience might have affected your design thinking.' Both graduate and undergraduate architecture students are represented through their unedited quotes.
6   The editors of *Grand Tour: Perspecta 41* have assembled a collection of essays that explore "how the practices inscribed by the tour have evolved, maybe unrecognizably so".
7   These books range from theoretical treatises such as Robert Venturi's *Complexity and Contradiction in Architecture* (1966) to the personal journal of Le Corbusier, *Journey to the East* (written 1911, published 1966).
8   In *Routes: Travel and Translation in the Late 20th Century,* anthropologist James Clifford examines how contemporary transcultural conditions are influenced by communication technologies on the global movements of people and ideas. For instance, he considers 'how is a culture also a site of travel for others?' His insights are particularly relevant to a discussion of traveling studios and global architectural culture.
9   For more on constructed knowledge and a feminist theory of agency, see the work of Mary Belenky and Joan Hartman.
10 For more on critical pedagogy, see Paulo Freire's books, *The Politics of Education: Culture, Power, and Liberation,* and *Pedagogy of Freedom: Ethics, Democracy, and Civic Courage.* Thomas Dutton has examined the value of critical pedagogy for architecture education in his essay, 'Cultural Studies and Critical Pedagogy: Cultural Pedagogy and Architecture'.

Bibliography

Belenky, M., Tarule, J M., Goldberger, N. R., and Clichy, B. M. (1986) *Women's Ways of Knowing: The Development of Self, Voice, and Mind,* New York: Basic Books.

Brainard, G., Mehta, R., and Moran, T. (2008) *Grand Tour: Perspecta 41,* Cambridge, MA: MIT Press.

Clifford, J. (1997) *Routes: Travel and Translation in the Late 20th Century,* Cambridge, MA: Harvard University Press.

Crisman, P. (2007) 'Working on the Elizabeth River', *Journal of Architectural Education,* 61, 1: 84–91.

Crisman, P. (2010) 'Environmental and Social Action in the Studio: Three Live Projects along the Elizabeth River', in *Agency: Working with Uncertain Architectures,* F. Kossak, D. Petrescu, T. Schneider, R. Tyszuk, and S. Walker (eds), pp. 32–46, London: Routledge.

Dutton, T. (1996) 'Cultural Studies and Critical Pedagogy: Cultural Pedagogy and Architecture', in *Reconstructing Architecture. Critical Discourses and Social Practices,* T. Dutton, T. and L. Mann (eds), pp. 158–201, Minneapolis, MN: University of Minnesota Press.

Freire, P. (1985) *The Politics of Education: Culture, Power, and Liberation,* D. Macedo (trans) South Hadley, MA: Bergin & Garvey.

Freire, P. (1998) *Pedagogy of Freedom: Ethics, Democracy, and Civic Courage,* P. Clarke (trans) Lanham, MD: Rowman & Littlefield.

Hartman, J. (1991) 'Telling Stories: The Construction of Women's Agency', in *(En)Gendering Knowledge: Feminists in Academe,* J. Hartman and E. Messer-Davidow (eds), pp. 11–31, Knoxville, TN: University of Tennessee Press.

Iliescu, S. (2008) 'Beyond Cut-and-Paste: The Promise of Collage in Contemporary Design', in *Places: Forum of Design for the Public Realm,* 20,1: 60–69.

Jones, K.B. (2001) 'Unpacking the Suitcase: Travel as Process and Paradigm in Constructing Architectural Knowledge', *The Discipline of Architecture,* A. Piotrowski and J. Williams Robinson (eds), pp. 127–157, Minneapolis, MN: University of Minnesota Press.

Kelly, D. (2009) 'Semiotics and the City: Putting Theories of Everyday Life, Literature and Culture into Practice', in *Integrating Study Abroad into the Curriculum,* E. Brewer and K. Cunningham (eds), pp. 103–120, Sterling, VA: Stylus Publishing.

Le Corbusier (2007). *Journey to the East*, trans., ed. and annotated by I. Žaknić. Cambridge, MA: MIT Press.

Leach, N. (2002) 'Belonging: Towards a Theory of Identification with Place', in *Perspecta* 33: 126–133.

Lefebvre, H. (1991) *The Production of Space,* Oxford: Blackwell Publishers Ltd.

Mosley, J. and Sara, R. (2013) *Architectural Design 226: The Architecture of Transgression,* London: John Wiley & Sons.

Ruf, F. (2007) *Bewildered Travel: The Sacred Quest for Confusion,* Charlottesville, VA: University of Virginia Press.

Schumacher, P. (2008) 'Parametricism as Style – Parametricist Manifesto', presented and discussed at 11th Architecture Biennale, Venice 2008. Accessed online at http://www.patrikschumacher.com, 10 Feb. 2013.

Schumacher, P. (2013) 'Transgression Innovation Politics', in *Architectural Design 226: The Architecture of Transgression,* J. Mosley and R. Sara (eds), pp. 103–120, London: John Wiley & Sons.

Solnit, R. (2007) 'Finding Time: The Fast, the Bad, the Ugly, the Alternatives', in *Orion Magazine,* Sept/Oct.

Traganou, J. (2009) 'For a Theory of Travel in Architectural Studies', in *Travel, Space, Architecture,* J. Traganou and M. Mitrasinovic (eds), pp. 4–26, Burlington, MA: Ashgate.

Van den Abbeele, G. (1992) *Travel as Metaphor: From Montaigne to Rousseau,* Minneapolis, MN: University of Minnesota Press.

Venturi, R. (1966) *Complexity and Contradiction in Architecture*, New York: Museum of Modern Art.

Chapter 9

Transgressing established contemporary boundaries

In the Footsteps of the Filid: the crime novelist as true chronicler in Ulster

Keith McAllister and Colm Donnelly

Introduction

Ulster,[1] whilst familiar in name to many, has historically been a region unfamiliar in detail to most. Long-insulated against external forces, the region consequently developed a rich lineage of poets and writers by way of a respected voice specific to the region. Ulster is therefore a distinct example where the craft of the poet and writer have very definitely helped contribute to a 'collective memory' that can be passed down from generation to generation (Bevan 2006: 15).

Literature can be considered an appropriate means of expression when describing place, as both writing and location are composed largely of language and text. Thus, when we look at a place, it is often the stories in our heads that suggest to us what we do and do not see. As a record of experience and event, stories help create a shared social identity located in both time and place. It is then by the accretion of such stories over time that places can become better understood and read. The Ulster poet Peter McDonald in his poem *Eclogue* (2012: 112) recognises the narrative inherently latent in place when writing.

> It's as though the fields around these parts
> Had been written over as well as worked
> For generations.

McDonald contends that landscape, like literature, is composed of text imbued with sense and meaning. Therefore, to facilitate understanding, there is genuine value in the poet or storyteller who can comprehend, read, chronicle and translate for others, the manuscript that is our environment.

The Gaelic tradition

Historically in Medieval Gaelic Irish culture, the role of reading and recording the landscape was undertaken by the poets (*filid*),[2] a profession that was greatly valued as a central and integral part of society. One of the most important of the professional classes (*aos dána*; 'people of the arts') within Gaelic society, poets had to undergo lengthy and rigorous training[3] in bardic schools to ensure skill in language and composition before undertaking their role (O'Riordan 1986: 74). Proficient in their art, the poets helped safeguard identity and provided reassurance for Gaelic aristocratic lineages by authenticating them temporally and spatially into their landscape. As the recognised literary elite of Gaelic society, the poets were authorised to compose official works and enjoyed a recognised social and political position within the Gaelic world. In a society dominated by the oral tradition and not the written word, theirs was a duty to accurately chronicle place and event for contemporary and subsequent generations. This was not just to help in compiling a continuous historical narrative, but also in collating material that could be used, if required, in legal disputes. These could include land challenges, providing proof of inheritance, in affirming existing or new borders between families and in recording agreed payments by vassals to overlords (Simms 2009: 32).

The decline of Gaelic society from the seventeenth century onwards[4] led to both the loss of patronage for the poet and the disappearance of the bardic schools. But we can still get a sense of the importance of the Gaelic poets when studying those works that were recorded before being lost. Among the recovered works are the topographical poems of Seán Mór Ó Dubhgáin (d. 1372) and Giolla na Naomh Ó hUidhrín (d. 1420), which help provide a comprehensive record of the genealogical branches of families allied to place, collated and edited in the nineteenth century by John O'Donovan (1862).[5]

Those poems are an extensive grouping of one thousand and six hundred four-line stanzas that cover all parts of Ireland. By way of illustration a (translated) example of just two stanzas is provided below taken from a section relating to Ulster and the *Cróeb Ruad* (*Red Branch*)[6]

> Chief over noble Clann-Aedha
> Is Mag Aenghusa, lofty splendid,
> They have chosen the warm hill
> They have taken all Uladh.

> MacArtan has by charter
> The steady-stout Cinel-Faghartaigh
> Who never refuse gifts to the poets
> They are the treasury of hospitality.

The first of these details the prominence of the Magennis clan in the twelfth century in becoming chief lords over the territory of Iveagh in what is now west County Down while the second informs the reader that the MacArtans (or McCartans) were the rightful hereditary lords over Kinelarty, a barony in County Down between Dundrum and Slieve Croob, in addition to proclaiming their generosity and sponsorship of the arts.

Thus the illustrated topographical poems map Gaelic ownership and activities, and link families directly to place throughout Ireland. By recording what was important in the region – boundaries, landmarks and ownership – the poems help, when used alongside other documents, in piecing together a more comprehensive picture of Medieval Ulster's Gaelic society. Continuity and preservation of the past were important; firstly in terms of language, with the poets being trained in Old Irish so that they could access older texts, and secondly in terms of identity with place. Importantly, as stressed by Simms (2009: 15), the demanding training undertaken by the poets at bardic school was intended to produce 'creative works of art, wisdom and knowledge rather than mere records'. Instead of being simple academic genealogies or chronologically compiled annals, the works had to be well constructed, where language, meter and rhyme could all be celebrated. Entrusted with the duty and responsibility to truthfully record place and event, the poets, by virtue of the patronage and prestige bestowed upon them by Gaelic ruling lineages, had the unique freedom to roam beyond man-made and geographical borders, travelling throughout the land, ensuring exactness when writing with authority, and weaving their histories into the very fabric of society. This responsibility was arguably all the more important in a society where ruling succession and leadership followed a system of tanistry[7] (*Tánaiste*) rather than that of primogeniture.

The challenge today

Today, however, in Ulster, with the historical and political situation so markedly complex, the setting is immediately difficult and nuanced. Born of pain and hurt, spectres dwell in the shadows of Ulster's histories. Whilst being rich in mythology and narrative, its people remain guarded by a wariness made real by fear and experience. It is a place where it is often better to say nothing than to say anything at all. Alternatively, in a place where little differences matter and where residents celebrate 'the narcissism of small differences' (Bevan 2006: 172). what is said can be purposely false to mislead, protect and camouflage.

Even everyday elements such as the spelling of names, attended primary schools and addresses are all labels that can betray a person's identity and supposed affiliation. As a result, verbal smokescreens and figurative borders may be purposely established to shield against the stranger and outsider. This reticence and guardedness continues today as exemplified by Ciaran Carson, when he begins his novel *Exchange Place* by stating: (2012: 1)

> Like most citizens who have lived through the troubles I have learned to be wary. I look and listen, since you never know who might be watching you.

Hence the outsider in Ulster is immediately disadvantaged in often being viewed with suspicion and distrust by locals. Despite having the potential objectivity in being freed from the baggage of past experiences, the lack of familiarity of a region can compromise the outsider's ability to comment on the real texture and feel of a place. With reference to crime fiction, the County Down novelist Colin Bateman wrote his first novel *Divorcing Jack* in 1992[8], (albeit when the worst of the Troubles were over) as a result of what he considered a misrepresentation of the actuality of the times.

> If it [*Divorcing Jack*] was anything, it was a rebellion against other books dealing with the North – the Troubles written by journalists who'd spent a few weeks here, who'd maybe got their facts right but didn't get the feel of the place.
>
> (Bateman 2011: 176)

Bateman was able to write about the Troubles by showing the absurdity of the situation with caustic black humour, a welcome antidote to living in sad and hurtful times. As an insider, Bateman makes the observation that he can have insight and knowledge beyond that of the outsider by being more intimate with people and place. Moreover, as suggested by Carson, if growing up in the Troubles, where one had to be alert and vigilant, the local writer as insider has had to develop important perceptive skills, by watching and listening to people. The insider then has the acuity and heightened observational skills to accurately witness, negating the risk that can befall many people in their locality of being blinded by habituation, as identified by Vidler when stating:

> We seldom look at our surroundings, streets and buildings, even those considered major monuments are in everyday life little more than backgrounds for introverted thought.
>
> (Vidler 2000: 80)

However, an immediate difficulty for local writers is that by being insiders, they are involuntarily implicated into past histories. Thus whilst having first-hand knowledge and comprehension beyond that of the 'outsider', the 'insider', or local writer, is automatically damned by association, happenstance and geography, inherent in a region where identity is immediately aligned with political and religious standpoint. This then tarnishes their voice in comparison to the perceived impartiality of an 'outsider'. Alternatively, the 'outsider', whilst freed from the difficulties of preconception and being able to bring a fresh perspective to the subject, is faced with the challenges of having to overcome the distrust and defensive attitudes of a wary society. Hence the ability and opportunity to truthfully chronicle can be problematic for both the 'insider' and 'outsider'.

The insider-outsider transgressor

Although the Gaelic poets are no longer with us, their authorised responsibility to assist memory and identity is one still shared by many artists today; even if this task is on occasions challenging and distressing. There is the need to act as both insider and outsider, taking the strengths of both roles and combining them in order to purposely transgress beyond the established boundaries that constitute man-made borders and prejudices. In the past, the Gaelic poets were able to do this as the patronage and prestige of their profession were guarantors of passage throughout the land. They could therefore fulfil the challenging intermediary role of insider-outsider with the knowledge and intimacy an insider gained after up to twelve years of arduous training in their craft, language and heritage, coupled with the neutrality and objectivity of an impartial outsider, demanded by their solemn responsibility to provide accuracy in their work.

Whilst this nowadays might seem an impossible conundrum to solve, the dichotomous role of transgressing insider-outsider has arguably been successfully employed by the poet and writer who has tackled the subject of the Troubles most acutely in his writing, Ciaran Carson. By use of both prose and verse, he has written about recent times while still resident in his hometown of Belfast. In his book *Belfast Confetti* (1989), Carson records shifting identities and perspectives from the position of an armchair *flâneur*, mapping the streets and non-streets of his childhood, including those that have been changed, altered, eroded, barricaded and curtailed since before the start of the Troubles. In doing so he is facilitated by the *aislinn* – a visitation of the Gaelic muse that transports the writer to an alternative worldliness. The confusion and changing perceptions are translated by Carson, who from the otherness of the *aislinn* is an outsider, but with the groundedness and intimate knowledge of the insider. Like the *filid* before him and the crime writers after him, Carson has to mediate and negotiate his way through the landscapes of memory and actuality, the real and the imagined, the known and unknown, between mythology and fact. Crucially, as a translator, Carson demonstrates the value of being able to fulfil both roles as 'insider' and 'outsider', and can successfully chronicle and confront rather than ignore the menace and threat redolent in the labyrinthine streets of Belfast's past.

The authors contend that now, following in the footsteps of the medieval *filid,* there is a new chronicler – the young modern Northern crime novelists who by use of the crime fiction genre, creation of character and choice of setting are carrying on the Gaelic poets' tradition of transgressing boundaries in being able to commentate accurately on contemporary times in the most difficult of terrains, Ulster. The crime novelist has the freedom to choose a place well-known to them as setting and the inventiveness to choose characters with different worldly views and standpoints as protagonists in their novels. In doing so they combine the qualities of the outsider-insider, can cross across problematic and obtuse boundaries and approach subjects and viewpoints that can otherwise be difficult and challenging to access.

Moreover, crime fiction itself is well suited as a genre to aid in critiquing contemporary society. By its questioning and investigative nature, crime fiction arguably offers more opportunity for insight into the present than other forms of literature; a position advocated by Scottish novelist Ian Rankin who has stated 'if you want to find out about a country … read its crime fiction' (Wroe 2006: 11). Accuracy is valued because good crime fiction, according to the Finnish novelist Antii Tuomainen, 'is always about the truth' (2013). Hence, if they are to be truthful and subsequently 'good', the novels (as espoused by Raymond Chandler in his 1950 essay when demanding realism in crime fiction, *The Simple Art of Murder*) should be made up with *real* places and *real* people. Crime fiction therefore can be realistic and accurate as evidenced by the contemporary Swedish crime novelist Arne Dahl[9], who described them as 'the perfect tool to investigate and tackle current situations in contemporary society' (2013).

Those current situations would include themes such as identity, place and territories, the very elements composed and recorded centuries ago by the Irish Gaelic poets. Furthermore, the settings and tensions that are all implicit and woven into the pages of the crime novel have parallels with the basic act of architecture in helping provide an understanding of the vocation of a place since both arguably 'gather the properties of the place and bring them close to man' (Norberg-Schulz 1980: 23). Such a crucial skill is clearly evidenced in the work of two current Ulster crime novelists, Stuart Neville and Brian McGilloway.

Stuart Neville

The novelist Stuart Neville, when contextualising his own work, makes the acute observation that if wanting to be contemporary in Ulster, any author has to deal with the very difficult subject of post-conflict Northern Ireland (Neville 2013). This straightaway is no easy task. There has never been a Truth and Reconciliation Commission in Northern Ireland. Instead the 'ghosts of the past'[10] dwell in the shadows, helping ensure that Belfast continues to suffer in that it 'is a city that has been stereotyped to death' (Dawe 2003: 207). Hence the all-too-common assumption is that it remains a city rigidified by unchanging territorial boundaries solely dividing and separating two opposing tribal factions. This subdivision of the city into what Aaron Kelly (2003) poignantly termed 'terror-tories' was arguably most frighteningly depicted in fiction in Eoin McNamee's novel *Resurrection Man* (1994), the harrowing story of Victor Kelly and a group of accomplices who systematically preyed on, kidnapped and then tortured abducted citizens; their choice of prey and getaway route often chosen by cognitively mapping street boundaries before driving at night and seizing innocent passers-by. The importance of knowing the boundaries and their immediate impact upon those times is graphically portrayed by McNamee's description of the office of news reporter Ryan, a journalist working in the city.

> There was a cellophane-wrapped ordnance map of the city above Ryan's desk in the newspaper office. He spent hours in front of it. Locations of sectarian assassinations were indicated by red circles .... There were lines on the map too, indicating rivers, areas which had been demolished, suggested escape routes following a bomb, zones of conflict, boundaries, divisions in the city.
>
> (McNamee 1994: 13)

Most cities, if not all, have fault lines, often along economic, class or social lines (Sennett 1994: 21). However, what distinguishes Eoin McNamee's depiction of

Belfast is that the divisions and boundaries being drawn appeared to be enduring and constant. The writer Glenn Patterson tellingly expressed this point when reviewing *Resurrection Man*, making the analogy that McNamee's novel depicts the city as a cadaver, lifeless and unchanging (Patterson 1994: 43–4). That depiction of Belfast sadly still remains today, an outdated obituary of the perpetual and persistent memories from the past.

Nevertheless, when describing Belfast in his novels *The Twelve* (2009)[11] and *Stolen Souls* (2011), Neville starts to depict the city differently, by taking the reader into parts of the city spatially and temporally that have hitherto previously been largely ignored. There, he starts to show that Belfast is no longer an unchanging putrefied city. In *The Twelve*, written at a time when the economy was healthy and house prices were on the rise, well-established tribal boundaries are starting to socially dissolve. Belfast is now a place where nightclubs are full of the 'young and affluent, young enough to have no memory of men like Fegan,[12] affluent enough not to care' (Neville 2009: 14). The economic boom and subsequent rises in housing prices, wages and disposable incomes meant that people were so keen to get a foot on the housing ladder that they were moving across long established social and traditional boundaries.

> The property boom had driven the young middle classes into parts of the city they had never contemplated before.
>
> (Neville 2009: 45)

Thus the fixed preserve of the former 'terror-tories' start to be challenged by a gradual influx of young professionals now priced out of the customary desirable areas to live in the city. This is however only the start of an ongoing process of change and variation, and one that continues in Neville's third published novel, *Stolen Souls* (2011). Three years on, Belfast is now not mapped and identified in terms of tribal boundaries but instead in terms of what was most pressing in the city at that time, the falling house prices and negative equity endemic throughout the British Isles following the global economic downturn. Accordingly, Neville, when describing real-life Belfast streets, writes that Connolly, a uniformed policeman, can only afford to rent in Ulsterville Avenue; Rugby Avenue is primarily quiet in the city because it is too expensive for students, and isolated dwellings can be found off Cavehill in a state of dilapidation and disrepair, because they are no longer of interest to the property developer. Moreover, rather than concentrate on the stereotyped inherited tribal neighbourhoods, Neville's characters inhabit the residential streets around the Holylands,[13] Lisburn Road and Stranmillis in South Belfast, frequented by large shifting transient student and migrant populations (Figure 9.1).

It is where his characters can freely come and go, reminding the reader that Belfast, as a port with its incoming waves of immigrant populations and different cultures is, after a period of previous population stasis, now maturing and graduating into being increasingly like its sibling cities of Glasgow and Liverpool. This is highlighted by Neville, who navigates and records the city of Belfast, not in terms of established and stereotypical tribal boundaries, but in terms of housing patterns, economic mobility and social class, bringing a new and real perspective to the city for the reader.

Figure 9.1
Palestine Street, part of the 'Holylands' in South Belfast, with its proliferation of lettable properties for transient populations

Brian McGilloway

The transgressor of boundaries as a means of recording the contemporary social and spatial condition is also frequently employed by author Brian McGilloway. In his choice of setting of the border between Northern Ireland and the Irish Republic in and around Letterkenny, McGilloway places his chief protagonist, detective Benedict Devlin, a member of the Republic of Ireland's An Garda Síochána[14], automatically in a place where two different jurisdictions meet. McGilloway then guarantees that he can explore the differences between the two by ensuring mutual co-operation and passage between Devlin and his counterpart across the border in Northern Ireland, Police Service of Northern Ireland (PSNI) Inspector John Hendry.

One of the very real and well-documented results of the economic downturn following the collapse of the Celtic Tiger[15] has been the proliferation of 'ghost estates' throughout the Republic of Ireland, unfinished and often derelict housing estates, built when times were good in the expectation and hope that the good times and increasing house values would continue to rise. Instead the crash and collapse in house prices meant that many thousands of people are now trapped in negative equity, with many paying for houses that remain unfinished. Many others are now residing in housing estates that will never be completed. Figures suggest that in 2009 there were as many as 120,000 vacant homes and flats in the Irish Republic, with ghost estates in every county contributing to that total (Kitchin et al. 2010: 21).

In *The Nameless Dead* (2012) McGilloway takes the reader to rural Donegal where his protagonist Devlin is investigating the discovery of a baby's remains during an archaeological dig in connection with the 'Disappeared'.[16] In the course of his travels, Devlin visits Christine Cashell in Islandview, a ghost estate overlooking the River Foyle. McGilloway's description of Islandview is telling and informative. Not only does he give the reader a description of the estate, where only thirty of the eighty houses are completed, he also describes their chronological sequence and the very real effects living in such an environment can have.

> In addition to the four hundred thousand euro each of the thirty buyers had paid for their homes, there were unforeseen costs; the empty houses further back in the estate were a magnet for couples seeking quiet spots for half an hour, or kids, too young to get into bars, looking for a shelter as they drank their carry-outs on a Saturday night.
>
> (McGilloway 2012: 88)

Built of poor materials (unlike, according to a later description, the showhouse on the estate) and with sewage effluent being directly discharged into fields behind the estate due to a broken sewage-pumping station, McGilloway paints a depressing view of what life must be like at Islandview (2012: 89, 181). Moreover, what he can do as a crime novelist is outline the factual processes and scams associated in the ghost estates along the border, by providing the reader with a greater understanding of the social context in which events occur. In part this is manageable due to the genre of crime fiction, which often explores the subject of criminality. This goes beyond explaining how developers could simply leave the jurisdiction of the Republic of Ireland in relocating across the border in Northern Ireland by also explaining the social security dodges that would take place, with people supposedly 'moving' to empty houses in the ghost estates to take advantage of a more favourable benefits system across the border in the Republic of Ireland (McGilloway 2012: 137).

The ability to record very real criminal activity associated with the built environment was highlighted again by McGilloway's then stand-alone book[17] featuring PSNI officer Lucy Black in *Little Girl Lost* (2011). Set in Derry-Londonderry, the plot revolves around the disclosure that a perceived terrorist attack during the Troubles on a public house was actually intended, not as an attack on security forces, but instead in order to purposely demolish a collection of listed dockside buildings for financial gain. Bought cheaply because of their listed status, after significant damage had been inflicted by the bomb explosion, the developer (McLaughlin) was hopeful of being freed from the financial burden of then having to comply with stringent planning restrictions. Thus the site became potentially extremely valuable until the following economic downturn, a fact conveyed by PSNI officer Lucy Black when briefing her superior:

> The Planning Department wouldn't authorise him [McLaughlin] to raze the place after the bombing, even though the buildings were unsound. He had been going through the courts for the best part of a decade. He got the all clear last year and got planning permission and everything, but by that time the value of the land had dropped with the recession.
>
> (McGilloway 2011: 238)

Figure 9.2
Two highly visible empty sites sit either side of the gateway Craigavon Bridge into the city of Derry-Londonderry
Those of the former Tillie & Henderson (demolished on 4 January 2003) and Hamilton shirt factories (demolished on 15 January 2012).

It is poignant and meaningful that McGilloway's choice of backdrop for the book, the destruction of listed buildings, is not without historic precedence in Derry-Londonderry. The historically important and prominent listed Tillie & Henderson shirt factory,[18] while in planning for change of use to a hotel and museum, was damaged when empty in a series of arson attacks (*Architects' Journal*, 2003: 5). Allegedly, in the interests of public safety, the owner then demolished the building on 4 January 2003 without permission, before a mandatory survey could determine the extent of the fire damage, thereby negating the need to adhere to expensive and restrictive planning legislation requirements (UAHS 2003: 5–7).

McGilloway is therefore reminding the reader of an ongoing problem currently blighting Ulster, that of the erosion of its architectural heritage. (*Architects' Journal*, 2004a: 5; 2004b: 18–19). Even in the UK's first City of Culture, with its peace bridge, investment in public art and reimaging of the city, importantly sited industrial buildings in a city with a rich industrial heritage[19] continue to be lost.

As recently as January 2012, the prominent former Hamilton Shirt Factory, seen as visitors crossed the Craigavon Bridge into the city, was demolished rather than be refurbished or reused (*Derry Journal* 2012). The loss of this historic built fabric as described by McGilloway is one that signifies a major ongoing irony throughout Northern Ireland, noted by Sheeran, who posits that whilst concentrating efforts on allegiance to a place, its residents and authorities are prepared to let its historical buildings go to 'wrack and ruin ... demonstrating an almost total inability to care or cope with them' (Sheeran 1988: 194) (Figure 9.2).

Conclusion

Both Neville and McGilloway do transgress by advancing into and crossing the established boundaries of stereotype and prejudice, thereby helping provide an authentic portrait of the changes and layers of post-conflict Northern Ireland. Through the genre of crime fiction, both novelists combine the knowledge of the insider freed from association, with the critical eye of the outsider, in being able to interrogate and bring focus on what is actually rarely portrayed. Their choice of protagonist allows them to operate with the intimacy of the insider and as an outsider freed from loyalties or obligations, other than those of self-imposed accuracy. Hence by grounding his novels in place and time Stuart Neville depicts the city of Belfast as one of flux and change and much more beyond that of clichéd rigidified brick sanctuaries and peace walls. Brian McGilloway sheds light on the social and environmental effects of a society dismissive of its own built heritage, both in rural Donegal and in Derry-Londonderry, our 2013 UK City of Culture.

Their work shows the potential value of the contemporary crime novel deeply engaged with place. It can help encourage an active sociological understanding by the reader and is therefore a resource worthy of serious consideration. It is our environment after all, according to Pallasmaa (2005: 78), which tells us who we actually are. Literature is an appropriate vehicle to employ in this interpretation because like place, landscape and the built environment, all are instruments of communication and also creations of social and cultural production (Sheeran 2003). Therefore it is this potential inherent *inter-textuality* that alludes to the latent richness of seriously considering the contemporary crime novel as a potential informative resource. By helping record contemporary society, the crime novel becomes like the works of the poets in Medieval Gaelic Ireland, an important cultural record. But it is one that should always be cross-checked and evaluated. Thus when looking back at the topographic poems of Seán Mór Ó Dubhgáin and Giolla na Naomh Ó hUidhrín it is informative that, although composed in the late fourteenth to early fifteenth centuries, they do not make any mention of the many well-established Anglo-Norman (also referred to as Anglo-Irish) families in Ireland at that time and instead concentrate only on the principal Gaelic lineages.[20]

Similarly, it would be wrong to think that crime novels should be taken unaccompanied as stand-alone documents. Instead what they can do is complement and add to other text, in no small part due to the inherent investigative qualities of crime fiction. The Scottish crime novelist Louise Welsh reinforces this observation when describing her professional life as one 'all about interrogation' (2011: 233). Hence, the introspective character of the crime novel, grounded in realism, can help us recognise our place through the potential of cross-fertilisation with other texts, not just written, but also evident in the built environment and landscape. The Ulster poet John Montague in his poem, *The Rough Field* (2012), not only advocates that place itself is a potential treasury, but one that today needs to be translated for society, stating that 'The whole landscape [is] a manuscript/ We had lost the skill to read.' That skill, one that necessitates transgressing beyond the limitations of perceived and real boundaries and borders is now being continued today by writers such as Stuart Neville and Brian McGilloway. It is therefore the authors' contention that as narrator and chronicler, the new breed of Irish crime novelists are continuing the mantle of the Gaelic *filid* in acting as custodians of cultural knowledge in Ulster. And if possible in the complex and difficult terrain that is Ulster this then may well be a role that their contemporaries, writing crime fiction centred on other places, may also share.

Acknowledgements

Lines from 'The Rough Field' from John Montague, *New Collected Poems* (2012) by kind permission of The Gallery Press.

Lines from 'Eclogue' from Peter MacDonald, *Collected Poems* (2012) by kind permission of Carcanet Press Ltd.

The authors wish to thank Andrew English for the use of his images

Notes

1. The modern province of Ulster is comprised of nine counties, six in Northern Ireland (Antrim, Armagh, Down, Fermanagh, Londonderry and Tyrone) and three in the Republic of Ireland (Cavan, Donegal and Monaghan).
2. *Filid* is the Old Irish plural for poets – the singular term is *fili*. These equate to the modern Irish nouns *fili* (plural), *file* (singular) and Scottish Gaelic *filidhean* (plural) and *filidh* (singular).
3. Training required for the highest grade of poet could take upwards of twelve years.
4. The collapse of the Gaelic hierarchy in Ulster followed from the Nine Years' War (1594–1603) against the Tudor crown, the Flight of the Earls (1607 – when the Gaelic lords fled to continental Europe for safety), and the division of their estates amongst newcomers from England and Scotland in the years after 1610. The (re)organisation of Ulster's society in the aftermath of these events led to profound social, legal, religious and economic changes and – as part of this process – the old Gaelic poetic tradition became all but extinct by the end of the seventeenth century.
5. Lengthy and detailed Medieval Gaelic poems composed in the fourteenth and fifteenth centuries, first edited by John O'Donovan in 1862 for the Irish Archaeological and Celtic Society in Dublin. There is a more recent edition (without translation) by James Carney, Dublin: The Institute for Advanced Studies (1943), with a helpful preface in English.
6. The Cróeb Ruad (Red Branch) refers to the families ruled from the court of the king of Ulster at Navan in County Armagh.
7. Tanistry was the system used in Gaelic society of appointing a lineage's successor. Unlike the system of primogeniture where the eldest in line would succeed the ruler upon their death, the Tanist system would see an heir apparent to a Gaelic lord elected during the lord's lifetime.
8. Although written in 1992, with publishers repeatedly declining Colin Bateman's submitted manuscript, *Divorcing Jack* was not published until 1995,
9. Arne Dahl is the pen name of the Swedish crime novelist and author, Jan Arnald.
10. The 'ghosts of the past' are recognised clearly in the works of Stuart Neville, who highlights this as a thread in *The Twelve* (2009) by including a quote from John Hewitt's dramatic poem 'The Bloody Brae' (written in the 1930s but not broadcast until the 1950s) which states *'The place that lacks its ghosts is a barren place'*, as the introduction to the novel.
11. *The Twelve* (2009) was published in the United States with the alternative title of *The Ghosts of Belfast*.
12. Gerry Fegan, a former paramilitary killer released following a prison sentence, is one of the main characters in Stuart Neville's novels *The Twelve* (2009) and *Collusion* (2010)
13. The 'Holylands' are a collection of terraced streets in South Belfast, so termed by most Belfast residents because many of their street names are derived from Middle East place names, including Jerusalem Street, Damascus Street, Cairo Street and Palestine Street.
14. An Garda Siochána (literal translation 'Guardian of the Peace') is the police force in the Republic of Ireland.

15   The 'Celtic Tiger' is a term used to describe the rapid economic growth in the Republic of Ireland from 1995–2007 before the dramatic reversal in its economy from 2008.
16   'The Disappeared' are murdered victims of the Troubles who have yet to have their bodies located.
17   Following the success of *Little Girl Lost* (2011), Brian McGilloway has since written a second book featuring PSNI officer Lucy Black. Titled *Hurt* (2013), the book is also set in Derry-Londonderry.
18   The Tillie & Henderson Shirt factory was not only the largest shirt factory in Derry-Londonderry but renowned on a global context as evidenced by it being referenced by Karl Marx in *Das Kapital* (1867).
19   During the nineteenth century Derry-Londonderry developed as an industrial powerhouse through employing in excess of 8,000 factory workers in the main shirt-making centre in the British Commonwealth. (*Derry Journal* 2008)
20   The Anglo-Normans settled in Ireland from the late twelfth century onwards, both marrying into and on occasions replacing Gaelic Irish land-holding families as the most powerful ruling elite in a region, as was particularly the case in Leinster.

References

Architect's Journal (2003).'Locals fume at illegal demolition of Irish landmark',16 January, 5.

Architect's Journal (2004a). 'Government slammed over illegal demolitions in Northern Ireland', 26 August, 5.

Architect's Journal (2004b). 'Are you being conserved?', 16 September, 18–19.

Bateman, C. (1995). *Divorcing Jack.* London: Harper Collins.

Bateman, C. (2011). 'The troubles I've seen', in D. Burke (ed.) *Down These Green Streets.* Dublin: Liberties Press.

Bevan, R. (2006). *The Destruction of Memory: Architecture at War.* London: Reaktion Books.

Carney, J. (1943). *Topographical Poems by Seán Mór Ó Dubhgáin and Giolla na Naomh Ó hUidhrín.* Dublin: The Institute for Advanced Studies.

Carson, C. (1989). *Belfast Confetti.* Winston-Salem, NC: Wake Forest University Press.

Carson, C. (2012). *Exchange Place.* Belfast: Blackstaff Press.

Chandler, R. (1950). *The Simple Art of Murder.* New York: Vintage Books.

Dahl, A. (2013). In conversation; book launch of the *The Blinded Man.* The Ulster Museum, Belfast, 24 September.

Dawe, G. (2003). 'Belfast and the poetics of space', in N. Allen and A. Kelly (eds) *The Cities of Belfast.* Dublin: Four Courts Press.

Derry Journal (2008). 'Thriving industry is no more: Glory days of shirt factories recalled', 13 June, 17.

Derry Journal (2012) 'Hamilton's demise requires city's built heritage debate', 27 January 2012, 25.

Kelly, A. (2003). 'Terror-torial imperatives: Belfast and Eoin McNamee's Resurrection Man', in Allen, N., & Kelly, A. (eds), *The Cities of Belfast.* Dublin: Four Courts Press.

Kitchin, R., Gleeson, J., Keaveney, K. & O'Callaghan, C. (2010). *A Haunted Landscape: Housing and Ghost Estates in Post Celtic-Tiger Ireland.* NIRSA Working Paper No. 59. Maynooth: NUI.

Montague, J. (2012). *New Collected Poems.* Loughcrew, Co.Meath: Gallery Press/

McDonald, P. (2012). *Collected Poems.* Manchester: Carcanet Press Ltd.

McGilloway, B. (2011). *Little Girl Loss.* London: Macmillan.

McGilloway, B. (2012). *The Nameless Dead.* London: Macmillan.

McNamee, E. (1994). *Resurrection Man.* London: Picador.

Neville, S. (2009). *The Twelve.* London: Harvill Secker.

Neville, S. (2010). *Collusion.* London: Harvill Secker.

Neville, S. (2011). *Stolen Souls.* London: Harvill Secker.

Neville, S. (2013). In conversation; book launch of *The Healer* and *The Blinded Man.* The Ulster Museum, Belfast, 24 September.

Norberg-Schulz, C. (1980). *Genius Loci: Towards a Phenomenology of Architecture.* New York: Rizzoli International Publications.

O'Donovan, J. (ed.) (1862). *The Topographical Poems of Sean Mor O'Dubhgain and Giolla-Na-naomh O Huidhrin*. Dublin: Irish Archaeological and Celtic Society.

O'Riordan, M. (1986). 'Historical perspectives on the Gaelic Poetry of "The Hidden Ireland"', *The Irish Review,* No.4 (Spring), Cork: Cork University Press.

Pallasmaa, J. (2005). *Encounters*. Helsinki: Rakennustieto Oy.

Patterson, G. (1994). 'Butchers tools', in *Fortnight* 331, September, 43–44.

Sennett, R. (1994). *Flesh and Stone: The Body and The City in Western Civilisation*, London: Faber & Faber.

Sheeran, P. (1988). 'Genius fabulae: the Irish sense of place', *Irish University Review*, Vol. 18, No. 2 (Autumn), 191–206.

Sheeran, P. (2003). 'The narrative creation of place: the example of Yeats', in T.Collins (ed.) *Decoding the Landscape.* Galway: NUI.

Simms, K. (2009). *Medieval Gaelic Sources.* Dublin: Four Courts Press.

Tuomainen, A. (2013) In conversation, book launch of *The Healer*. The Ulster Museum, Belfast 24. September.

UAHS (2003). *Heritage Review* (No.6). Spring, 5–7.

Vidler, A. (2000). *Warped Space*. Cambridge, MA: MIT Press.

Welsh, L. (2011). 'Afterword', in L.Wanner, *Dead Sharp,* Uig: Two Seasons Press.

Wroe, N. (2006). 'Northern exposure.' *The Guardian*, 9 September, 11.

Chapter 10

Architecture in the material space of possible transgression

Nathaniel Coleman

Upturned boat: the possible utopianism of the new Scottish Parliament building

> In Scotland's parliament I'd like to see
> the corridors of power awash
> with glacial slush
> descended from the heights
> of gleaming Sirius.
>
> [...]
>
> Scotland's parliament would be composed
> from drops and lines of lyric wisdom
> from epic poems
> as memorably by heart
> we'd make our turn our part.
>
> (Ransford 2000, p. 47)

Emptying Utopia

In contradistinction to typical conceptualizations of Utopia, especially in relation to architecture, Utopia's radically transgressive dimension is emphasized in this chapter, in particular with regard to the proposition of distinct spatial forms within which radically new social and political forms could be elaborated as alternatives to present conditions. Indeed, in most instances, architectural novelty (primarily visual) is taken as a form of 'difference', equivalent to transgression and Utopia. Such a view is ultimately limited because it disregards Utopia's chief vocation for mounting sustained critiques of the given, which is also a way of charting the first steps in the direction of transformation in tandem with apparently unimaginable alternatives.

By seeming to be always and everywhere in the eye of the beholder alone, Utopia, like beauty, has been denuded. Utopia can now seem of little value beyond shoring up relatively facile declarations of superficial difference, which is why terms like 'transgressive' can seem more useful. Often enough, Utopia is little more than a descriptor of easily perceptible difference, which makes claiming it hardly worth the effort in the face of the myriad negative estimations of the concept accruing to it since the nineteenth century. Indeed, when unhinged from its radical socio-political vocation, all that remains of Utopia is a street-level aesthetic sense of it that turns on the relative presence of apparent *otherness*, in much the way any term of resistance or transformation – *transgression* for example – is at risk of when associated with the fine arts or architecture. While difference is as key to Utopia as to transgression, it is disobedience with given conditions and its value as a method for exceeding the limitations of the given that is Utopia's greatest transformative potential, rather than unusual appearance, or technological innovation. Ultimately, a Utopian ethos endures as the most promising source for counter-projects in these times of austerity.

Rather than accepting Utopia as necessarily and impossibly relativist, in the context of this chapter Utopia is employed in a specific way, denoting a particular position, related directly to establishing the first buildings of a better nation, with the aim of providing a better civilization with a space to evolve. Along these lines, Utopia is deployed here as both critique and method. In this regard, superficial difference, in the form of apparent otherness, is of little interest, such as prevails in most books on architecture that include the word 'Utopia' in the title. The value of Utopia as method and its radical project is emphasized here through a discussion of Enric Miralles's (1955–2000) new Scottish Parliament building (1999–2004) in Edinburgh, and the Scottish Parliament itself. A number of the ideas on Utopia introduced here are returned to throughout this chapter, and in particular the section under the heading of 'The upturned boat and "The Skating Minister"'.[1]

It is important to state at the outset that the prevailing idea of Utopia as inevitably absolutist and as always charting non-possibility, especially in relation to architecture and the city, is set aside here in favour of an idea of Utopia that is provisional and hopeful, thereby emphasizing possibility as central to the concept.

Identifying Utopia's exhaustion as an inevitable outcome of an aesthetics of Utopia, as I have done above, should not be seen as a cover for a desire to return to some universal definition of Utopia's vocation or possibility, any more than it would be possible to recuperate a Classical conception of beauty as wholeness and truthfulness, no matter how much an individual work might be recognizable as worthy (beautiful) in just these ways. The diversity and conflict of communication that characterizes our epoch makes it difficult to say what truth, beauty, or wholeness would (or must) be in every instance, the capacity of individual works to instruct us in the relevance of this in unique ways on a project-by-project basis notwithstanding. It is with this in mind that tolerance and inclusivity are indeed profound strengths of contemporary discourse. However, Italian philosopher Gianni Vattimo's conception of 'dispersal'– multiple voices/ perspectives valued, but always with a politically and socially progressive agenda – is more promising (even for the abnegation Vattimo's position seems to embody) than the at times nearly complete absence of rigorous definition that dominates the use of Utopia, especially in considerations of architecture.

Although architecture seems an obvious companion of Utopia (as of change and transformation), in particular because both provide frameworks for speculation about alternative social arrangements, the association between them is under-theorized, despite a degree of growing interest in the relationship between architecture and radicality. As methods for hypothesizing concrete *Not Yet* conditions, architecture and Utopia are manifestly cognate, thus the relative invisibility of Utopia's transgressive socio-political project to architecture, and the minimal concern of so many architectural practices with philosophical reflection on the nature of the 'good life' and its settings reveals the problematic of architecture and Utopia as one of clarifying (and emphasizing) what it is that architects and students of Utopia might find of value in reflecting on the two together.

The upturned boat and 'The Skating Minister'

With the above reflections in mind I will now turn more directly to a consideration of Miralles's new Scottish Parliament building, with the primary objective of determining the degree of utopianism that might reasonably be ascribed to it. Ultimately, in making this determination, emphasis must be placed on 'utopian' potential, rather than the certainty of 'Utopia'. Indeed, the best a building (or city) can ever hope to achieve is the provision of a setting amenable to social dreaming, rather than exhausting or crushing it. Although authorial intent, relative to a work harbouring a verifiably Utopian content (resulting on occasion in an equally utopian form), is significant, more valuable is how the constructed environment, or aspects of it, could support – contain and facilitate – the social dreaming of Utopia (as an acceptably never achievable ultimate goal that is nevertheless necessary for shaping action and giving it a purpose). While the distinction between 'utopian' and 'Utopia' might seem equivocal, even evincing a retreat from searching out Utopia realized, it is actually in-line with the inevitability that Utopia is never fully achievable, and that this is not so much a sign of failure, as it is precisely the point: the greatest value offered by reflection on Utopia is not completeness of achievement but rather the awakening of desire and the giving of direction to it. At this juncture, it is worth noting that my interest in the Scottish Parliament building is far less a matter of taste (or should I say, form) – I like it so it must be utopian (or transgressive) – than it is a matter of gauging its usefulness for the work of inventing a nation that could be better than is imaginable. In this way, it could be said that my preoccupation is with function, or content, rather than form, though I think this dichotomy misses what I am after. The building is of interest as a certain kind of setting that might be said to

Figure 10.1
Scottish Parliament,
Edinburgh, Scotland
(1999–2004), near the
former public entrance,
looking west

Figure 10. 2
Scottish Parliament,
looking north along
Holyrood Road

enable potential; something of a utopian machine, or tool, if you will (accepting that it is an error to ask too much of architecture in accomplishing the work of transformation).

Although commonly associated with political processes and their settings, a national parliament building ought to be an ideal location for social dreaming and political possibility. As it turns out, certain specific aspects of its program – architectural as well as political – encourages just such a reading of the new Scottish Parliament building.

Motivated by Scottish poet and artist Alasdair Gray's motto: 'Work as if you live in the early days of a better nation', which was inspired by a line from Canadian author Dennis Lee's long poem *Civil Elegies*: 'And best of all is finding a place to be in the early years of a better civilization'), the Parliament building might well be the first building of a better nation, an at present devolved Scotland that may soon have its independence.

Despite being ridiculed for taking longer to construct than anticipated and costing much more than allowed for in the original budget, the Parliament building is a compelling manifestation of Scotland's assertion of difference (no university tuition fees, free prescriptions, etc.) from its dominant southern neighbour (in terms of social justice, for example). Gray's borrowing of his motto – which adorns the building – from a Canadian poet preoccupied with the dominance of Canadian consciousness by the USA, suggests that the Parliament is an expression of civic (rather than ethnic) nationalism, an assertion encouraged by the building having been designed by a Catalonian, rather than a British, or Scottish, architect.

Figure 10.3
Alasdair Gray's famous motto (paraphrased from Dennis Lee's 'Civil Elegies'), adorning the Canongate Wall of the Scottish Parliament

Figure 10.4
Looking up Canongate, toward Canongate Entrance, and the Canongate Wall, which includes Gray's motto, amongst numerous others by Scottish cultural figures

Arguably, the relation between Scotland and England is analogous to the relationship between Catalonia and Spain, and between Canada and the USA. As a European building with a regional accent, the Scottish Parliament is paradoxically more assertively cosmopolitan (international in spirit and culturally inclusive) than the Palace of Westminster, for example, which is so thoroughly identified with a nostalgic vision of Englishness. The famous Houses of Parliament in London (begun in 1840 and finally fully completed in 1870), with its distinctive tower and clock, is best known for its assertion of Englishness, embellished with a distinctly native Perpendicular Gothic decorative program, inside and out, designed by Augustus Welby Northmore Pugin (1812–1852), albeit laid over a more Classical plan by Charles Barry (1795–1860), as an expression of a distinctly national character of a racial sort.

To understand why the expressive and organizational audaciousness of the Scottish Parliament is justified, necessary actually, it is important to keep the Englishness of the British Parliament in London in mind. At the very least, to assert the difference of national character it is meant to craft and represent, the design of the Scottish Parliament had no option but to look beyond the shores of the Green and Pleasant Land to be liberated from the long dominance of English governance and English monarchs. While looking toward Europe may have been a logical choice, not least as a reflection of Scotland's enduring ties with France (another assertion of difference from England), selection of an architect from a distinct native minority in the shadow of a more dominant nation was a clever and subversive move (even if not an entirely conscious aspect of the selection process). Arguably, the characteristics of difference attributed to the Scottish Parliament above make it utopian as well, even if the Utopia it suggests is never realized or even embarked upon. Moreover, as an audacious step toward dissolving the Articles of Union, the Parliament is decidedly transgressive.

But is It Utopian?

In the preceding section, I have encouraged a reading of the new Scottish Parliament building informed by Alasdair Gray's oft-repeated motto, cognizant of its origins in Dennis Lee's elegy of Canadian nationalism, understood also through the building architect's Catalonian origins, and the relation of his work to Catalan's nationalist claims. But is this enough to ascribe a credible utopianism to the building, or to make it transgressive? More to the point, can the ethos embodied in the building be ascertained and read out of it through sustained use or more casual encounters with it? Perhaps even more importantly, how active is the building in enabling the possible utopianism of the Scottish Parliament as a legislative body?

Along these lines, is the strangeness of the building, its novelty and wildness, enough to confirm its utopian-ness? Or is the degree to which the building overwhelms (or amuses, or angers) simply a testament to its general gratuitousness? While it might be possible to interpret the location of the building in the shadow of Arthur's Seat (the main peak of the group of hills which form most of Holyrood Park, where the building is located) as either a lame or excruciating attempt to link the new Parliament with the wildness of Scotland's land, perhaps even with banal representations of this, such as in the film *Braveheart*, I think it is fair to say that the building is more sophisticated than that. The building's own wildness, or savageness, might associate it with popular imaginings of the Scottish Highlands, its rugged, rough-and-ready character relates more to its status as a work of landscape design appropriate to its general context, rather than as simply representing some overheated narrative aspirations.

In light of the statements above and the questions raised at the beginning of this chapter, the utopian-ness of the New Scottish Parliament building is by no means irrefutable. Frustrating as such an admission might be, for the moment it will have to do. It is worth reflecting on the continuing condition of Scotland as a nation but not yet a state, in the sense that while its independent identity and geographic sovereignty are not questioned (it even prints its own banknotes), it remains largely governmentally and economically dependent on the highly centralized British government in London. But a Scottish Parliament building as audacious as the current seat of the partially devolved Scottish government (but not yet independent state) is, reveals the very existence of the parliament (building and political assembly) as at worst an ameliorating fiction and at best as a claim to statehood. In this sense, the audacity of the New Scottish Parliament building is particularly well-suited to the 'not-yet' condition of the Scottish State, assuring in equal measure its ultimate (inevitable?) achievement and the assumed certainty that this will never come to pass. However, accepting the emergence of a Scottish state as a real possibility, reflecting on the building and the operations it houses, continuously reveals that something of the utopian-ness of its originating desire persists, even in the face of encroaching managerialism and short-sighted economic preoccupations.

Figure 10.5
Upturned boat
Miralles was inspired by local and regional landscape and other elements in the region: the roof lights in this photo (near the staff canteen) are abstractions of the famous upturned boats on Lindisfarne (or Holy Island), in Northumberland, just south of the Scottish–English border.

Rather than being an indication of incompetence or profligacy, the excessive cost of the Parliament building, and its late completion, confirm that it embodies values other than time, money, or economics. Arguably, it is about much more than any of those. It is simultaneously a separatist building and a European one as well. The complex asserts an independent identity in the shadow of a dominant neighbour to the south, both symbolically and literally. Symbolically the Scottish Parliament rejects the form and expression of democracy represented by the Houses of Parliament in London, in favour of an assembly (more consultative than adversarial), and literally, by being an extravagant statement of difference in the shadow of the British monarch's Edinburgh Palace across the road. The building's design by a Catalonian architect links it to the aspirations for an independent Catalonia and to all such claims wherever they are expressed. At the very least, this associates the building with Europe, over and above identifying it with England, Britain, or the United Kingdom. In one sense, this makes it

Figure 10.6
The Skating Minister'
Window seat in a member of the Scottish Parliament's (MSP) office, an abstraction of the famous painting of the skating minister, which depicts the Reverend Robert Walker (1755–1808), skating on Duddingston Loch (1795), by the Scottish painter Sir Henry Raeburn (1756–1823), on display in the Scottish National Gallery, Edinburgh.

a Catalonian building (but not a Spanish one) because of its architect, but also because of that architect's cultural association with Barcelona and Antoni Gaudí (1852–1926); also a Catalonian architect who believed that expression of the region's distinctiveness in its art and architecture is a necessary adjunct of claims to independence. In this way, the building is built out of the spirit of asserting the independent identity of a minority population, or of a subservient (dominated) culture, in the shadow of a stronger one. But if the Parliament is a Catalonian building it is also a Celtic one, not simply for being in Scotland (or for the overtly Celtic motifs found in the building), but also historically, in the sense that the Celts made forays into Catalonia. In consideration of all of these influences and associations, the building is inevitably more distinct than an actual independent Scotland could likely ever hope to be.

Overall, the new Scottish Parliament subverts conventional Western expectations of a parliament building – it is neither Classical – or monumental, nor does

it rehearse some historic national style. As such, it is intentionally a counter-parliament, most explicitly in response to the Houses of Parliament in London (all English Perpendicular decoration on a classical plan). It is also a clear statement of difference in proximity to the monarch's Holyrood Palace across the road. The point here, however, is not to argue for the utopian status of the new Scottish Parliament building as somehow equating to a declaration of its worth in terms of architectural style or taste. In fact, one need not even admire the building to acknowledge it utopianness. Doing so neither contributes to, nor detracts from the potential utopian-ness of the building, which can be assessed according to more precise evaluative criteria, little prone to personal taste. Like many a Utopia, the building intrudes upon the consciousness in such a way as to open up possibilities, not only of perception but of alternative practices as well. In this way, the building is transgressive but also generative, evocative, and resonant: it is less a blueprint or recipe Utopia, than an interrogative Utopia. It is alien but not alienating, largely because it encourages a wide range of associations far more sophisticated than the literal references built into the building by its architect and read out of it by its current curators: Celtic symbols, reference to upturned boats in Lindisfarne, and 'The Skating Minister'.

Although overwhelming for not lending itself to being easily grasped – largely because of its expansiveness and strangeness – the building ultimately makes a cogent statement, challenging how we think of a serious institutional building. And it is precisely this that makes it a platform of possibility, apart from its sillier propensities that on occasion border on kitsch. Perhaps even these qualities, that lend

Figure 10.7
Celtic crosses adorn the vaulted ceiling of the main public area of the building near the entrance

Figure 10.8
General view of the Parliament, looking northwest

themselves to being read as childlike, indulgent, or cartoonish, and which could make the building appear toy-like or silly, are in fact indicators of a very serious attempt to articulate a platform of otherness at the very heart of organizational tendencies toward homeostasis. The tensions raised by such manifest dichotomies are touched upon in the sections that follow.

Architecture in the material space of possible transgression

> Surely there comes a moment when formalism is exhausted, when only a new injection of content into form can destroy it and so open up the way to innovation.
>
> (Lefebvre 1991 [1974]: 145)

Arguably, transgression in architecture is all but impossible to achieve, unless transgression is understood in formal terms alone. For German philosopher Ernst Bloch (1885–1977), for example, architecture is too much of a cultural production to permit any substantive disobedience, in the sense of being so profoundly ensnared within the hollow space of late capitalism as to foreclose on noncompliance with the controlling sweep of the dominant system of conception and construction. Italian architectural historian Manfredo Tafuri (1935–1994) and, to a somewhat lesser degree, political theorist Fredric Jameson, recognize that putative acts of architectural transgression are little more than either exercises in the prison yard of late capitalism, or futile, amounting to rattling the cage of what for all intents and purposes is a closed system.

However, unlike Tafuri, who saw little more than self-delusion in attempts to escape given conditions, Jameson acknowledges that thinking beyond the limitations of the present is tantamount to at least some recognition of the limits of our imagination, which, after all, is something of a start in the direction of being able to actually think of alternatives. Nevertheless, Jameson's optimism about the transgressive possibilities of architecture is tempered by its necessary engagement with the material out of which it is made (including its organizational complexity and cost, or 'economic necessity'). It is a condition that separates it from, say, literature, 'in which the negative is lodged in the very medium and the material'; 'distance' is secured 'in literature' because words 'can never become things', whereas 'architecture becomes being itself'; meaning that it is all but impossible for 'the negative' (the transgressive?) to 'find any place in it' (Jameson 1997 [1995]: 246). In comparison to Bloch, Tafuri, and Jameson, French philosopher Henri Lefebvre's (1901–1991) position is the most optimistic. He was adamant that even under conditions of apparent total closure established by the hegemonic spaces of neocapitalism (neoliberalism), cracks can be located and counter-projects mounted. In fact, he goes so far as to argue that 'to change life ... space ... must change', in the surprising sense that a space that challenges the status quo of entrenched spatiality really does prepare the ground, or even sets it, for the emergence of a new life (Lefebvre 1987: 11).

But Lefebvre is quite clear that formal play or visual novelty are not enough. Rather, challenges to the current situation (one can infer from him), can only go against prevailing conditions if what is proposed and built achieves something qualitatively superior at the level of use (in a sense that exceeds the limitations of technical functionalism by providing a far more sophisticated setting). Following Lefebvre, geographer David Harvey, asserts that new social forms – new ways of being – require new spatial forms (Harvey 2000). According to him, relatively open social processes, even radical ones, require relatively closed spatial forms in which to, as it were, take shape. Or, as Lefebvre puts it:

> the creation of 'a new space [is] the precondition of a new life (not that the mere invention of space is the sufficient condition of a new life). ... The fact is that the space which contains the realized preconditions of another life is the same one as prohibits what those preconditions make possible. ... To change life, however, we must first change space.
>
> (Lefebvre 1991[1974]: 306; 189–90)

Although substantive disobedience in architecture can seem a relative impossibility (because of its entrenchment within the dominant culture), the problem may actually lie in the fact that there is a general satisfaction with representations of transgression as though they were the real thing, in the sense that products that break formal rules are seen as equivalent to works that violate social expectation by transcending it. In this regard, Lefebvre alerts us to the inevitable failure of substituting 'communication for revolution'. He also returns the conversation to content, and to social practices, away from form (alone), which for him amounts to inevitably alienating abstraction, constrained to reproducing the conditions of consumption and accumulation that must seek to neutralize transgression, or conflict, of any kind, not least by apparently providing spaces for such endeavours.

Thus, in no small way, Lefebvre suggests a route through the closure suggested by, amongst others, architectural theorist Anthony Vidler, who asserts that a transformation of consciousness as much as of content must precede transgression – or the possibility of a revolutionary or utopian moment – in architecture; novel forms or techniques just won't suffice, any more than novel materials will (Vidler 2011). Yet, even if transgression at the level of content demands liberation from the social processes and economic forces that actually shape architecture, as introduced above, Lefebvre turns the usual order of things on its head by suggesting that space comes first.

Shifting the argument from a more strictly theoretical one to the consideration of concrete form can provide the discussion with a substantive object of inquiry – Miralles's new Scottish Parliament in this instance – particularly in terms of its relative transgressiveness. More precisely, probing the explicit disobedience of the Parliament building – relative to expected modes of practice in a heritage context, but also relative to the anticipated (monumental) form or organization of a profoundly important governmental building, or even the apparent disregard for budget reveals it as a counter-project to the banality of conventional architectural practices of the sort PFI procurement, for example, all but assures. As proposed earlier, the putative transgression mounted by the new Scottish Parliament building is much more profound than simply being an essay in novel form, overheated metaphors, decorative indulgence, or profligacy.

If the parliamentarians in Scotland can meet the challenge of the building, it arguably provides them with a space of new possibilities in which to advance counter-proposals of governance that resist the prevailing 'bureaucracy', which, Lefebvre observed, may have 'already achieved such power that no political force can successfully resist it' (Lefebvre 1991 [1974]: 51). It might even be enough for the building to raise such questions for those who work in it and visit it. Moreover, these questions need not be the same as either the task or accomplishing it; but in consideration of the current state of governance, dominated as it is by a mania for management in the absence of ideas, a building with a surfeit of them, dripping off every inch of it, may indeed constitute a first step. By providing anything but a banal environment, or a monumental one, the intensity of the Parliament building – decorative as much as tectonic – hints at how the bureaucratic dominion of governance without ideas could be eclipsed.

An obvious question – especially in light of the doubts raised by the failures of orthodox modern architecture (particularly in its deterministic social science mode) – is whether or not the challenge the Parliament building sets for itself (or that I am setting for it here) is too much for one eccentric work of architecture, or even an ascendant Scotland, to contend with. Although offering a definitive response is undeniably beyond the scope of this chapter, it is worth considering nonetheless. If Lefebvre is correct, that the 'precepts ... "Change life!" "Change society!" ... mean

Figure 10.9
West wall of MSP offices
External expression of abstraction of the skating minister – the numerous elements individually fitted to the building obviously translated into increased costs.

nothing without the production of an appropriate space' and that 'To change life, … we must first change space', consideration of the Scottish Parliament building turns on whether or not it is an appropriately changed space for the emergence of a changed life or society (Lefebvre 1991 [1974: 59, 190]). Now, it is unlikely that Lefebvre imagined that the relationship between changed spaces and changed lives or societies is quite as causal as his comments might suggest, especially when read against his sustained critique of orthodox modern architecture and the urban space it produced. In this sense, 'the production of an appropriate space' would be unlikely to occur unless at least some prospect onto a changed life and changed society had opened up by way of a transformed consciousness, such as art can provide access to. The quality – architectural as much as conceptual – that would make such an opening possible is what Bloch called the 'anticipatory illumination' that a work of art lights up, which is also a description of that work's utopian dimension, inasmuch as this describes 'a configuration closely tied to concrete utopias that are lit up on the frontal margins of reality and illuminate … possibilities for rearranging social and political relations' (Zipes 1988: xxxiii).

The challenge raised by the Parliament building turns on the degree to which – as a product of the culture (broadly speaking) that produced it (or it is at least born of

Figure 10.10
Parliament Debating Chamber
Less adversarial than the Chamber in the House of Commons in London.

the desires of that culture) – it is even possible that the sort of space produced by it is anything more than simply a representation of the culture that produced it. In short, is the Parliament building transgressive, has it produced a new space as the precondition of a new life, or is it simply just another already consumed product that legitimizes the very system apparently being disobeyed, albeit veiled in the self-serving language of autonomy or genius? In one sense, the answer to this last question is less relevant than the possible interpretations (of self-governance and self-determination) the building opens up. Alasdair Gray offers another way of considering this apparent impasse that is at once clarifying and paradoxical:

> I … think a new Scottish parliament will be squabblesome and disunited and full of people justifying themselves by denouncing others – the London parliament on a tiny scale. But it will offer hope for the future. The London parliament has stopped even pretending to do that. I believe an independent country run by a government not much richer than the People has more hope than one governed by a big rich neighbour.
>
> (Gray 1992: 63)

In an age of austerity, in which there appear to be no alternatives to a bankrupt and increasingly brutal system (for its increasing inequality), that is also soul destroying (for the despair it fosters and thrives on), the 'hope' Gray speaks of is about as disobedient a proposition as one is likely to formulate. This raises again the crucial question about the Scottish Parliament building: is it viable to see it as a setting in which the first steps might be taken toward realization of 'a better nation', and if so, could it reasonably be understood as the locus of the 'early days' of that 'better nation'?

Or is the new Scottish Parliament building, to say nothing of the Scottish Parliament, simply an extravagance, audacious but in no way utopian – noncompliant with but rather related to the logic of spectacle and advertising and simply just another setting for the arid bureaucratic habits of management that characterize modern political practice. Put another way, is Miralles and his audacious building a child of Antonio Gaudi (by giving form to separatist aspirations), or a nephew of Frank Gehry (by being simply formalist)? In answer to this last question, my proposition is as follows: surely an English architect could not have been permitted to design the building, but might its distinctive foreignness, as an eccentric work by a 'willfully imaginative Catalan' architect, introduce a degree of necessary and tonic distanciation (in Paul Ricœur's productive sense of the term as 'the condition of understanding') right into the centre of Scottish self-governance that might just be disruptive enough to stand as a challenge to mainstream ideological and institutional structures (Ricœur 1991: 88).

Overspending as the most transgressive act

> They eat and drink out of vessels of earth or glass, which make an agreeable appearance, though formed of brittle materials; while they make their chamber-pots and close-stools of gold and silver, and that not only in their public halls but in their private houses.
>
> (More 1901 [1516]: 58.)

In the first section of this chapter I examined the new Scottish Parliament building in terms of its relative utopiannesss, and Utopia as a method of transgression. In the second section I considered the degree to which the building might actually be transgressive. In this concluding section I consider the cost overruns the building is famous for also as its most utopian and transgressive dimension. A challenging and unique building, the new Scottish Parliament, completed in 2004 (after five years of construction), and formally opened by Queen Elizabeth II on 9 October that year, is perhaps best known for its eye watering cost overruns.

It is worth noting that in what follows, issues of authorial intent, or the lack thereof, are raised relative to the building's architect and most ardent supporters alike during its design and construction. In particular, my inverted reading of some of the project's most apparently glaring shortcomings – dramatic cost overruns and excessive delays – as positive attributes is not an assertion that they were intended as such, or at all, from the outset. Nevertheless, Donald Dewar (1937–2000), founding first minister of Scotland, understood that the parliament building would have to be special, not just as an emblem of Scottish self-government but as the setting for its emergence as well. The selection of Miralles for the project was a step in this direction. And as a Catalonian, Miralles was profoundly aware of symbolic and practical significance of the Parliament building. Thus, while all parties may have believed in good faith that such an important edifice could be built for the paltry sum budgeted for it in the short time allocated to its construction, Dewar and Miralles, amongst some others, understood the sensitivity of the task at hand from the start and were willing do what was necessary to realize their shared vision, which the *The Holyrood Files* (2005) documentary makes abundantly clear.

A lamp of sacrifice budget: busting as good utopianism at the Scottish Parliament building

Originally estimated as costing between £10,000,000 and £40,000,000 to complete, the final cost of construction rose to an impressive £414,400,000. A source of embarrassment for all involved (perhaps save the architect), the virtues of such apparent profligacy are little discussed; no surprise in the dominion of quanta where such apparent excess will be seen as first, last and always an extravagant waste of money, even worse because taken from the public purse. Although the Parliament's fortunes have shifted somewhat, before being 'regarded as a masterpiece' and becoming 'a tourist attraction' on account of its novel forms and quaint local cultural references, the building was considered a 'national scandal', previously having been 'voted one of Britain's 12 most vile buildings' (Kennedy 2005). In this regard, Wikipedia offers a good overview of the story of the building:

> From the outset, the building and its construction have been controversial. The choices of location, architect, design, use of non-indigenous materials (granite from China instead of Scotland), and construction company were all criticized by politicians, the media and the Scottish public. … A major public inquiry into the handling of the construction, chaired by the former Lord Advocate, Peter Fraser, was established in 2003. The inquiry concluded in September 2004 and criticized the management of the whole project from the realization of cost increases down to the way in which major design changes were implemented. Despite these criticisms and a mixed public reaction, the building was welcomed by architectural academics and critics. The building aims to conceive a poetic union between the Scottish landscape, its people, its culture, and the city of Edinburgh. This approach won the parliament building numerous awards including the 2005 Stirling Prize and has been described as 'a tour de force of arts and crafts and quality without parallel in the last 100 years of British architecture'.

Obliquely related to the interesting fact that both Miralles and Donald Dewar (b. 1937), founding First Minister of Scotland and the building's greatest champion, died in 2000, nearly four years before the Parliament was completed, I assert that amongst all of its latent utopian aspects, the willingness to stay the course and see the project through to completion has produced a monument not so much to folly or hubris, but to sacrifice. In these times of austerity and radically diminished expectations, the achievement of the Scottish Parliament building is inspiring. If it really is easier to 'imagine the end of the world than it is to imagine an alternative to capitalism', conceiving of value in terms other than money is indeed a utopian achievement, and an exceedingly transgressive one at that.

Sacrifice

My defence of the putatively extravagant cost overruns associated with the realization of the Scottish Parliament building makes a direct appeal to John Ruskin (1819–1900), in particular the first chapter of his famous *The Seven Lamps of Architecture* (1849), 'The Lamp of Sacrifice', and his 'Nature of Gothic' (1853), the most famous chapter from his *The Stones of Venice* (1851–1853), to provide the conceptual framework for this endeavour. In the 'Lamp of Sacrifice', Ruskin makes a distinction between building and architecture, according to which building is pure necessity whereas architecture concerns the unnecessary (which, interestingly, endures as generally accepted).[2] He continues by arranging architecture under five headings: devotional, memorial, civil, military, and domestic (Ruskin 1989 [1849/1880]: 10). The idea of sacrifice will likely strike many today as strange, especially in an architectural context. Arguably less so if one considers the building industry's immense daily consumption of economic and natural resources in its operations; what other word but sacrifice could possibly suffice?

What makes sacrifice useful for developing an understanding of the Scottish Parliament building is Ruskin's requirement that our buildings should evidence an offering of 'precious things simply because they are precious; not as necessary to the building, but as an offering, surrendering, and sacrifice of what is to ourselves desirable' (Ruskin 1989 [1849/1880]: 10). Granted, the material and labour sacrificed to the production of the Parliament building in Scotland are significant, but in our day, there is no greater value in the measure of all things than money. Thus, in the production of the most important civic building in a nascent nation, no symbol could be more powerful than a willingness to invest whatever money it takes – and it took a lot – to construct the material expression of a desire (albeit not universally shared) for self-rule.

In Ruskin's mind, sacrifice is relevant to devotional and memorial buildings alone but in our secular age I think his limitation can bear expanding to include at least civic and institutional buildings as well, such as hospitals, terminals, schools, museums, governmental buildings and civil engineering works, amongst other structures that adorn public life, something Italian Renaissance architect and theorist Leon Battista Alberti (1404–1472) would have surely supported. Building entailing necessary sacrifice for the good of the psyche and the community alike stands in defiant opposition to, as Ruskin argued, 'the prevalent feeling of modern times, which desires to produce the largest results at the least cost' (Ruskin 1989 [1849/1880]: 11). In light of this, the Scottish Parliament building breaks the bonds of the existing order, which, in the name of economy, revels in the general degradation of the public realm (Abensour 2008: 413). While it might seem eminently justifiable to argue that all, or part, of the Scottish Parliament building's final cost of over £400 million would have been better spent on social programs to improve the lives of Scottish people, this would be to miss the point by falling into the self-serving logic of scarcity that prevails in political discourse. Rather, as Alberti observed, cities ought to be projected 'by way of example' and 'the whole commonwealth … should be much embellished', without losing sight of either 'time or necessity' (Alberti 1988 [1485]: 96, 155; Coleman 2005)

Accordingly, for the purposes of the argument developed in this chapter, the Scottish Parliament building is a sacrifice, and required sacrifice for it to be constructed,

Figure 10.11
Garden Lobby

which arguably can be read out of it, revealing it as something much more than a problem of simple necessity. In Ruskin's terms, the building embodies 'the desire to honour or please someone else by the costliness of the sacrifice', ideally the Scottish people. Such sacrifice is public in nature, intended to honour that which is held in common. As such, extravagant displays of wealth – ostentatious corporate headquarters or private homes for example – do not constitute a sacrifice.[3] For the Lamp of Sacrifice to be upheld, as its own reward, and as a virtue, the sacrifice must adorn that entity beyond family made by individuals when they come together: the community. Ruskin asserts that for the 'Spirit of Sacrifice' to be manifested, 'we should in every thing do our best; and … we should consider increase in apparent labour as an increase of beauty in the building' (Ruskin 1989 [1849/1880]: 20–1). In an age of assembled, rather than crafted, buildings, the nature of labour in construction is somewhat peculiar; its value primarily determined by its cost and quantity. And yet, one imagines construction workers must derive a different sort of satisfaction in their labour when a building is both challenging to construct and of great significance, like the Scottish Parliament, for example.

It is important to keep in mind that for Ruskin, 'Doing one's best' has little or nothing to do with modern work culture in which economy – efficiency return on investment and some myth of perfection – dominates. Explicitly, as spelled out by Ruskin in the Stones of Venice, apparent perfection as a product of completeness is of little value, because what has been attempted requires only limited mental and physical effort.[4] Making the point, he argues that 'better our work unfinished than all bad.' Furthermore, we should always prefer 'what is good of a lower order of work or material, to what is bad of a higher; for this is not only the way to improve every kind of work, and to put every kind of material to better use; but it is more honest and unpretending' (Ruskin 1989 1849/1880]: 22). With this, Ruskin illuminates the predicament of mass production, modular construction and the dominance of assembly over craft that

Figure 10.12
Garden Lobby roof below, Queensberry House to the left, the Committee Tower in the centre, and Holyrood park beyond

bedevils architects and reduces the emotional charge of the constructed environment. To its credit, the Scottish Parliament building shows how, as Ruskin asserted, 'if we are to have great men working at all, or less men doing their best, the work will be imperfect, however beautiful. Of human work none but what is bad can be perfect, in its own bad way' (Ruskin 1905 [1853]: 171, para. XXIV).

There are two things I would like to emphasize at this juncture: first, the Scottish Parliament is far from a perfect building, and in this it opens up the possibility of achievements beyond itself, in terms of architecture, but also relative to the politics it houses now and might in the future, particularly if the referendum on Scottish independence is successful. Second, those aspects of the Scottish Parliament building that are actually handmade, or convincingly appear to be so, respond to our hunger for something better, in response to that something that is missing from our individual, family, community, civic, and political life, as well as from cities and the public realm more generally. In these ways, the Scottish Parliament building arguably makes good on one of Ruskin's key definition of architecture: 'Architecture is the art which so disposes and adorns the edifices raised by man for whatsoever uses, that the sight of them contributes to his mental health, power and pleasure' (Ruskin 1989 [1849/1880]: 34).

The contentiousness of the Scottish Parliament building reveals it as utopian and transgressive in a further way. The building adheres to no conventional architectural representation of Utopia; it is neither circular nor spherical in shape or form, or organized according to some other perfect or ideal geometry predictably associated with Utopia. The building challenges perception every step of the way, and is positioned as far apart from the Palace of Westminster, or Houses of Parliament in London, as is conceivable. In these ways, and others too numerous to name here, the Scottish Parliament building is evidence of the possibility of what philosopher Miguel Abensour calls 'another utopia' that permits us to think 'utopia otherwise' by engendering 'a new intelligence of utopia' in which 'only a thought of utopia that does violence to itself, that includes the critique of utopia, acquires the hardness necessary to destroy the myths that ruin utopia' (Abensour 2008: 415). If the possibility is entertained that a single building can do all of these things, or can at least suggest them, even for a moment, then it would also be permissible to say that the Scottish Parliament building challenges the reactionary idea that Utopia spoken must be fulfilled, and that Utopia apparently achieved must be eternal and disastrous, which is but a cover for myriad actions against hope. Charges of eternal Utopia aim to divert attention away from what is missing, and from attempts to redress this, effectively veiling a conservative impulse to maintain what is at any cost, while disregarding the unhappiness and inequality preserved by the existing order.

Notes

1 For more on the conception of Utopia that informs this chapter, see Coleman (2005, 2007, 2012a, 2012b, 2013a, 2013b, 2013c, 2013d, 2014a, 2014b)
2 Apart from Ruskin, perhaps the best-known expression of the apparent dichotomy between building and architecture is Pevsner's declaration that 'A bicycle shed is a building. Lincoln Cathedral is a piece of architecture' ([1948] 1990: 16).
3 See for example, 'I do not understand the feeling which would arch our own gates and pave our own thresholds and leave the church with its narrow door and foot-worn sill', or, 'I do not want marble churches for their own sake, but for the sake of the spirit that would build them' (Ruskin 1989 [1849/1880]: 17, 18).
4 See Coleman (2005: 128–32) for an extended discussion of how Ruskin's conceptualization of ambition and fallibility can assist in developing an understanding of Le Corbusier's work (as an example of a modern architect).

References

Abensour, M. (2008), 'Persistent Utopia', *Constellations*, vol. 15, no. 3, pp. 406–21.

Alberti, Leon Battista (1988 [1485]), *The Art of Building in Ten Books* (*De Re Aedificatoria*), trans. J. Rykwert, N. Leach, and N. Tavernor. Cmabridge, MA: MIT Press.

Coleman, N. (2005), *Utopias and Architecture*, Abingdon: Routledge.

Coleman, N. (2007), 'Building dystopia', *Rivista MORUS – Utopia e Renascimento* (Brasile), no. 4, pp. 181–92.

Coleman, N. (2012a), 'Utopia and modern architecture?', *Architectural Research Quarterly*, vol. 16, no. 4 (December), pp. 339–48.

Coleman, N. (2012b), 'Utopic pedagogies: alternatives to degenerate architecture', *Utopian Studies*, vol. 23, no. 2 (December), pp. 314–54.

Coleman, N. (2013a), 'Utopia: beyond amelioration', *Boundaries International Architectural Magazine*, no. 8 (December), pp. 4–11.

Coleman, N. (2013b), 'Utopian prospect of Henri Lefebvre', *Space and Culture*, vol. 16, no. 3 (August), pp. 349–63.

Coleman, N. (2013c), '"Building in Empty Spaces": is Architecture a "Degenerate Utopia"?', *Journal of Architecture*, vol. 18, no. 2 (April), pp. 135–66.

Coleman, N. (2013d), 'Recovering Utopia', *Journal of Architecture Education*, vol. 67, no. 1 (March), pp. 24–6.

Coleman, N. (2014a), 'On "Where are the Utopian visionaries? Architecture of social exchange"' (review article), *Journal of Architectural Education*, vol. 68, no 1 (March), pp. 118–19.

Coleman, N. (2014b), 'Architecture and dissidence: Utopia as method', *Architecture and Culture*, vol. 2, no. 1 March, pp. 45–60.

Gray, A. (1992), *Independence: Why Scots Should Rule Scotland*, Edinburgh: Canongate.

Harvey, D. (2000), *Spaces of Hope*, Berkeley, CA: University of California Press.

Holyrood Files, The (2005), DVD, BBC Scotland, directed by Stuart Greig.

Jameson, F. (1997 [1995]),'Is space political?', in Leach, N. (ed.), *Rethinking Architecture*, London: Routledge. Reprinted from C. Davidson (ed.) *Anyplace* Cambridge, MA: MIT Press.

Kennedy, M. (2005) 'Scottish parliament wins Stirling prize', *The Guardian* 17 October, available at: http://www.theguardian.com/uk/2005/oct/17/scotland.artsnews (accessed 5 February 2014).

Lefebvre, H. (1987), 'The everyday and everydayness', trans. Christine Levich, *Yale French Studies*, no. 73, special issue on Everyday Life, pp. 7–11.

Lefebvre, H. (1991 [1974]), *The Production of Space*, trans. D. Nicholson-Smith, Oxford: Blackwell.

More, Sir Thomas. (1901 [1516]), *Utopia*, London: Cassell & Co.

Pevsner, N. (1990 [1943]), *An Outline of European Architecture*, London: Penguin.

Ransford, T. 2000, 'Without day', in A. Finlay (ed.) *Without Day: Proposals for a New Scottish Parliament*, Edinburgh: Pocketbooks.

Ricœur, P. (1991), 'The hermeneutical function of distanciation', in *From Text to Action: Essays in Hermeneutics II*, trans. K. Blamey and J. B.Thompson, Chicago, IL: Northwestern University Press.

Ruskin, J. (1905 [1853]), 'Nature of Gothic', Chapter VI. *Stones of Venice Vol. II*, in *The Complete Works of John Ruskin, Vol. VIII*, New York: National Library Association.

Ruskin, J. (1989 [1849/1880]), *The Seven Lamps of Architecture*, second edition, New York: Dover Publications.

Vidler, A. (2011) Response to 'Crisis of Utopia? Editorial Questionnaire', *Autoportret*, available at: http://autoportret.pl/wp-content/uploads/2011/09/A34_01_Questionnaire.pdf (accessed: 3 April 2014).

Wikipedia (2014) 'Scottish Parliament Building', Wikipedia, The Free Encyclopedia, available at: http://en.wikipedia.org/wiki/Scottish_Parliament_Building (accessed: 3 April 2014).

Zipes, J. (1988) 'Introduction', in E. Bloch, *The Utopian Function of Art*, Cambrdige, MA: MIT Press.

Intervention 4

Rogue Game

An architecture of transgression

Can Altay

Rules of the game

Take a look at any multi-purpose sports hall, you'll notice different lines and geometries that are color-coded and overlaid on top of one another. The color-coding would indicate spatial regulations for different games (sports), to be played at varying time intervals. The sports hall allows each game to take place; offers the potential and the spatial indicators for them to be played. The common sense or convention remains that each game is to be played separately, one at a time, and most commonly as a competition between two teams of players, who are often composed of same-gender athletes.

   Rogue Game (2007–ongoing) by Sophie Warren and Jonathan Mosley, in collaboration with Can Altay, takes its cue from here, and proposes to exhaust the field (or to reveal its inherent excess) by opening it up to the various games that the overlaid lines 'regulate', simultaneously. For example, in the same field, two teams of football compete against one another, while the same happens for two teams of basketball and volleyball. This superimposition of sports at once forces the players to negotiate their pace, rhythm, demarcation, as well as coming to terms with the other lines and regulations they were formerly 'unseeing' on the field. A new game arises, with the introduction of multiple teams, a game where not everyone is in competition with one another, but still get face-to-face in the field.

   Sophie Warren and Jonathan Mosley summarize the situation as 'the soft logic of play and the soft body are applied to the planned and regulated as a way of writing in new possibilities for how we may inhabit or perceive these spaces' (Altay *et al.* 2011: 9).

Figure 14.2
Rogue Game Replay
2012 by Sophie Warren
and Jonathan Mosley
with Can Altay
Rogue Game transgresses
the rules and spatial
regulations of the sports
field by rendering visible
the layers of lines and
other indicators. The
'social choreography' that
enables this transgression
is not prescribed by the
authors but negotiated by
the players.

The relatively pure (yet competitive), regulated and controlled game space is thus pushed towards hosting a situation more complex and to a point that neither the players nor the spatial setting can remain as true or as pure as initially planned.

Rogue Game involves clashes and negotiations of territories, rules, regulations, conflicts, speeds; blending the games into one another (who can stop a basketball player from kicking a football?). Yet there is a partnership of shared goals (for each team) and a partnership over space. The habitual rhythms of each team change through the game, they settle, adjust, the bodily proximity of so many players in the field generate a new rhythm. As Franco 'Bifo' Berardi suggests 'a new rhythm makes it possible to see a new landscape…[with] a new landscape you discover new ways' (Berardi 2012: 35). These 'new ways' suggest a sense of cohabitation that is closer to the urban condition, where layers of people, practices, and structures clash and overlap. *Rogue Game* posits the struggle of a 'social body' within a set of boundaries that are being challenged.

The emergence of the new game is the result of choreographing colliding collectivities. Choreography here should not be thought of as a set of dictated moves based on a prescribed manual,but as 'social choreography'. As Gabriele Klein suggests

> [as] a performative structuring of body practices, as an analytical category that allows reflection on social order, as well as a concept that permits exposure of the relationship between the aesthetic and the political in all social fields.
>
> (Klein 2012: 90)

The language of choreography suggests 'a moving arrangement of bodies in space and time' (Brandstetter 2012: 45), an organization of bodies in space, or an organization of space for bodies to be in movement. It is notable how 'movement' and

Figure 14.1
Rogue Game First Play
2011 by Sophie Warren
and Jonathan Mosley
with Can Altay
Rogue Game reveals
the inherent excess
in the playing field by
superimposing three
matches from three
sports, where the
simultaneity of the games
lead to the emergence of a
new game.

various other descriptions of physical displacement such as 'revolution', 'uprising', 'strike' are used in reference to a social body in pursuit of a collective goal (Latronico 2012: 55).

This new game also requires that a collective refereeing process is at stake, so besides the keeping of time, there is no external authority. With the mixed-gender teams formed on voluntary basis, *Rogue Game* further challenges the preconceptions on competition, gender, and homogeneity evident in spectator sports.

Rogue Game thus 'transgresses' various games and the game space, through challenging the existence of perceived limits and rules, and the spatial indicators and boundaries, making them visible through play, both in the sense of being-at-play and staging this play to an audience.

Transgression's power as a concept lies in its processes of 'rendering visible'; of 'forcing the limit to face the limit of its own being' as Michel Foucault (1991: 28) argues, building on the work of Georges Bataille. Most often, the existence of boundaries are acknowledged and challenged simultaneously at the moment of transgression, forcing the limit 'to face the fact of its imminent disappearance, to find itself in what it excludes' (Foucault 1991: 28).

Architectures of the game

Inhabitation, cohabitation, movement, and proximity in the *Rogue Game* provide 'tools' with which the limits of architecture can be revealed and exhausted; as well as prescribing the possibility of 'an architecture' that can intervene and contribute to other social processes and urban spaces in similar manners. Space expands through inhabitation and movement, since there is always a 'spatial excess' contained within architecture, existing 'beyond the relevance for the present, and into the realm of the future' as defined by Elizabeth Grosz (2001). The ways in which we occupy given

Figure 14.3
Rogue Game First Play
2010 by Sophie Warren
and Jonathan Mosley
with Can Altay
Team portrait after the re-inauguration of a disused pitch in the Eden House Estate, Penfold Street, London, 2010.

systems, structures, and spaces are crucial, for any attempt to activate this excess, and to challenge, alter, or transform our given reality. *Rogue Game* thus suggests ways in which other architectures and urban contexts can be occupied.

Yet, how does *Rogue Game* itself inhabit its given architectures? To understand this, it is important to look at how *Rogue Game* is situated. Over a period of five years, four different incarnations of the game has occurred. The context for each incarnation is as important as the content. Three remarkably different architectures have hosted the game until now.

The first is the standard, professional multi-purpose Sports Hall (Bristol, 2007 and Utrecht, 2011). Here the game presents itself against the conventions of the sports environment, the spatial framework of colored lines forming the primary architecture. The action, the social choreography in itself and by itself transgresses: the expected use and boundaries within the field are subverted by an additive process, more games, more people, more action leads to a collective activity beyond the singularity of a competitive game.

The other two contexts provide further glimpses for the possibility of an architecture of transgression. The game here not only inhabits, but transforms the space physically by borrowing the spatial framework of colored lines, and superimposing it to an existing site. One of these sites is an unused pitch in a council estate in the Church Street neighbourhood in Edgware Road, London. The social housing context reveals the intention of the planners and policy-makers of placing sports as a social and recreational activity. However, the actuality of the pitch, a sunken concrete plot, caged

Figure I4.4
Rogue Game First Play
2012 by Sophie Warren
and Jonathan Mosley
with Can Altay
Installation view of *Rogue Game* from Spike Island, Bristol where 'fitting' the gamespace into the gallery space causes further challenges.

and closed for further use, and surrounded by a car park, draws a different social reality. Due to antisocial and unwanted behaviour from youth in the neighbourhood, the site has been closed down, turning the pitch into an inaccessible space. The proposition of *Rogue Game* here, includes painting lines on the pitch, and re-opening it for play as 'part of the interface and legacy ... within the community' (Altay *et al.* 2011: 13). As the game ventures outside of the sports environment and into socially controversial settings such as former public recreation areas that are no longer in use, it strives to affect its context as much as its players and its audience.

The third type of architecture, and architectural gesture in the *Rogue Game* series, is set in a gallery context. Spike Island in Bristol has been altered to become the playing field for the game in this incarnation. Since spatial configuration plays such an important role in sports, for *Rogue Game* in such a context, a further negotiation was being made: that of superimposing the field on to the given space, in a way that alters both of them. The lines and movement of the game are now further restrained; as the space of the sports field does not fit the floor space of the gallery, they start expanding towards its walls. This transformation in a way makes the limits of the space not only visible but also bodily experienced, and brings further effect into play, the potential and capacity of subjects and objects to affect and be affected.

The situated games, thus overlay social compositions and spatial reconfigurations towards an architecture that involves time, movement, process. This architecture reflects on its context, as much as it reflects on the clashing bodies and rhythms that make it happen.

Transgressions of architecture

Architecture is at once a generator of performative collectivities (through inhabitation and cohabitation) and the operational tool for regulating and restricting movement and action (through physical control and spatial composition). As the professional practice of architecture eventually finds itself in the domain of authoritative command or prohibitions (i.e. no access and homeless proof designs), there is once again a growing need to think towards an architecture of transgression (Tschumi 1996: 77). This dual nature of both setting the grounds for relations and controlling them, necessitates thinking about choreography, and its collective potentials as well. An architecture of transgression cannot simply operate on physical spatial compositions, it has to involve collective movement, and inhabitation, to the point that such movement can also exhaust the limits of its own being.

Rogue Game is subversive through adding things rather than taking them apart. The crowding of the field leads to higher proximity and towards a different kind of tolerance. Simultaneity of the multiple games bring the process closer to the urban reality of space, in comparison to the abstraction that sports usually suggest. Rogue Game transgresses both the sports and their spatial configurations. They also provide a (mostly sensory) experience of cohabitation, and of generating a new rhythm collectively.

The value and responsibility of transgression lies in how it activates the inherent excess within any space, structure, or system; forcing them to face their

Figure I4.5
Rogue Game First Play
2012 by Sophie Warren and Jonathan Mosley with Can Altay. Spike Island, Bristol
The crowding of the field leads to higher proximity and tolerance within clashing collectivities.

boundaries, and making us face our preconceptions and expectations from them. *Rogue Game* offers an architecture of transgression in the way it works through time and space, questioning and revealing the socio-political constructs surrounding the sports, the social formations, as well as the architectures that are being 'played'.

Bibliography

Altay, C., Warren, S., Mosley, J. and Pethick, E. (2011) *'Rogue Game*: Conversation between C. Altay, S. Warren, J. Mosley and E. Pethick' in *Soon All Your Neighbors Will be Artists,* Birmingham: Eastside Projects, 9.

Berardi, Bifo F. (2012) 'Automation and infinity of language: poetry versus financial semiocapital' in E. Basteri, E. Guidi and E. Ricci (eds.) *Rehearsing Collectivity: Choreography Beyond Dance,* Berlin: argobooks.

Brandstetter, G. (2012) 'Choreography beyond dance' in E. Basteri, E. Guidi and E. Ricci (eds.) *Rehearsing Collectivity: Choreography Beyond Dance,* Berlin: argobooks.

Foucault, M. (1991) 'Preface to Transgression' in F. Bolling and S. Wilson (eds) *Bataille: A Critical Reader*, London: Wiley-Blackwell.

Grosz, E. (2001) *Architecture from the Outside*, Cambridge, MA: MIT Press.

Klein, G. (2012) 'Micro-politics of social choreography' lecture cited in E. Basteri, E. Guidi and E. Ricci (eds.) *Rehearsing Collectivity: Choreography Beyond Dance,* Berlin: argobooks.

Latronico, V. (2012) 'A bijection can also be referred to as an equivalence' in E. Basteri, E. Guidi and E. Ricci (eds.) *Rehearsing Collectivity: Choreography Beyond Dance,* Berlin: argobooks.

Tschumi, B. (1996) *Architecture and Disjunction*, Cambridge, MA: MIT Press.

Part IV
Art practice

Chapter 11

Modes of transgression in institutional critique

Gunnar Sandin

Relational Aesthetics and double institutional articulation

The transgressive impact of artistic acts is usually measured in terms of the current values, rules or expressions that constitute the tradition with which the act is associated. The eventual effect of a transgressive act – its altering capacity – may come later, or remain obscure, or even be completely hidden from the eyes of non-experts. However, sometimes a transgressive act is judged more in terms of its direct societal impact, as a possible leak in, threat to, or actual change of normal circumstances. At times, explicitly stated shifts of interest appear with transgressive intent, such as when Relational Aesthetics was declared in the 1990s as a contemporary movement of institutional reconsideration by its lead theorist Nicolas Bourriaud, breaking with a traditional order of passive spectatorship in museums and galleries. Relational Aesthetics stood for a more problematized, but also a more physically and socially engaged relation between artist, work and public. The break was also stated in relation to the Situationists' ranks as a main anti-institutional movement of modern art. Bourriaud (1996) saw their lead figure Guy Debord as trapped in a negative Marxist understanding of 'exchange', associated with the economic value of trading labour in a market economy, and implied instead that in current times of blurred economies and ownerships, 'exchange' could in a subversive account be understood more in terms of human encounter. Even if this emphasis on 'exchange' and 'relational' was meant as a counter-force against the hierarchical standards of subjectivity-making (including passive onlookers to well-framed geniuses' artworks), it was also criticized for repeating the usual kind of role patterns and for masking societal conflicts in sensuous encounters with an art-specific content. Since its appearance, Relational Aesthetics has been regularly debated and criticized, probably in large part because the concept was originally tied to certain artists in a certain period in time, ignoring other, or earlier, relationist works. The term itself also became disputed because it came to represent – in a less scrupulous account, beyond Bourriaud's control and intentions – a more common institutionalized ambition with programs for 'social art' taking place outside the walls of galleries and museums. In his critique of relational art, Jacques Rancière (2009) pointed out that even if radical change was proclaimed, a self-defining discourse in fact restated its own communicational consensus. Judging in retrospect, there is some obvious truth in Rancière's view that Relational Aesthetics instantly became an institution in its own right, but one must also understand Rancière's claim here as emanating from his own particular demand for politics in aesthetics. He defended the classical 'inactive' viewer's position, to a certain extent, as long as the work produced the effect of 'dissensus', giving the viewer at least two perspectives of one and the same circumstance (Rancière 2010). The art theorist and historian Claire Bishop (2004) pointed to other examples of what she viewed as more radical artistic intervention, or as it were, more 'participatory' activation of the social realm than those artists represented by Bourriaud. For Bishop, 'participatory' means not 'a relational aesthetics, [but] a politicized working process' (Bishop 2012: 2). This declaration could, taken in isolation, be the theme of this text as well. However, in what follows I will be less concerned with the records of participatory projects in the perspective of a recent history of art, and I will avoid ranking art as more or less successful in its critical effect. This text is instead devoted to principal ways of dealing with the issue of *double institutional articulation*, or how an artistic action concerns, and potentially influences, not only the art institution but other institutional contexts as well. Hence I will take 'institution' to mean any regulated collective framework or instance that has a public function and an established position of some relevance in society. 'Transgressive' acts in this respect are those that have the capacity to alter the rules, mechanisms or comprehensions of institutions. This does not preclude that institutions themselves can be transgressive. A double institutional articulation, or action, would then not only concern two (or more) institutional frameworks as its subject matter, but also, consequently, put to the test the artistic identity upon which the transgression itself rests.

Historiography as a disciplining agent

The controversy concerning 'relational art' reflects the complexity of institutions' perpetual making of spectatorship, including claims of owning the issue of what is to be considered transgressive. The recent diversity of critical art practices (in the last half-century or so) also indicates the difficulty of maintaining any reasonably clear-cut conception of what constitutes practical criticism, or what is generally in art discourse labelled 'institutional critique'. One reason is also that contemporary art institutions may claim their own role as themselves critical, appearing as increasingly scattered, networked, subversive, or run under umbrellas of radical policy, sometimes by few people and sometimes only temporarily (Möntmann 2009). We may then ask: what really is transgressive in such a complex state of affairs? Gerald Raunig, for one, maintains that institutional critique – after its modern invention in the 1960s and 1970s in the United States and Europe – is still a valid concept. He sketches how clear-cut critical or antagonist practices in the early phases of this period evolved into a merging of transgressive and alternative strategies, leading lately to more constructivist and autonomous forms, or what he labels 'instituent practices' (Raunig 2009). Raunig is primarily concerned with how artists, and the art world, can work in a politically progressive manner. His position can thus be seen as a stance against the more existential, and in a sense dystopic, opinion raised by, for instance, Andrea Fraser, which holds that artistic criticism is essentially impossible because the artist's identity carries the institution inside (Fraser 2005). Raunig aligns his reasoning to some extent with a general tendency in art theory of viewing the recent historical narrative in these matters as categorizing the intentions of the 1960s and 1970s as radical, the 1980s and 1990s as mixed and introspective, and the current period as more autonomous (Sheikh 2006; Bryan-Wilson 2003). This type of historiographical periodization, however, to some extent covering discernible trends and struggles of critical art in post-Fordist economies, also runs the risk of becoming a disciplining force in itself, grouping and streamlining diverse types of art criticism. Departing instead from the basic idea that societal contexts are never uniform and stable, but force institutions and artists to reconstitute themselves in several different ways, my intention in the following will be to regard individual acts of institutional critique as showing varying modes of antagonism, varying positions of autonomy, and varying types of institutional support. Hence, in order to allow our modes and even methods of critique to be transferable, they could preferably be seen as comprising elements of historical periods that are too often seen as separate and contrasting.

The institution as a spatial Agency

In the latter part of twentieth century, social media and discursive artistic and cultural modes of expression started to conquer, and in some instances replace, the physical and multi-sensory aesthetic encounter. Despite a general preference for screen-orientation today, artistic display is still often conceived in spatial terms: belonging inside/outside given frameworks, establishing cooperational sub-agencies or satellites, using physical matter, operating at certain locations in an urban context, etc. On a theoretical level, attempts to capture institutional transgression may therefore benefit from viewing 'the institutional' as a spatial entity, without of course diminishing the issue as being a simple matter of the division between inside and outside the walls of the institution. Nor should we return to a mere site/non-site distinction, notwithstanding Robert Smithson's profound efficiency in stating, and staging, the interdependence between site-specific activity and (geographical, cognitive, scientific and institutional) space of display.

Architectural approaches may be of analytical and methodological help here. In its most radical appearance, architecture could be seen to break with its own tradition's procedures, though usually it has no intention to do so, nor even struggles to do so. More than fine art, architecture is traditionally a genre inherently 'relational' in the sense that the receiver's physical and social encounter with the resulting product is unavoidable. While 'instituent practices' in the art world are seen as recent and radical entrepreneurial types of commitment (Raunig 2009), subversive and autonomous, but sometimes not hesitating to join methodological force with some capitalist principles, architecture is already constituted as a commissioner- and user-oriented practice, and more used to handling such complexes. And even if radical so-called 'paper architecture' could be considered similar to art practice in terms of visual conceptualization of radical ideas, there is still a difference in expectation in that architecture has an implied second step in the project realization. In her view of architecture as a dissident practice resisting obfuscated and elusive hegemonies, or slippery political situations, Keller Easterling has suggested a repertoire of 'sneaky' techniques of less transcendent and less automatically oppositional resistance. These techniques include 'gossip, rumours, gifts, exaggerated compliance, meaninglessness, misdirection, distraction or entrepreneurialism' (Easterling 2013: 31). This repertoire suggests that institutional critique and transgression have to acknowledge modes of communication intertwined with those of the institution or hegemony in question. Without here diving into the specificity of these 'dissident' modes, taking them instead as exemplifying a heterogeneity of subjectivities that both contrasts and aligns with Raunig's notion of 'instituent practices', I will next discuss a range of para-institutional artistic work. This work spans from smoothly negotiated projects to intra-institutional controversy and to more direct confrontation. The artists discussed vary greatly in experience and level of career, reflecting different types of artistic and human persistence, but also thereby contributing to the complexity of the issue of transgression.

Conjoining two institutions

In 1983 the American artist Mierle Laderman Ukeles turned a garbage truck into a shining vehicle running on the streets of New York City. This act, reflecting not only the life and looks of the city in a literal sense, but also attitudes towards the handling of waste, was one in a range of works by Ukeles that directly addressed the conventions and labour of maintenance at both societal and domestic levels.

Another work in this series was *Touch Sanitation* (1978–80), in which the artist commissioned herself to shake hands with 8,500 New York sanitation workers. It took her eleven months to accomplish. Ukeles has only recently been recognized in a broader international context for her consistent work on maintenance issues. For decades she was most known for her early work *Hartford Wash* (1973), executed at Wadsworth Atheneum in Hartford, Connecticut, where she spent the days of the exhibition period cleaning the floors and entrance stairs of the museum building. In this work, important for the early feminist American art movement, she addressed in a

Figure 11.1
Mierle Laderman Ukeles,
Touch Sanitation,
1978–80

public act the notion of maintenance as tied to specific social groups or categories. This performance was accompanied by a written manifesto about her role as a woman and mother, the first version of which appeared in 1969. Ukeles thus became a relational artist in a period when most conceptual art was dominated by a more introspective reflection or archival aesthetic. Her works directly involved people that otherwise had nothing to do with the art world, and rules and issues belonging to institutions outside the art world.

Ukeles's works with sanitation issues led to her being co-opted as a member of New York City's Sanitation Department, as an unsalaried artist-in-residence, starting in 1977. The relationship grew into a long-term affiliation as part of the remaking of the vast Fresh Kills landfill on Staten Island.

As artist-in-residence, Ukeles's intention was to work artistically with the material of non-art institutions and corporations. Her position was in a way reminiscent of the collaborations with industry and government by the British APG (Artist Placement Group), conceived by Barbara Steveni as early as 1965. APG was jointly run with John Latham and other artists for two decades, and after 1989 they were known as the networking and archival organization O+I. Apart from making actual 'placements' in non-art contexts (Tate 2014), APG sought to establish programmes and theories to define specific working concepts like 'incidental person' and 'event structures' (Slater 2000) for the sake of negotiating types of transgressive agency other than the conventional and in their view insufficiently introspective labels 'art' and 'artist'. Ukeles, in comparison, set rather as an individual artist driven by a passionate urge to transgress certain lines of division between the art and non-art worlds. Ukeles opened some ways of merging art activity with corporate activity, while often maintaining a clearly mediated distinction between art work and other work, such as when mimicking the movement of sanitation workers or staging a play with caterpillars, in order to symbolically recognize the lesser known and under-appreciated qualities of labour. Ukeles's works are an example of freedom lying 'less in the solipsistic ideal of doing whatever one wants, and more in the accomplishment of "bringing into relationship"'(Gablik 1991).

On the whole, Ukeles's work is an example of undertaking a critical project in relation to two different social domains and institutions: art and maintenance. Her work is done in collegiality with both, and thus is transgressive not in the sense breaking the rules or causing a dispute, but as a patient occupation with the disciplinary frames of those institutions. Thus she works *with* the institutions rather than against them in order to achieve a change in the way they are viewed. Alteration of perspective, does, as we shall see, not even require a positioning on the outside, but may be achieved in works that remain completely within the context of the institution physically but that use the institutional architecture itself as working material, as will be shown in the next case.

Institutional framing as a working material

The American artist Michael Asher transformed in 2008 the Santa Monica Museum of Art by filling the interior space with a series of bare metal stud walls. The floor-to-ceiling studs partitioned the rooms in seemingly random ways, but showed at the same time a certain repetitive pattern. This metal framing pattern showed the positions (forty-four in all) of the temporary walls that had been built for all the various exhibitions the museum had held over the years. It revealed a preference for certain wall locations, but also deviations indicating specific artistic demands. As a poetics of institutional space – poetics being a genre-specific reflection of its own tradition – the piece was accomplished literally through the vanished material used by that tradition. This minimal work could thus be seen as a material merging of 'history' and 'institution'. Even if the meaning of the work has an evident conceptual side – the fact that we know how it was done is enough to grasp the idea – the full and immediate sense of the historical-material collapse also includes an experiencing embodied presence (Rondeau 2008).

Asher often works, as in Santa Monica, together with the governmental organization and the physical context of the institution, sometimes including its public relations staff. 'Asher's methodology is precise: his work is always crafted from the existing contingencies that make its presentation possible' (Rondeau 2008). He is, in other words, making context into theme, context here comprising the immediate material circumstances as well as the commonly assumed policies for art display, communication, and, not least, ownership. Who has the right to (the display of) a work of art?

The particular issue of ownership was given another consideration by Asher in a work conducted at the Museum of Modern Art in New York in 1999, a work that generated wider public interest in the mass media, and a general debate of civic rights in relation to museums. He was invited to participate in a group exhibition called *The Museum as Muse: Artists Reflect*. The premise of the exhibition, from the curator's perspective, was to render the 'museum as subject'. This theme seemed to imply, in Asher's own words in an interview, 'a visual representation of the museum' rather than

Figure 11.2
Michael Asher, *Santa Monica Museum of Art*, 2008

a 'critical inquiry into its mechanisms' (Pascher 1999:24). Nevertheless he accepted the request as a great challenge to reveal and articulate the ideological difference between these two aspects in a work that addressed the most fundamental function of a museum, namely the practice of collecting. Asher had found out that MoMA regularly published information about their acquisitions but never about their habit of transferring works of art out of their collections. His interest then became focused on the 'secret' de-accessions recursively made by the museum. He managed, with hesitating assistance from the museum, to produce a list of de-accessions, a list that became his contribution to the exhibition. However, the chief curator of the museum wanted to make a written statement accompanying Asher's list, saying that it was 'unofficial' and did not 'meet the criteria of completeness or accuracy that we would require in a museum publication' (Pascher 1999: 24). This statement was made in spite of the fact that the museum had compiled the list itself after working on it for six months. Asher did not have access to the contents of the statement in advance of the exhibition, so he hesitated to take part, and his name was deleted from the list of names of participating artists. The announcements for the exhibition therefore did not include his name. Before the opening he was encouraged by a curator of lower rank to participate, and through her secured a copy of the museum's written statement. However, Asher did not see the finished work (the list printed as a catalogue) until he picked it up himself at the opening of the exhibition. The work caused institutional fear of losing trust beyond this internal curatorial situation. After the opening, in an attempt to reassure potential donors, another museum director wrote a letter to the editor in the *New York Times* (Miller 1999) saying that 'most American museums acquire far more than they remove'. The artist Allan Sekula commented on this statement, meant to reinstall institutional integrity, by pointing to its 'Borgesian character of [implying the existence of] a Museum that removes more works than it acquires' (Sekula 1999: 13).

The public critique of the museum's de-accession policy made by journalists, critics, and public figures, along with the museum's response, reflect the political train of relations between society and artistic space. In a reflection on the societal implications, Asher commented on the public protests against MoMA's politics, saying that the collections in museums must be seen as part of 'a consciousness of the community' (Pascher 1999: 26). The exposure of this way of dealing with public property without informing the citizens – the essential owners – raised the general awareness of collective ownership.

The head of an institution, as its representative in society, has the legal ability to define the border between what in the institution is public and what is not. But moving that border implies political action. This is part of what we may call the institutional production of societal space. Maybe we must acknowledge two kinds of 'public' domain here, as far as institutions that are wholly or in part funded by taxpayers are concerned: one mediated space (*to* the public) and one administered space (*for* the public).

A last detail, and an explicitly spatial turn in this museo-political event, casts light on the phenomenon of authority as well as on the general problem of positioning something 'critical' inside a 'neutral' institution. When Asher's catalogue eventually was incorporated into the exhibition, it deviated in various ways from his wishes and instructions. Apart from being installed differently and formed differently both in terms of graphics and content, it was, in Asher's words 'placed exactly the opposite of what I had wanted, in a completely different location within the museum' (Pascher 1999: 25). These reorganizations of space and matter and the previous fights for authorization show the status and power of spatial possession. They also show the importance of two 'essentials' of an event, namely the duration and the division of time. The preparation periods in the daily running of an institution reveal how its policies are articulated.

It has been suggested that Asher's preoccupation with the fundamental matters of institutions are 'supportive' (Peltomäki 2010) of or 'encouraging' (Rondeau 2008) to the institution. For instance, in the end he improves the spatial conditions for other artists or improves the quality of the promotion of an exhibition. Asher's works often evoke negotiation troubles or outright conflict with an institution, but the acts themselves are not confrontational in a societal or legal sense; they are meticulously performed to question the social constructions of customary institutional behaviour. Asher's intra-institutional way of working, engaging a multiplicity of institutional actors, may as indirect effects bring about changes in society. In order to also render a more direct addressing of societal institutions outside the art world, we will look into a type of intervention that, in contrast to both Ukeles's and Asher's firmly negotiated approaches, works more by an unannounced provocation of social rules and etiquette.

Institutional intervention and the exposure of tacit and legalized rules

While still a student at Konstfack, the University College of Arts, Crafts and Design in Stockholm, the Swedish artist Anna Odell meticulously prepared an event in which she would appear to be about to jump from a bridge. She chose Stockholm's Liljeholm Bridge, known locally for suicide attempts, and on the evening of 21 January 2009 Odell appeared on the bridge acting suspiciously desperate. Passers by noted her actions and somebody called the police. They picked her up by force and admitted her into protective medical custody in the psychological emergency ward at St Görans Hospital. When she eventually revealed that her act had been a part of an art project, the hospital staff was enraged and the head of department reported her to the police, and it became news matter. When people found out, she was quickly denounced in the mass media by journalists, medical professionals, and even people in the art world, but above all by the general public for having done nothing more than waste hospital resources and show contempt for the rescue service personnel.

This action became one of the most mass-mediated art projects ever in Sweden. Odell appeared on the prime-time evening news to explain it as a work of art about human rights in general and healthcare policy in particular. She referred to an experience early in her own life when she met with violence in a psychological treatment situation. The act of threatening to jump and being taken into custody thus expanded into media discussions about why and how this could be considered a work of art, and how the art school that supported her could sanction such an action. This initial phase of the debate focused almost solely on the rights and restrictions of art, and on ethical and legal judgements of what were considered 'fake' or 'destructive' actions.

A couple of months after the bridge action, Odell followed with a video-based installation in a traditional art context (as part of the annual students' exhibition). She showed a symbolic bed with restraining belts alongside documentation of the act itself (film and photos shot from a distance by friends), and a filmed documentary of Odell's preparatory process including consultations with lawyers and psychiatrists.

Figure 11.3
Anna Odell, video still,
Unknown, Woman **2009-**
349701, 2009

The bridge action led to legal action, and Odell was convicted of violent resistance and fraudulent practice. She and her solicitor objected to the verdict of fraudulent practice, but she also declared herself reasonably comfortable with the outcome and with the support given to her by her supervisors: 'My institution [Konstfack] has supported me all the way. I am not disappointed' (Öjemar and Bergbom 2009).

One year later, speaking on a popular talk radio programme, Odell gave a detailed, explanatory, and self-confessional account of the whole process (Odell 2010), including polemic comments towards people in power positions. Other public events followed: talks, interviews, panels, and lectures at schools and institutions.

Odell showed in this work, *Unknown, Woman 2009-349701*, an order of transgression opposite to pre-announced and institutionally supported art projects. Operating unannounced, provoking tacit rules in society, and only thereafter revisiting the art institution as well as the hospital institution in the communications that followed, Odell had to rely initially on the decency of common societal reasoning, something she could not really control herself. The only institutional support she had came from her school's supervisors. This 'weak' institutional framework could be compared with the context of another act debated fiercely a few years earlier in the Swedish media, namely Alfredo Jaar's work *Public Safety* (2000), in which the artist built an art gallery in Skoghall out of locally produced building material, then burned it to the ground on the day of its inauguration. While symbolically addressing art institution politics, this work was part of a larger advertised group show, and thus already placed inside a safer institutional frame.

In the public debate about Odell's work, a subtle shift occurred in media coverage from being preoccupied with art definitions and the ethics of the artistic act itself to more direct questioning medical care policies. But the polemic tone was also altered. In a series of recurring vignettes about the case in the leading newspaper *Dagens Nyheter*, the events were first depicted as having caused a 'scandal', then a 'debate' (Anders Marner, quoted in Söderberg 2009). Thus in relation to the ambivalent but strong public response, Odell's act may be seen as trans-contextual in several ways: apart from having a direct impact on the debate and regulation regarding psychiatric care, and in particular the use of restraints and the reporting procedures (Björling 2009), it also influenced the debate and the protocol regarding the role of authorization and ethics in art education. And not least, as the change in the debate showed, it managed to evoke questions about investigating and journalistic ethics.

Transgressive architectural practice in institutional space

The works discussed here reflect the transgression of rules in art institutions as well as in other contexts, such as sanitation, civic ownership, and medical care. All of them appeared, in one phase or another, within the physical framing of institutions, whether that framing was treated as an unproblematic spatial resource for display or as the material thematically addressed in the work. This dichotomy reflects the general architectural problem of redefining institutional habits through the medium of spatial design. Architecture that moreover takes on a double critical approach – to the traditional process of accomplishing a building as well as to the societal institution it hosts – faces in principle many of the same problems as the artists mentioned above. One may in this respect recall the seminal examples of Matrix Feminist Design Cooperative in the 1980s, with their daycare architecture for multi-ethnic neighbourhoods. Their unorthodox design approach allowed both the institution and the parents to participate in the design process (in drawing, 3D modelling and construction). This led to a thinking that allowed sequential movements through the interior division of space, a mix of working groups, and group care for children of different ages instead of a static separation and a more dictatorial spatial canalization of activities and users (Dwyer and Thorne 2007). Needless to say, this type of partial integration, reflected and realized in Matrix's projects, has in recent decades revolutionized day care and nurseries in many Western countries, and thus also changed the way children are integrated into adults' cultures and worldviews.

Matrix's transgressive and self-defining architectural agency exemplifies a kind of productive disregard for institutionalized procedures. So do also some of the instituent practices and autonomous agents that not only reinvent the habits of a practice but also the professional identification with it. One example is CUP (Center for Urban Pedagogy), whose engaged consultation in visual communication, writing, and law is at the centre of their aspiration to improve civic engagement and demystify urban policy and planning issues (CUP 2014). These ways of incorporating public engagement into the planning process could be compared with another recent example of an unorthodox client relationship, namely the Norwegian architect Beate Hølmebakk's transgressive handling of prison spaces, which also transgresses traditional building design procedures. In order to trigger solutions for spatial improvement of prisons, her office, Manthey Kula, sent letters to the leaders of forty-two state prisons in Norway (Payne 2010) to gather information about their spatial qualities (or lack thereof). Hølmebakk used these letters as sources of inspiration for design proposals, supporting her office's on-going work with institutional spatial hierarchies and regulation. It led, for

Figure 11.4
Beate Hølmebakk/
Manthey Kula, *Outdoor*
Area, Juvenile Unit,
Bergen Prison, 2010

example, to altered conceptions about what kind of views of the outside should be offered to prisoners and staff. It also generated an unorthodox architectural response to what kind of messages the fencing – i.e. material raised primarily to keep groups of people apart – conveys to those on the inside and to those on the outside as well.

A common feature in the work of Hølmebakk, CUP, and Matrix, apart from their interest in the physical aspects of common institutional space, is their unorthodox way of handling not only the subject matter of institutions, but the practical procedures of invitation and decision-making. They avoid the modes of internal professional institutionalism others take for granted. This also aligns them, though they belong to different communities of practice, with Asher, Ukeles, APG, and Odell. A degree of autonomy in relation to their own tradition is a common transgressive feature, though they handle it very differently.

Conclusion: institutional critique as double articulation

In this reflection on artistic institutional critique we have been able to discern at least five principal forms of what has here been labelled *double institutional articulation*: 1) acts that conjoin different types of institutions, thus activating otherwise separate types of societal agency; 2) acts that make spatial alterations to existing design of institutions, hence influencing institutional administration as a general issue; 3) acts that initially operate unannounced in one institutional context, and later have a postponed effect in other contexts; 4) acts that contrast hermetic institutional decision-making with public participation; and 5) acts that temporarily disregard normal institutional existence in autonomous practice. These modes of transgression illuminate not only the institutional regulatory framework and its material features, but also the societal task of hosting, representing, and ordering human subjectivity. In this respect they serve, by making visible and tangible, a general right to alter our societal conditions.

Bibliography

Bishop, Claire (2004), 'Antagonism and relational aesthetics', *October* Magazine, 110, Fall, 51–79.

Bishop, Claire (2012), *Artificial Hells, Participatory Art and the Politics of Spectatorship*, London/New York: Verso.

Björling, Sanna (2009), "Den slutna vården", *Dagens Nyheter*, 22 August, http://www.dn.se/nyheter/sverige/den-slutna-varden/ (accessed 4 February 2014).

Bourriaud, Nicholas (1996), 'Relational Aesthetic' (Part two), *Documents sur l'Art*, 8, 42–46, Dijon: Les presses du réel.

Bryan-Wilson, Julia (2003), 'A curriculum for institutional critique, or the professionalization of conceptual art", *New Institutionalism, Verksted # 1*, 89–109, Oslo: Office for Contemporary Art.

CUP (2014), *The Center for Urban Pedagogy*, New York, http://www.welcometocup.org (accessed 2 April 2014).

Dwyer, Julia and Thorne, Anne (2007), Evaluating Matrix: notes from inside the collective," in Doina Petrescu (ed.) *Altering Practices: Feminist Practices and Poetics of Space*, 39-56, London: Routledge.

Easterling, Keller (2013), 'Inadmissible evidence', *Architecture and the Paradox of Dissidence*, paper abstract at AHRA conference London 2012, http://www.dissidence.org.uk/downloads/Architecture-Paradox-Dissidence-Nov12-Conference.pdf (accessed 2 April 2014).

Fraser, Andrea, (2005), 'From the critique of institutions to an institution of critique', *Artforum*, Vol. 44, Issue 1, 278–96.

Gablik, Suzi (1991), *The Reenchantment of Art*, New York/London: Thames & Hudson.

Miller, Steven H. (1999), 'Letter to the editor', *New York Times*, 3 June.

Möntmann, Nina (2009), 'The rise and fall of new institutionalism: perspectives on a possible future', *Art and Contemporary Critical Practice: Reinventing Institutional Critique*, 155–160, London: Mayfly.

Odell, Anna (2010), Sommar 19 August 2010, radio broadcast, Sveriges Radio, http://sverigesradio.se/sida/avsnitt?programid=2071&date=2010-08-19 (accessed 2 April 2014).

Öjemar, Fredrik and Bergbom, Kalle (2009), 'Odell dömd till dagsböter', *Dagens Nyheter*, 31 August, http://www.dn.se/sthlm/odell-domd-till-dagsboter/ (accessed 2 April 2014).

Pascher, Stephan (1999), 'Cave notes', an interview with Michael Asher, *Merge*, 5, Summer 23–26.

Payne, James R. (2010), 'Norwegian architect Beate Hølmebakk of Oslo-based Manthey Kula', *Building Design, bdonline*, 7 May 2010, http://www.bdonline.co.uk/norwegian-architect-beate-hølmebakk-of-oslo-based-manthey-kula/3162947.article (accessed 2 April 2014).

Peltomäki, Kirsi (2010), *Situation Aesthetics: The Work of Michael Asher*, Cambridge, MA: MIT Press.

Rancière, Jacques (2009), *The Emancipated Spectator*, London: Verso.

Rancière, Jacques (2010), *Dissensus: On Politics and Aesthetics*, London: Continuum.

Raunig, Gerald (2009), 'Instituent practices: fleeing, instituting, transforming', *Art and Contemporary Critical Practice:Reinventing Institutional Critique,* 3–11, London: Mayfly.

Rondeau, James (2008), *Frieze Magazine*, issue 113, March, http://www.frieze.com/issue/article/thinking_space/ (accessed 2 April 2014).

Sekula, Allan (1999), 'Michael Asher, down to earth', *Afterall*, #1, London: The University of Chicago Press.

Sheikh, Simon, (2006), 'Notes on institutional critique', *Transversal: Do You Remember Institutional Critique?*, eipcp: European Institute for Progressive Cultural Policies, http://eipcp.net/transversal/0106/sheikh/en/#_ftn1 (accessed 2 April 2014).

Slater, Howard (2000), "The art of governance: The Artist Placement Group 1966–1989", *Variant*, Vol 2, No 11, Summer, 23-26.

Söderberg, Marianne (2009), 'Ett lugnt samtal kring årets hetaste konstdebatt', *Norrbottens-kuriren*, 12 October, http://www.kuriren.nu/nyheter/ett-lugnt-samtal-kring-arets-hetaste-konstdebatt-5093165.aspx (accessed 30 March 2014).

Tate (2014), 'APG: Artist Placement Group', Learn, Online Resources, http://www2.tate.org.uk/artistplacementgroup/default.htm (accessed 2 April 2014).

Chapter 12

We-Minotaur-Labyrinth-Root

Talking transgression with Beuys and Bataille

Victoria Walters

Introduction

This chapter has emerged from a set of reflections and a body of work produced by myself and Professor Rebecca Krinke for the AHRA conference on Transgression. In it, I would like to tease out a number of issues arising from our work together and to bring in other, related questions I have been reflecting on, in an attempt to address the leading question of 'what architecture might be' (Troiani, Ewing and Periton 2013: 7). Rebecca has been working mainly through visual arts practice, thinking of herself primarily as an artist who teaches landscape architecture and I have been operating largely through theory as a researcher in visual culture, investigating the work of German twentieth-century artist Joseph Beuys. While Rebecca opted not to co-author this piece, I hope that I have honoured our experience here and indicated clearly where observations are not my own. However I accept that my authorship has led me to focus on elements that particularly interest me.[1] I have a strong sense that questions I have been grappling with around Beuys' transgressive legacies constitute a still pregnant aporia that might have some relevance for architecture. These relate to issues around meaning and related anthropological notions of the human being that had initially led me to work with Rebecca. I will begin by discussing the journeys that we made, then give a brief introduction to Beuys and philosopher and anthropologist Georges Bataille's respective positions with regard to form and meaning and finally, in the third section, consider how our work and these related critical debates have affected my thinking about architecture and transgression.

Working in an expanded field

Professor Krinke and I both share an interest in issues of trauma and representation and in working within an expanded field of practice.[2] We saw the call for papers as an opportunity to discuss and make work relating to transgression over an extended period. We were clear at the outset that we wanted to work through both theory and practice and explore notions of making and thinking; to draw from one of the dictionary's definitions of transgression, we sought to step across (or, arguably, overstep) the confines of our general practices and processes. This was not a new impetus for either of us; Rebecca had come to see her practices within the context of an expanded field, a synthesis which, as she explained, 'was not a smooth journey for me – there was a fairly long and tumultuous period of finding it difficult not to fit neatly into any one practice and not being able, until recently to see this as a strength' (Krinke in Krinke and Walters 2013).

Although written research was my main form of practice, I had made numerous attempts to make visual art work, with varying degrees of success, and had first encountered and become fascinated by Beuys' work while on an art foundation course. I began to study this artist, whose call for an expanded, anthropological notion of art continues to haunt contemporary practice, and became interested in border crossings between art and anthropology. It was an 'inner hearing' encounter I had had with Beuys' work that had initiated my own research and it was this that had particularly interested Krinke and caused her to want to work with me:

> I heard Victoria talk about an encounter she had with the work of Joseph Beuys in a museum – and the visceral reaction she felt in her body – which she described as an inner hearing that enabled her to experience the pain that the work was addressing. The fact that she talked about this in a public lecture, in a scholarly lecture – was something I found most compelling, unusual, and brave, and indeed it felt transgressive and powerful to me, and signalled a place where our interest overlapped.
>
> (Krinke and Walters 2013)

There was also an emphasis on dialogue as part of our process and a sense of warmth in the interaction between us that could be seen as Beuysian.

We began by reading shared texts and talking about transgression using Skype, asking ourselves a variety of related questions: What forms of transgression are beneficial for people? What risks are worth taking and for what reasons? What should cross the threshold of language and what remain unspoken? Other issues that engaged us were: animal–human transgression; the unspoken/unsayable and silence; people and the body in relation to particular sites; the sense that certain elements of reflective processes are not all about the intellect; and the degree to which meaning is out of our control. We both found that speaking aloud to a trusted colleague was a potent form for creative and intellectual growth. However, we came to the point where we felt we needed to undertake a defined activity to stimulate practice. There was a temptation to 'revert to type', and for me, as 'theorist', to ask Rebecca, the 'practitioner', questions about her visual arts practice. But this binary was not what we had sought in the process, which we hoped would integrate our wider capacities. A colleague suggested we consider reading Tim Ingold's book *Making: Anthropology, Archaeology, Art, and Architecture* and we decided to obtain a copy of the book and move forward from there.

Aligning with a particular approach in anthropology

Ingold's book argues that anthropology, archaeology, art, and, notably here, architecture, are not positive sciences, but that each constitutes an 'art of enquiry'. That is to say that they are all making processes that involve 'knowing *from the inside*', rather than just knowing about. Ingold suggests that the way in which 'the 4 As' connect knowing and being, and allow practitioners to learn from and with the world and other living beings rather than about them, is seldom acknowledged or understood. He argues that this lack of understanding causes anthropology and ethnography to be wrongly conflated, explaining that anthropology distinguishes itself from ethnography in its transformative focus on learning with and from the lives of the people worked with, rather than just about them: 'Anthropology is studying with and learning from; it is carried forward in a process of life, and effects transformations within that process' (Ingold 2013: 3).[3] Despite the influence of anthropology on the discipline, perhaps visual culture could be said to occupy a similar position in relation to art and the visual in the everyday; arguably it seeks to study visual events and their reception by audiences in the context of everyday life, rather than to inhabit the space of creating the visual from within.

Ingold proposes that allying anthropology with art, archaeology and architecture as arts of enquiry, allows us to perceive the way in which these disciplines seek a correspondence with the world. He encourages a resistance to the tendency to conceive of art, or indeed architecture, as objects or compendia for study – as in, for example, the anthropology of art – arguing in favour of anthropology with art. He explains:

> To carry out anthropology with art is to correspond with it in its own movements of growth or becoming, in a reading that goes forwards rather than in reverse, and to follow the paths along which it leads. And it is to link art and anthropology through the correspondence of their practices, rather than in terms of their objects, respectively historical and ethnographic.
>
> (Ingold 2013: 8)

With respect to architecture's inclusion in the '4 A', Ingold comments:

> In combining it with art and anthropology, I propose instead to think of architecture as a discipline that shares with art and anthropology a concern to explore the creative processes that give rise to the environment we inhabit, and the ways we perceive them. Taken as the practice of such a

discipline architecture is not so much about as by means of buildings. It is, in short, an architecture of inquiry. Included in it are questions concerning the generation of form, the energies of force and flow, the properties of materials, the weave and texture of surfaces, the atmospheres of volumes, and the dynamics of activity and of rest, of making lines and making place.

(Ingold 2013: 10)

This embodied notion of anthropology, art, architecture and archaeology interested both Rebecca and I in the context of our attempts to discover what it means to transgress in architecture – in a sense it offered a transgressive position that contested positivistic understandings of the discipline, an acknowledgement that architecture constitutes an invitation to do, rather than solely know about, in order to understand.[4]

Ingold's thinking had inspired, and evolved with, several university seminars and courses, and Rebecca and I decided to follow a project the anthropologist sets his students as part of a course called 'The 4 As'. He asks them to select a 'thing' located outdoors and spend an hour a week there. Each week, they are to focus on a different aspect of this object or living being, its history for example, or the way in which people and other living beings move around it. This is a means to encourage them to sharpen their observations and to learn through doing, to understand in practice. Through a combination of error and artistic license, we undertook a hybrid of this exercise, because we also set ourselves the task, connected to another exercise Ingold asked his students to do during the same course, of collecting materials from the environs of the thing we had chosen and making an object out of them, in order to learn about the nature of materials and their flows as well as the role of our own corporeal gestures in the making process.[5] The only concession we made to the fact that we were not anthropology students, and were both interested in sculpture, was that we gave each other permission to make a 3D object or objects, and to introduce a new material if we felt we needed to. However, we saw this very much as an experiment, rather than a means to produce anything approaching a finished piece. In this way, we both selected our 'thing' to focus on, and went on separate journeys.

Journey 1 – Working with a labyrinth (Rebecca Krinke)

These are Rebecca's presentation notes about her project:

I chose a labyrinth for my site for the exercise – it is five minutes from my house, between a church and a park. I had never been there and I chose it because I was sceptical of labyrinths. It seemed to me that they were a kind of pat solution to public art or place making or to spiritual ideas of space – and I was judging without experiencing. A labyrinth is relaxing because unlike a maze you don't solve it – you follow the one path. This one is about 40 feet in diameter and takes about 10 minutes to walk or less. I did notice that in 5 minutes of walking it I could feel a shift in my body and mind as if my blood pressure was going down to healthy levels.

Figure 12.1
Labyrinth

Figure 12.2
Process piece that
emerged from the work

Your focus is on following the path, wide enough for one person. You look down, seeing the simple textures and also feeling a lot of space, and being aware of moving in a measured way. Not just sitting at a park or sitting to relax – moving to relax.

Made of concentric circles – the space is simple and seemed to etch itself into my mind and body. I had dream about it – iPad map [Rebecca dreamed that a labyrinth form appeared across a conventional map displayed on her iPad screen]...I walked it in my mind. I craved going there it worked so well to settle me down and shift my state which I did not expect for me – a new reading of space by simply challenging myself to spend time with it, and to challenge my assumptions.

Lifting your head you see a larger context which is something the labyrinth reminded me of.

Since the labyrinth is on my way to and from work, it's interesting to notice now how often I feel as if I don't have the 10 minutes it takes to walk it. Made me wonder – how often do we take time out of our supercharged lives to spend time with a building or space? And what would be the impact for architecture if we did?

What I made – I collected materials from the site and placed them into these glass vessels I found.

I set them up as a sequence along a wall to engage the act of walking and the quality of space in between. Brings the textures of the ground to eye level (Krinke in Krinke and Walters 2013).

Journey 2 – Working with a tree (Victoria Walters)

My journey focused on an old beech tree standing in Winchester Cathedral garden, a tree I had drawn previously for another project. I had initially been so impressed by its sheer physical scale and the beauty of its trunk. The exercises I chose included writing about the tree's roots; observing and documenting how living beings moved around it and free writing about the tree while sitting at a distance, to examine how that affected my perception of it. Over time, I noticed I was building a real sense of connection to the tree and becoming more aware of the diverse living beings it sustained. Birds sang from branches or pecked at the ground, a squirrel climbing its trunk regarded me with curiosity and caution. Homeless people congregated nearby regularly, just outside the spread of its canopy. A child hid behind the tree during a game of hide-and-seek and a woman posed for a photograph, leaning against its trunk. And there was me, of course, affecting the field, observing and being observed by people, other animals and perhaps the tree itself, writing or drawing under its shelter which at one point saved me from a soaking.

It felt wonderful to visit the tree once a week, and particularly moving to reflect on its roots. I could physically feel a kind of energy emanating from them. Perhaps I was just imagining their activity of drawing substances from the soil and extending out. Clearly the tree did not have eyes, but it felt so responsive to its environment that I started to feel that the entire tree was almost like a kind of giant sensing eye. I reflected, what does it mean to sense the energy of a tree, to intuit or

Figure 12.3
Beech tree in Winchester Cathedral Gardens

imagine it, and can this be accepted in a positivistic enquiry? Could Ingold's notion of anthropology as an art of enquiry, and my journey learning with the tree, allow me to accept intuition as part of understanding? I loved the beautiful forms around the bottom of its trunk where the roots appeared slightly above the ground and had developed a hard, bark surround. They enabled me to see that the roots of this old beech extended over a great distance.[6]

Was this living 'thing' architectural in any conventional sense? Looking at academic papers, I noticed that work had been done on what is referred to as 'the architecture of trees'. However, it appeared that the spatial structure of the roots seldom factors in these studies. Reflecting on the roots led me to see the architecture of a tree as more of a circle than a view from ground up would suggest, or perhaps operating within a kind of circular configuration, since of course the roots are not identical to the trunk, boughs and canopy of a tree. I asked myself – do architects working in relation to the built environment, or even landscape architects, have a full image of the architecture of a tree and its role as a shelter and home in their minds when they plan?[7] If they did, as Rebecca mused later in our discussion of the work, would they be less inclined to take out trees in their building projects? Or, could they, I would now add, design newly built elements that come into the proximity of, and sit alongside trees in ways that recognise them as a fully sensing part of a hybrid built environment? What does it mean to see trees as part of the architecture of a site?

I felt there was something spiritual going on during this whole exercise and not simply because the tree was situated in the gardens of a cathedral. This is touched on, if only obliquely, by Ingold's notion of knowing from the inside. As living beings, trees sustain an abundance of life and are often extremely beautiful, so it is understandable that we feel a primal link to them, but these factors alone do not seem to fully explain the strong sense of connection between people and trees. The UK

Figure 12.4
**Process piece that
emerged from the work
(plaster and diverse
materials collected from
around the tree)**

government's recent proposed destruction of forests has led to huge public outcry; there is a real sense of trees reaching into people's interior space, into something very core, almost archetypal. I started thinking of a kind of soul architecture, an architecture that perceives the boundary between the 'external' world and the 'interior' world of the human being as more porous.

I began to reflect on how to use the materials I had collected around the tree to understand the way in which materials can be restored, as Ingold puts it 'to the currents of life' (Ingold 2013: 19). Initially I re-fired a ceramic tile I had picked up, seeing its copper colour emerge once again from the grey dust it had gathered over time. I realised I very much wanted to draw attention to the materials as they expressed the connection between the tree and the life processes going on in and around it. An initial idea was to create separate ceramic vessels and place them in a configuration, so that the gap between them indicated where the tree's visible, but absent roots were, as a kind of inverted representation of a tree. But that did not lend itself to the medium which, as Ingold had indicated in his book, had its own designs. The materials had particular propensities; I had to collaborate with them in order to find appropriate 'correspondences'. I started forming the materials into a tree shape and this expressed the connections between the tree and its environment, albeit rather clumsily. In the process I was reminded of Ingold's observation about the necessity of getting dirty when working with materials during this exercise:

> Materials do not, of themselves, stay in place or hold to the bounds of any form, and have an inherent tendency to run amok. We are all familiar with Mary Douglas's (1966: 44) celebrated definition of dirt as matter out of place, and sure enough, we quickly got our hands very dirty.
>
> (Ingold 2013: 18)

Finally, it occurred to me that a white plaster cast of the roots themselves would provide a kind of ghost image, with spaces into which I could place the materials. To do this, I enlisted the help of a local sculptor and ceramicist, Jerzy Mazur. When we went to cast a small area of the tree roots, I was concerned that we might harm the tree I had become so attached to, perhaps a sign that there was some form of boundary there. We created an alginate cast and then a plaster mould, from which Jerzy cast a white plaster form for me in his studio.

Looking at the process piece, I had an impression of issues I had been grappling with at the beginning of the project, which had led me to work with Rebecca. Focusing on what was around the tree could be seen as focusing on waste; old leaves, detritus, dirt, old bottle tops, diverse elements that could be seen as the unusable remains of commodities, thus lying outside signification within capitalism. But for me those materials were a qualitative expression of the interchange between a tree and its wider environment, telling me what goes on in and around it and the incidences and relationships the tree's energy and activities pull into its sphere of influence. In a sense, then, these connections could be seen as part of a larger ecology of meaning and it is to the issue of meaning that I would now like to turn in relation to the respective positions of Beuys and Bataille and the issue of why I feel comparative discussion of the respective positions of these two twentieth-century figures may have relevance for architecture.

Beuys and Bataille – the struggle for meaning

As suggested previously, I wanted to start experimenting through practice again and to do some reflective work with Rebecca concerning transgression, materials and meaning, because of an impasse I was experiencing both in relation to my theoretical concerns and visual practice. This had come to a head in relation to a well-known critique of Beuys' work. In the catalogue of the exhibition they curated in 1996 entitled *Formless: A User's Guide*, art historians Rosalind Krauss and Yve-Alain Bois make use of Georges Bataille's notion of *l'informe* (the formless) as a means to analyse, or rather, to operate upon, works of art.[8] In a section of the book entitled *No...To Joseph Beuys*, Krauss uses the formless to discuss Beuys' 1964 work *Fat Chair*, a chair onto which Beuys had moulded a triangular slab of fat, visible in cross section at the sides, to reveal the chaotic nature of the substance. She comments, 'the scatological nature of the materials, the insistence on the sacred – might strike one as textbook Bataille' (Krauss 1997: 145). However, she points out that on closer examination, Beuys' argument that every human being is an artist transcodes, or collapses the figure of the bohemian into that of the proletarian in a way that is antithetical to Bataille's stance.

Krauss observes that for Bataille, the bohemian, which she translates in Marxist terms as the lumpenproletariat or proletarian, is interesting precisely because it cannot be assimilated into Marx's logic of history and society, which revolves around the relationship between the proletariat and the bourgeoisie, and is thus able to 'void the economy of representation' (ibid.). Making a clear reference to Bataille's theory of *dépense* (expenditure), Krauss argues that while Bataille recognises that 'homogeneous society … produces waste that it cannot assimilate', Beuys' notion of social sculpture differs, and indeed is dangerous, because it subsumes everything into meaning: 'Beuys' notion of total recuperation connected to a system from which nothing escapes being impressed into the service of meaning is thus involved in an idea of the sacred that is as far away as possible from that of Bataille's [sic]' (ibid.). Krauss rejects Beuys' artistic position and what she sees as the artist's adoption of the roles 'of shaman, of wandering Jew, of scapegoat, of Martyr', concluding that his approach constitutes a drive to the transcendental, a position with which the formless is hostile, because it 'always tries to recuperate the excremental, or the sacrificial fall, by remaking it as a theme' (Krauss 1997: 146).

Krauss' argument with respect to Bataille and Beuys is a complex one, grounded as it is in an analysis of their respective positions in relation to Marx's historical materialism. When I started working with Rebecca, I had come to a standstill with regard to my own feelings about Beuys' legacies in the light of Krauss' vehement critique, and felt at a loss as to how to respond to them. It seemed to me that revisiting this constructed critical 'standoff' between the two figures might be important for me, but also for understandings of transgression within architecture (and visual culture more broadly). Bataille's ideas have had a major influence on what transgression is understood to constitute in the discipline.[9] In his keynote speech at the AHRA conference, architect and educator Bernard Tschumi elaborated on architecture in terms of Bataille's notions of eroticism and desire, evoking the way in which the architect is bound by (increasingly) narrow contexts within which she/he is expected to create and innovate.[10] Yet with the greatest of respect for Tschumi as a leading international architect, I could not avoid a sense that, in the current context, the use of this kind of notion of transgression, or at the very least, the way in which it had been interpreted within architecture and allied fields, had become tired, that the very frameworks and contexts architects were operating in within late capitalism were now so constrained that to operate within such limits no longer seemed even painfully pleasurable. At the same time, just as Bataille figured large at the conference, there was also the occasional glimpse of the figure of Beuys.[11] It felt problematic to entirely dismiss either figure's position. There was something about the two figures' respective stances with respect to language, the human being and transgression that, it appeared to me, required reconsideration in contemporary contexts.

Bataille famously outlined the concept of *l'informe*, or the formless, in an article of the same name submitted within the dissident surrealist art journal *Documents*. In the article, he explains the term in relation to the broader project of *Le Dictionnaire Critique*, which outlines a new role for the dictionary:

> A dictionary begins when it no longer gives the meaning of words, but their tasks. Thus formless is not only an adjective having a given meaning, but a term that serves to bring things down in the world, generally requiring that each thing have its form. What it designates has no rights in any sense and gets itself squashed everywhere, like a spider or an earthworm. In fact, for

academic men to be happy, the universe would have to take shape. All of philosophy has no other goal: it is a matter of giving a frock coat to what is, a mathematical frock coat. On the other hand, affirming that the universe resembles nothing and is only formless amounts to saying that the universe is something like a spider or spit.

(Bataille 1985 [1929]: 382)

For Bataille the important question is not what words mean, but what they do, and what they do is labour.[12] The theorist argues that words are tools that actively give form, and that the world itself is only given the false appearance of form by words, when in fact it is formless. With the concept of the formless, Bataille, in a sense, brings words low, debases them, but at the same time he highlights what they bring into being; as Hollier puts it, for Bataille 'the word is the locus of an event, an explosion of affective potential, not a means for the expression of meaning' (Hollier 1992: 30). As a result, through his *Dictionnaire Critique* (the wider language project the article *L'Informe* relates to), Bataille also debases notions of the human soul; Hollier notes Carl Einstein's statement in another article in *Documents*: 'What is called the soul is, for the most part, a museum of signs devoid of meaning' (Einstein, cited in Hollier 1992: 29). For Bataille, the mystical element of words for human beings relates to their essential emptiness of meaning.[13]

What is particularly intriguing, in relation to the work Rebecca had undertaken, is that this emptiness of meaning is developed by Bataille in relation to the image of the labyrinth. Bataille argues that because people *are* only in relation to language, they are never sufficient in themselves; language is the reason why people wrongly consider themselves as individuals when they cannot, in fact, escape their relational connections to others. Benjamin Noys explains:

Bataille chooses the image of the labyrinth to describe this state because it captures the effect of disorientation caused by insufficiency, but at the same time the labyrinth is never sufficient and is always in relation to an exterior which cannot be completely specified in advance. The most powerful example of the principle of insufficiency is language, because language imposes itself on us and puts us in relation to others. To be in language is to be in relation to others, a relation that can never be fully mastered or controlled.

(Noys 2000: 20)

It occurs to me that Bataille's notion of the word as 'the locus of an event' rather than a vector of meaning, and the centrality of language for human shaping, may not be dissimilar to the position taken by Beuys with respect to language. However, it is clear that the conclusions Beuys draws about people's potential as a result have a very different emphasis. Beuys is renowned for a variety of controversial statements and actions, but perhaps most well known for the pronouncement 'everyone is an artist'. Rather than a glib statement about the ability of people to make paintings, 'everyone an artist' reflected Beuys' notion that all human beings demonstrate creative capabilities and a longing to journey beyond the surface of materials. From the artist's perspective, it is the human act of creative sculptural forming from chaos, including the forming of speech and language more broadly as part of an expanded notion of language, that is central to what it means to be human, and this shaping must be done with a sense of responsibility, it must be brought high.

This is to say, verbal language is seen to have substance as human thought shaped by the mouth and transmitted in vibrating air; in the post-war context in which Beuys was working, the message here seems to be: one could be pessimistic about people and their capability to shape materials given all that has happened historically, but they must engage their creativity and seek to form a better world, and do this both as individuals and as collectives, or humanity and many other species will not survive. It seems to me that Bataille and Beuys' respective understandings of language might, in some sense, represent corresponding facets of a similar notion of meaning, from which different conclusions about the human being have been drawn. While Krauss is concerned with Beuys' alleged attempt to subsume everything into meaning, it seems to me that *for both figures*, the human being engages with the chaos of materials and the key issue distinguishing their respective positions is their interpretation of the predicament of the human being.

For Bataille, this is essentially a pessimistic one. Hollier notes that for Bataille architecture is oppressive because of 'its anthropomorphism'; it is, in a sense, a prison because it is inescapably an image of the human being whose very form is 'his first prison' (Hollier 1992: xi-xii). Yet it could be argued that Bataille's image of people is grounded in anthropological notions that are highly suspect. For example, in *Alchemist of the Revolution: The Affective Materialism of Georges Bataille*, Gavin Grindon notes that Bataille put anthropological ideas, such as the concept of the pot-latch, to the service of his revolutionary schema, yet these models did not emerge from investigations he, himself, had undertaken, and were often based on presumptions of a commonality not borne out by detailed anthropological investigation. Indeed they could be seen as, themselves, part of a colonial discourse.[14] This is not to say that they constituted part of a right-wing project, however. Bataille's project in *Documents* related to an attempt by the dissident surrealist group to borrow from the approaches of the far right in order to work against fascism, provoking affect and violence, but putting it to the task of protecting the community, thus seeking to prevent people from falling under the hypnotic power of the dictator. Bataille calls for a sadistic revelry in violence and dirt which, for the theorist, must accompany revolution:

> Without a profound complicity with natural forces such as violent death, gushing blood, sudden catastrophes and the horrible cries of pain that accompany them, terrifying ruptures of what had seemed to be immutable, the fall into stinking filth of what had been elevated – without a sadistic understanding of an incontestably thundering and torrential nature, there could be no revolutionaries, there could only be a revolting utopian sentimentality.
>
> (Bataille, cited in Grindon 2010: 307)

Grindon notes that Bataille's thinking on the potential of affect to stimulate class struggle and social change were at work in developments on the far right, but clarifies that Bataille was never allied to the right and argued that the left must take the tools being exploited by the right-wing to stimulate affect into their own hands.

In 'Neither beast nor man: Qu'est-ce que c'est qu'un monstre?', Martyn Llewellyn explores Bataille's position with respect to fascism in relation to his development of a particular understanding of the figure of the Minotaur, and his related notion of Acéphale Man. Llewellyn notes that these figures 'illustrate the avant-garde's ambiguous response to fascism in the 1930s'. He explains that 'Bataille's consideration of the Minotaur effectively strips it of its cultural status, as a symbol of classical myth, and reconfigures it as an embodiment of the animal in the psychology of primitive humanity' (Llewellyn 2010: 123). There is not space here to elaborate the complex subtleties and distinctions between the Minotaur and the Acéphale Man for the Surrealists and for Bataille in detail, however it is significant that Bataille's thinking relates to a particular interest in sacrifice. He sees in the operations of fascism the hypnosis of the individual into believing that against any ethical sensibilities they may have, they must sacrifice themselves for their leader. Llewellyn explores Bataille's notion that fascism plays upon an inherent desire in the human being for the Other, a desire, in fact, to be the other in the sense of becoming animal; both the Minotaur and the Acéphale Man are framed by Bataille not as animals but as 'alter(ed) humans' which Bataille works with in order to explore how the desire and violence that fascism seeks to direct towards hero worship might be channelled towards the community. Llewellyn concludes that this human element 'allows for a new perspective to consider the place of the subject in relation to the Other, framed by desire' (Llewellyn 2010: 136). Of course, it was of considerable interest to me that Bataille had elaborated his understanding of language in terms of the image of the labyrinth and that the figure of the Minotaur had figured so heavily in his thought.[15]

In post-war Germany, after the fascist rhetoric of blood and iron I would argue that it was, in Beuys' eyes, no longer defensible to see transgression in these violent terms. Yet without this sadistic understanding of, and work with, 'natural forces' including dirt, was Beuys, following Bataille's assessment, indulging in a 'revolting utopian sentimentality'? Given the artist's use of abject materials and his relentless determination to look both backwards and forwards in relation to German history, to acknowledge what he referred to as the 'indescribable darkness' of the Holocaust, it is difficult to see sentimentality in Beuys' work, for all its apparent utopian feeling. Indeed Beuys clearly 'mucked in'. But his use of materials appears primed to initiate a memory process and to stimulate libidinal, spiritual energy in people that could be said to exist prior to language. There is a pre-symbolic process at work which stimulates affect, those 'visceral forces beneath, alongside, or generally other than conscious knowing that can serve to drive us toward movement, thought and ever-changing forms of relation' (Gregg and Seigworth 2010: publication abstract). Rather than channelling this towards extremist discourses as the fascists had sought to do or towards the communal, as with Bataille, Beuys sought to lead this energy in the direction of dialogue.[16] The 'incontestably thundering and torrential' force in

Beuys' vision appears to be the threat of imminent environmental catastrophe, those of the real elemental powers in the world, the thunder and torrents wrought by the weather.

For Beuys, architecture has to become a positive and productive endeavour, or humanity will not survive. In the context of his expanded anthropological art, human creativity is, whether knowingly or otherwise, being exercised in every discipline and could be developed even further, in a more self-conscious and purposeful way, to counter the increasingly technocentric and positivistic current that was destroying the environment and bringing people, and notably also their spiritual inner lives, to the brink of extinction.[17] Beuys' expanded notion of sculpture extends into the organic, even encompassing the way in which people shape their thoughts, their words and their societies, and indeed must come to do so self-consciously, as a matter of urgency, a methodology which Beuys called social sculpture, and also, on several occasions, 'social architecture':

> Only on condition of a radical widening of definition will it be possible for art and activities related to art to provide evidence that art is now the only evolutionary-revolutionary power. Only art is capable of dismantling the repressive effects of a senile social system to build a SOCIAL ORGANISM AS A WORK OF ART. This most modern art discipline – *Social Sculpture/ Social Architecture* – will only reach fruition when every living person becomes a creator, a sculptor, or architect of the social organism. Only then would the insistence on participation of the action art of FLUXUS and Happening be fulfilled.
>
> (Beuys 1993: 21, my emphasis)

For Beuys, this was the natural fulfilment of the work of Marcel Duchamp, whom he criticised for having understood the implications of the creativity of all, but still chosen to occupy a position of ironic silence, rather than extending art into the anthropological.[18]

Referring back to Krauss' critique again, it appears to me that her famous rejection of Beuys' position with respect to meaning reflects a partial misunderstanding of Bataille's notion of expenditure (*dépense*) and thus a degree of misrepresentation of the difference between the two figures. Her analysis is extremely astute, certainly, however its claim that Bataille was interested in the lumpenproletariat because it was able to 'void the economy of representation' and her suggestion that for Bataille, there are materials that cannot be recuperated or recycled seems somewhat at odds with Bataille's point. This is, it seems to me, an anthropological one; he argues that the human being experiences the need to feel that there is a loss and that this stems from an impossible desire to remain unsullied by impurity. In *Against Architecture: The Writings of Georges Bataille*, Dennis Hollier explains that *dépense* is:

> Primarily *a theory of the need for loss rather than a theory of loss strictly speaking*. It responds to the need to believe that there is a pure loss, that there is lost

time and there are waste lands, unproductive expenditures, things one never gets over, sins that cannot be redeemed, garbage that cannot be recycled.

(Bataille, cited in Hollier 1992: xiv)

Somewhat ironically, Krauss seems to use Bataille to maintain a discourse of purity, a normative proposition that 'homogeneous society … produces waste that it cannot assimilate' rather than the diagnostic one Bataille intended, that homogeneous society produces waste that it would prefer to believe it cannot assimilate in order to maintain a sense of being pure. Bataille celebrates the detritus, which of course, in his revolutionary schema, refers not just to materials but to people, the lumpenproletariat. However, he resolutely brings them back into the frame. Taking issue with Marx's ejection of the lumpenproletariat from his dialectical revolutionary framework and his reference to this group as 'offal' or 'scum', Bataille insists that the lumpenproletariat, the 'brothel-keepers, organ-grinders and ragpickers' should be valorised, and in so doing makes them signify the entirety of the working class; as Grindon puts it, 'Bataille returns these "moral" exclusions as a central quality of the working class itself' (Grindon 2010: 309). Certainly he 'makes of the entire working class a resistant other who are the excluded excess of capitalism' but capitalism itself does not constitute meaning, this is not to say that they 'void the economy of representation'.

Bataille insists that people acknowledge the myriad histories of a place, both sublime and sinister, that they face the blood of the abattoir as they do the apparent (but erroneous) purity of the Museum, breaking with the taboos of dirty and clean. I would suggest that, while Bataille and Beuys' positions certainly differ, there may not be the opposition that Krauss tries to establish; indeed that Beuys' position appears far more sympathetic to that of Bataille than her analysis would allow, for both figures hold the brightness and the darkness of the past firmly in mind. However, as has already been mentioned, Bataille's project champions the need for the return of the repressed, of the triumph of waste and 'offal'. For him, these are terms to be revelled in and reclaimed; the affect borne of the violence of the lumpenproletariat and their violation of taboos is the only transgressive force for radical change. Where Bataille sees a human being who experiences an innate need to maintain a notion of purity, Beuys' human being is defined by creative agency as central to what it means to be human, and demands a form of art that never fails to reflect on the 'indescribable darkness' of the German past, an art that acknowledges the trauma and materials of the past while seeking to channel affect in the direction of dialogue.

In light of the work Rebecca and I had undertaken with materials, the necessity of getting dirty due to their 'inherent tendency to run amok' and my desire not to conceal 'matter out of place' in my small process piece, this critical nexus gives me pause. It seems to me that the influence Bataille had exerted on post-structuralism must be handled with particular care. Given Krauss's rejection of Beuys' position in favour of that of Bataille – or as Gregory Williams puts it, 'Beuys as the anti-Bataille' (Williams 2008, n.p.n) – it is no surprise that her notion of the expanded field seemed to inherit its implicit pessimism, while constituting an extremely useful framework. In her famous *October* article 'Sculpture in the expanded field' (1979), Krauss notes the increasing 'elasticity' of the term sculpture since the late 1960s and the tendency to obfuscate how different these new forms were by trying to establish continuity between them and the forms of the past through historicising, at first in terms of more recent practice and then in relation to forms from increasingly distant pasts (Krauss 1979: 32–33). Krauss argues that sculpture is, in fact, 'a historically bound category and not a universal one' and that the time came, when the notion that 'the logic of sculpture' was 'inseparable from the logic of the monument' no longer held. For Krauss, this was the beginning of modernism, when sculpture entered 'the space of what could be called its negative condition – a kind of sitelessness, or homelessness, an absolute loss of place' (Krauss 1979: 34). Krauss argues that this was a limited state of affairs, so from the 1950s on, sculpture became an exhausted category, 'experienced more and more as pure negativity', that is to say 'something that was possible to locate only in terms of what it was not' (Krauss 1979: 34). She formulates a notion of the 'complex', whereby architecture constitutes that which is 'not landscape' and landscape that which is 'not architecture', explaining:

> Our culture had not before been able to think the complex, although other cultures have thought this term with great ease. Labyrinths and mazes are both landscape and architecture; Japanese gardens are both landscape and architecture; the ritual playing fields and professionals of ancient civilizations were all in this sense the unquestioned occupants of the complex ... They were part of a universe or cultural space in which sculpture was simply another part ... Their purpose and pleasure is exactly that they are opposite and different.
>
> (Krauss 1979: 38)

For Krauss, the 'expanded field' explains the new scenario where artists situate themselves in different places within the field at any given time, 'within the situation of postmodernism, practice is not defined in relation to a given medium – sculpture – but rather in relation to the logical operations on a set of cultural terms, for which any medium ... might be used' (Krauss 1979: 42).

Yet if Bataille's approach acknowledges that the world is formless and that language obscures people's inherent relational ties, that of Beuys seems to follow some of Bataille's findings to a radical conclusion in the context of a more hopeful set of suppositions. For if language has a central role in all shaping, then interdisciplinary working is the only way in which people can confront the inherent connections between things, obscured by the capacity of language to classify and divide. Beuys' anthropological 'expanded field' of art/architecture is arguably more progressive than that of Krauss, calling for interdisciplinary dialogue and engagement brought on by the recognition that specialist knowledge, while valuable, is not the only form of understanding required to face new contexts and environmental challenges. Indeed for Beuys, disciplinary methods are forms of sculpture, or architecture, in themselves, shaping our understandings of the world, and this must therefore be undertaken with a sense of responsibility as to their consequences. Further, Beuys' field is both an outer and an inner environment. The artist sought to encourage an understanding of the way in which people's perception of materials reaches into their inner, spiritual world, promoting the capacity to apprehend and work with materials in terms of these invisible, intuited qualities, as well as their visible external forms. The outer world relates to the inner world of the human being. Social sculpture/architecture stimulates an interior, expanded language that is felt from within. Beuys talked about entering into a living being, really observing another living being and allowing your rational and imaginative faculties to play a role in your understanding of it and thereby developing new powers of perception in yourself.[19] This is an approach that was very much influenced by Steiner's studies of Goethean science and points to the connection between people's inner and outer worlds. Beuys once declared, 'Die Bäume sind nicht wichtig, um dieses Leben auf der Erde aufrecht zu erhalten, nein, die Bäume sind wichtig, um die menschliche Seele zu retten' ('trees are important not simply to maintain life on Earth, but to save the human soul') (Fuhlbrügge 2007: 29).

Reflections on our journeys

When we first started to talk over our journeys together, Rebecca noted that we had looked at sites, a labyrinth and a tree, that could be seen as rather fairy-like and fey, but that these turned into important encounters for us both. We recognised that we were working with spaces that could be seen as archetypal and this made me think of Jane Bennett's book *The Enchantment of Modern Life*. Bennett argues for a process of re-enchantment and points to the way in which this affective process may have an ethical dimension (Bennett 2001). This is interesting in light of Bataille's conviction that affect was the route to revolution and Beuys' conviction that working with human creativity would lead to evolution. Rebecca and I would like to come back to this issue in a further iteration of our work together. In relation to my comparison of the respective positions of Bataille and Beuys, I had to reflect on the journeys Rebecca and I had undertaken. I started to consider, both humorously and earnestly, whether my feeling towards the tree I had worked with constituted a form of desire for the Other and to ask myself whether the connection between what I had learned with the tree, and my dialogue with Rebecca, constituted fields of affect. I reflected on Rebecca's exploration of a labyrinth, her initial concern that the construction of a labyrinth was a somewhat hackneyed attempt to create a spiritual sense of place in public space, but her subsequent experiential sense of the labyrinth as a form that calmed her down. Was this form cathartic because it constituted a reflection of the human being's predicament within language, as Bataille had surmised? If that was the case, it certainly did not seem to galvanise aggressive energy.

The figure of the Minotaur connected to our earlier discussions of human/non-human relations. One of the texts we had read in the early stages of our work was a book chapter by Jan van Boeckel entitled 'A point of no return: artistic transgression in a more than human world'. Van Boeckel, part of a research group in phenomenology and existentialism, writes about the challenges and value of ecological education and engaging people with the environment through art, but suggests that care needs to be taken with respect to methods. He asks whether some artists' work may go too far in transgressing human–animal boundaries to offer routes forward in this area and in order to investigate this, compares the human–animal transgressions of Beuys with those of Timothy Treadwell, who adopted the behaviour of a group of Alaskan grizzly bears in order to be accepted among them, an experiment that ultimately led to his death. Van Boeckel looks specifically at the Beuys action *I Like America, America Likes Me* (1974), sometimes referred to colloquially as the coyote action, where Beuys spent eight hours over three days with a live coyote. He argues that in this action, the artist was not transgressing boundaries between humans and other animals in a radical way, so much as proposing a way of thinking about the relationship between the 'earthly and spiritual realms' that was influenced by anthroposophy:

> Though it can be said that Beuys, in his actions, came close to testing the border between the human and non-human, it seems that after each experience he was able to retract safely from the liminal space ... Summarising, one can question whether Beuys's actions in essence constituted a deep probing of the boundary with the non-human Others. I suggest they should rather be taken as artistic performances, happenings, aimed at conveying a strongly held conviction to an audience.
>
> (van Boeckel 2011: 5)

In contrast, Treadwell seeks to become like a bear and van Boeckel concludes that as a result, he falls foul of a transgression that the indigenous populace would never entertain, because 'the bear represents something sacred'. He argues that the danger of 'non-indigenous postmodern longing' is its failure to respect taboos and cites Martin Drenthen:

> In the native view, a taboo regulates the relation with bears and orders not to cross the borderline between their world and ours. Bears and humans should keep distance from one another, because the gap between worlds is not merely factual but also a [sic] symbolic. On the other side of the gap exists an alien, sacred world of its own, inaccessible to humans, but with its own reason.
>
> (Drenthen, cited in van Boeckel 2011: 9)

This 'case study' resounded with Bataille's thinking, with Treadwell appearing as a kind of human sacrifice to his desire for the Other, but the comparison between Treadwell and Beuys was compelling. Beuys' artistic approach to treading into the realm of desire and communion with another animal appears to stimulate an affective response of association and desire in the audience and gets something moving. Whether this 'gap between worlds' is purely symbolic is a matter for discussion in another essay, but suffice it to say that in initiating the audience's traversal into the 'sacred world' of the coyote in the context of a ritual, imaginative action rather than seeking to *be* coyote, Beuys could be said to retain a degree of respect for the difference between human and non-human worlds.

Conclusion

At the end of our journeys, clear answers and strident positions were slow to emerge, but that has perhaps been of benefit to us both: we are interested in the vibrant questions arising from the work. The project we undertook may appear somewhat naïve, but I am glad that we did it with an open mind and focused on both theory and the experience of making, without letting theory outweigh practice too heavily in what we did together. Our exercise was an attempt to consider and work with our respective concerns but to experience them in a new and different way. Admittedly we adopted a particular notion of what anthropology was through drawing on Tim Ingold's ideas, but I tried to stand at one remove from Beuys' position during our work, and it was perhaps just as well that neither of us had been pulled into that of Bataille either as we were not familiar with his writings. It was a surprise to discover at the AHRA conference that a number of elements Rebecca had brought to our process, notions of the unspoken, for example, or an investigation of the labyrinth, had figured prominently in Bataille's thinking in relation to language and reflections on – and indeed against – architecture; the process of writing this chapter has allowed me to look into this more deeply.

Through considering these figures at arm's length, I have come to some awareness of how their investigations have come to frame a particular notion of the human being and taken a particular position with respect to Marx's thought, which have then impacted on notions of transgression playing out in architecture. The power of affect, for Bataille, derives its revolutionary force from the breaking of taboos. However, looking into Bataille's notion of transgression has raised a number of questions about the potentials and dangers of drawing on dubious anthropological understandings in making political pronouncements or constructing architectural positions, particularly where these are not the result of a lived process of learning with other people, in Ingold's sense.[20] In the context of discussions of transgression in architecture, Beuys' work with social sculpture/architecture, and his attempts to engender in people the ability to exercise and develop their own powers of perception appeared as an equally fascinating trajectory of thought, as did the artist's expanded thinking on materials. These seemed to point to a form of transgression that could enable people to see afresh in the context of their everyday perception, to engage their imagination and intuition while remaining safe, in psychic terms. Even at the beginning of our work together, there had already been a sense that, consciously or unconsciously, Rebecca and I might be working with, or at the very least open to, a broader notion of what objects and materials set in train for people. However, it was clear that it was unproductive to set Bataille against Beuys in a definitive way.[21] Bataille's brave and fascinating work is a vital trajectory of thinking and, as Noys warns, by attempting to reject and then appropriate it, there is a danger of repressing the shocking vitality of the writer's thought in order to maintain purity (Noys 2000: 2–5). At the same time, I would not also want to conclude that either figure's approach should be beyond question or critical reassessment in light of emerging understandings in anthropology or ecology, for example.

I am now less anxious about social sculpture/architecture than I was at the outset, but am still questioning. Disciplines, not unlike the lives of other species, have their own rules, and when we transgress their boundaries we need to be critically aware of why we are doing this and acknowledge that the rules are not familiar. This is as much in the interest of our own well being as it is in the clarity of our investigations. But at the same time, all disciplines and species are connected within a wider ecosystem, as emanations of life and thinking, and we need to find critical ways to move across them in order to act as translators and, like Hermes, ferry back messages. Of course, this begs the question: what position do we want to take with respect to these strands of radical thinking and acting in relation to transgression? What are the current requirements for social change? Despite the fact that architects work 'by means of buildings' in Ingold's sense, I wonder whether architects are now operating within a system that, all too often, requires them to turn their back on the 'counsel from the world itself' even as their focus is on process and materials. This irony had been suggested by Rebecca's journey, the joy of the work for her lay in the opportunity it afforded her to judge a labyrinth by experiencing it rather than knowing about it, and in the opportunity to learn about a site through encountering it. The increasing urgency of the environmental context impressed itself upon me and in the context of rapid climate change, I asked myself, is it finally becoming clear that the first and last architect is the ecosystem itself, in relation to which humans are always left to construct and build in whatever way they can?[22]

What new, or conversely old, approaches are needed? Clearly, drawing from Ingold, we need to glean lessons through doing, and to learn from knowing from within, rather than just knowing about. Referring back to van Boeckel, if Timothy Treadwell had spoken to the local populace about his experiments with bears, he may have come to an understanding of what role the taboo of the difference between human and bear serves in articulating the symbolic gap between them, thus protecting them both. Following Beuys, who was interested in revisiting the 'lost forces' worked with by the shaman, is the challenge that of transgressing the boundaries between ourselves and other living beings through observation and imagination in order to learn with and from them, developing new capabilities in ourselves and new architectural forms as a result? Or is this a naïve approach? If Bataille's articulation of the desire that humans feel for other animals is accurate, perhaps the role of the original Greek myth of the Minotaur, which he had reconfigured, is, in itself, a means to articulate human desire for other living beings poetically, in a way that maintains the dynamic in the realm of the psychic imaginary as a real but not literal experience, something only experienced in mythic time or non-rational consciousness? Perhaps recognising the hovering figure of the Minotaur in our own aspect, the 'zone of indecidability', between ourselves and other living beings, encourages us to respect those taboos that keep us safe, preventing us from being devoured, or indeed, devouring ourselves?

Notes

1. I also hope that some of my further reflections may touch on issues that are pertinent for Rebecca's practice.
2. We are both members of a research network called 'Mapping Spectral Traces', which looks at the way in which trauma can continue to affect places, and ways of working ethically with those residual issues through theory and practice. See http://www.mappingspectraltraces.org

3   For Ingold, ethnography is a more documentary-related task that cannot be seen in the same way. Thus his premise is constrained in that it focuses solely on the four stated disciplines.

4   As Ingold puts it in relation to a seminar he ran on the interface between art, architecture and anthropology, 'We had to be doing things ourselves' (Ingold 2013: 9).

5   For this project, Ingold asked his students to collect a selection of objects, then a selection of materials (to encourage them to reflect on how the terminology caused them to select and treat what they were working with), and to work with what they had found with glue and poster boards to understand 'on the one hand the manual and bodily gestures of ourselves, as practitioners; on the other hand the particular flow patterns of the mixtures we had made' (Ingold 2013: 18).

6   While reflecting on this, I remembered Deleuze and Guattari's use of the image/analogy of roots as part of discussions of ways of understanding culture when they contrast the rhizome root system with the tree root system. I find their concept of a tree root as an analogy for culture that charts causality along chronological lines, a theocentric culture, valuable but limited, because to me it is impossible to see a tree's roots as an image entirely abstracted from the tree as a whole – indeed that is my main criticism of the work I have made – there is not a linearity but a circular process in operation there.

7   In the textbook *Ecology*, T.J. King notes, 'The tree is like a house with many rooms, each offering a different meal and a different environment' (King 1989: 7).

8   The exhibition, curated at the Centre Georges Pompidou in Paris in 1996, was developed as a result of Krauss and Bois' observation that there were modern art works that could most fully be understood in relation to Bataille's notion of the formless and to explore what this might mean for contemporary and future debates about critical terms and categories. As they explain, 'The intent was to demonstrate the power of the conceptual tool, but would also pick apart certain categories that seemed to us increasingly useless – even as they had become increasingly contentious – namely, 'form' and 'content': and to explore what the formless might offer future understandings of modernist art. (Bois and Krauss 1997: 9–10).

9   Of course, my impression that Bataille's work has had a huge influence on understandings of architecture must be tempered by the fact that transgression was the aperture through which we were all viewing architecture at the conference.

10 Tschumi spoke about his encounter with Le Corbusier's Villa Savoye, a building whose decay appeared to Tschumi as sensual and architectural in its precarity, sitting between life and death. As somebody who was new to discussions of architecture, it intrigued me that Tschumi had been interested in architecture and representation from early on in his career. In *Against Architecture*, Denis Hollier cites Tschumi's discussion of his work at the Parc de la Villette in terms of its 'assault on meaning', and its attempt to 'dismantle meaning'. (Tschumi, cited in Hollier 1992: ix) In short, he frames this work in relation to what architecture means.

11 In his keynote talk, Didier Faustino mentioned Beuys' coyote piece and its resonance in the face of his anger and despair at hearing of a man who had climbed into the wheel hub of a plane in his desperation to find asylum in France, dying in the attempt. The coyote, the 'pest' animal, stands in for the 'other', the scapegoat onto which to project the inadequacies of the self.

12 Denis Hollier's translation of Bataille's original word *besogne* as 'job' or 'work' seems limited to me, because as Hollier himself notes, *besogne* implies a sense of obligation and 'drudgery' (Hollier 1992: 28) As a result I have used the word labour which I feel may be a more appropriate translation, especially given the political aspect of Bataille's position.

13 This understanding of words clearly relates to structuralist thought and signals a movement towards post-structuralism, the notion that meaning occurs as a result of relations of difference between terms, rather than their supposed content, but that as a result meaning is never resident anywhere, words are empty, a position that clearly influenced Derrida's thought.

14 Grindon gives a fascinating outline of the influence of the pot-latch and gift-giving economy on Bataille's notion of expenditure, yet notes that he was working with a false assumption that these forms of giving were identical in different societies. Grindon suggests that the term 'pot-latch' itself was a dubious term used to group and render illegal a variety of Native American practices. Grindon sees Bataille's thinking on the potential of affect to stimulate class struggle and social change at work in developments on the far right, although he clarifies that Bataille was never allied to the right and, indeed, that he argued that the left must take the tools of affect being exploited by the right-wing into their own hands.

15 Bataille's ideas about these two figures may provide an interesting focus for study in relation to contemporary notions of the cyborg.

16 For a more detailed assessment of Beuys' artistic strategies and their confrontation of what Gene Ray refers to as 'Nazi fantasies of purity and omnipotence', see Walters 2012: 190–6.

17 Beuys found his calling as a teacher of this expanded art and, during his lifetime, advanced the idea that art would soon emerge as the only approach to the challenges of a world in thrall to a scientistic mode of thinking, and arguing that his anthropological notion of art was one that would constitute the 'newborn child of all the disciplines' (Beuys, cited in Zurbrugg 1993: 60). The artist proposed that in the future, all human creativity would need to be put to the task of creating healthy social organisms. People would need to learn how to perceive the sculptural qualities in the world

around them and in themselves, and thus to diagnose where society had become unhealthy and (re)shape it self-consciously. In a sense, then, Beuys' resulting methodology, social sculpture, was an exercise in developing people's powers of perception and diagnosis, and encouraging them to act.

18 Indeed, it was this attempt to make these ideas function in a broader sense that signaled Beuys' break from Fluxus and which is also echoed in his claim that his work took Duchamp's work to its evident and ethical conclusion.

19 An excellent introduction to Social Sculpture and its theoretical underpinnings can be found in Shelley Sacks' 2011 essay 'Social sculpture and new organs of perception: new practices and new pedagogy for a humane and ecologically viable future'.

20 This being said, it is important to draw the distinction between Bataille's interpretations of anthropological understandings and the degree to which much of Bataille's work *was* based on a close relationship between his writings and his life. Indeed the importance of life experience to Bataille's work was paramount. (see Noys 2000: 5–14).

21 There was also an emphasis on dialogue as part of our process and a sense of warmth in the interaction between us that could be seen as Beuysian.

22 So many historically important buildings, Winchester Cathedral among them, have structural problems precisely because of natural forces that continually transgress human attempts to hold them in check. In the case of Winchester, there was a heroic and successful initiative to stabilise an area of the cathedral by William Walker during the Edwardian period when its foundations became waterlogged. This was due to its being built on a dry riverbed, the river having been 'relocated' in Roman times. But for how much longer will this part of the building withstand the challenges of its situation, reliant, as the caretakers of religious buildings often are, on donations and public funds? Is a teetering cathedral the ultimate image of the formless, of architecture against architecture? Conversely, is the example of William Walker the image of human creativity and resilience we have to encourage and hope for?

Bibliography

Bataille, Georges (1985 [1929]) 'Formless' ('L'Informe'), text translated by Allan Stoekl with Carl R. Lovitt and Donald M. Leslie Jr., in Georges Bataille *Visions of Excess: Selected Writings, 1927–1939*, Minneapolis, MN: University of Minnesota Press.

Bennett, Jane (2001) *The Enchantment of Modern Life: Attachments, Crossings, and Ethics*, Princeton, NJ: Princeton University Press.

Beuys, Joseph (1993) 'I am searching for field character', in Carin Kuoni (ed.) *Energy Plan for the Western Man – Joseph Beuys in America*, New York: Four Walls Eight Windows.

Bois, Yve-Alain and Krauss, Rosalind E. (1997) *Formless: A User's Guide*, New York: Zone Books.

Fuhlbrügge, Heike (2007) *Joseph Beuys und die Anthropologische Landschaft* [*Joseph Beuys and the Anthropological Landscape*], Berlin: Reimer Verlag.

Gregg, Melissa and Seigworth, Gregory J. (eds) (2010) *The Affect Reader*, Durham, NC: Duke University Press.

Grindon, Gavin (2010) 'Alchemist of the revolution: the affective materialism of Georges Bataille', *Third Text*, Vol. 24, Issue 3, May, 305–317.

Hollier, Denis (1992) *Against Architecture: The Writings of Georges Bataille*, Cambridge, MA: MIT Press.

Ingold, Tim (2013) *Making: Anthropology, Archaeology, Art and Architecture*, London: Routledge.

Krauss, Rosalind E. (1979) 'Sculpture in the expanded field', *October*, Vol. 8, Spring, 30–44.

Krauss, Rosalind E. (1997) 'No to … Joseph Beuys', in Yve-Alain Bois and Rosalind E. Krauss, *Formless: A User's Guide*, New York: Zone Books.

King, T.J. (1989) *Ecology*, second edition, Walton-on-Thames: Nelson.

Krinke, Rebecca and Walters, Victoria (2013) 'Talking transgressions', paper given at the 10th Architectural Humanities Research Association International Conference, 'Transgression', 21 November.

Llewellyn, Martyn (2010) 'Neither beast nor man: Qu'est-ce que c'est qu'un monstre?', in Amaleena Damlé and Aurélie L'Hostis (eds) *The Beautiful and the Monstrous: Essays in French Literature, Thought and Culture*, Oxford: Peter Lang.

Noys, Benjamin (2000) *Georges Bataille: A Critical Introduction*, Modern European Thinkers, London: Pluto Press.

Sacks, Shelley (2011) 'Social sculpture and new organs of perception: new practices and new pedagogy for a humane and ecologically viable future', in Christa-Maria Lerm Hayes and Victoria Walters (eds) *Beuysian Legacies in Ireland and Beyond: Art, Culture and Politics*, Berlin and Münster: Lit Verlag.

Troiani, Igea, Ewing, Suzanne and Periton, Diana (2013) 'Architecture and culture: architecture's disciplinarity', *Architecture and Culture*, Vol. 1, Issues 1 and 2, November, 7–19.

Van Boeckel, Jan (2011) 'A point of no return: artistic transgression in the more-than-human world', in Ane Faugstand Aarø and Johannes Servan (eds) *Environment, Embodiment and Gender*, Bergen: Hermes Text.

Walters, Victoria (2012) *Joseph Beuys and the Celtic Wor(l)d: A Language Of Healing*, Zurich/Münster: Lit Verlag.

Williams, Gregory (2008) Review of Claudia Mesch and Viola Michely: *Joseph Beuys: The Reader*, BookForum, January/December http://www.bookforum.com/inprint/014_04/1468 (accessed 8 April 2014).

Zurbrugg, Nicholas (1993) *The Parameters of Postmodernism*, Carbondale, IL: Southern Illinois University Press.

Chapter 13

Underground Urban Caretaking

Unearthing social knowledge through image and sound

Sara Brolund de Carvalho and Anja Linna

Our film *Underground Urban Caretaking* was initiated through an academic exercise at KTH School of Architecture, led by architect and assistant professor Meike Schalk. The task was to develop experimental forms and methods of mapping, and to question conventional architectural methods that privilege seemingly objective data over personal experience in site analysis and research. We wanted to find new tools, as architects, to gather and create knowledge, and to transgress the boundaries of what is valued as important in architectural projects. In making a short film, our intention was to unearth social knowledge that is usually not considered in planning and building processes. Our initial research question was: how can feminist strategies and tools together with the use of art practices help us go beyond the limits of mainstream architecture practices?

Underground Urban Caretaking portrays hands, filmed close-up, accompanied by stories from several non-profit associations and small-scale urban actors, such as a feminist tattoo collective, a drumming school and various handicraft associations. The setting is the Stockholm suburb of Bagarmossen, built mainly in the 1950s and inspired by the neighbourhood unit concept.[1] Apartment buildings, mostly three storeys tall, are oriented along narrow, circular streets with pedestrian walkways connecting them to the community centre with library, shops and a subway station. A very specific feature to the apartment houses is that most of them contain relatively hidden semi-subterranean rental spaces, which were originally designed as common spaces for the inhabitants to meet and socialize in. Each housing block had, in the 1950s, their own common spaces that were accessible for the tenants of that same block. The large number of non-residential spaces in the housing blocks was part of the

aim to create a sense of fellowship and community. Today these spaces are sublet, but not very suitable for commercial use due to their relatively small size, lack of visibility and non-existent shop front windows. Consequently, there is an exceptionally large number of small associations and cooperatives renting the semi-subterranean spaces in Bagarmossen today.

* * *

Inspired by feminist architects before us, such as Matrix and the founders of the Women's Design Service in Great Britain in the 1970s as well as contemporary architecture/art practice muf, we question norms and power relations in architecture, as well as pay attention to the unseen and seemingly trivial. Instead of abstracting reality according to dominant power structures, a feminist approach deals with the 'messiness' of the world, the political, social and bodily aspects of places. In other words, feminist strategies allow us to value the everyday and the personal as an important basis for knowledge in architecture. The embodied and lived experience is often forgotten or even openly put aside in favour of a theoretical or rather technical framework, where the quantifiable is treated as reliable while all other observations become curiosities or mere indicators. What we want to do is to focus on everyday and personal aspects of places, and find other stories and ways of representing them.

As Sandra Harding points out feminist research requires careful positioning. What happens when the researcher puts herself in the same critical plane as the object of study? Harding writes: 'Thus the researcher appears to us not as an invisible, anonymous voice of authority, but as a real, historical individual with concrete, specific desires and interests.'[2] By stressing our positions as architects and 'real individuals' we

Figure 13.1
'Maybe we take care of each other.'
'Many here have had worries, relatives that died and things like that. We can come here and cry, and there is nothing strange with that. This place is caring and warm. It doesn't have to be less of a place just because there are no men here; regardless this place works very well.' (quote from *Underground Urban Caretaking*, 2012, dir. Sara Brolund de Carvalho and Anja Linna)

also allow ourselves to engage in projects, places and people in a more personal way, demanding more of us.

We argue that the concept known as feminist ethics of care allows us to transgress our roles as architects. The ethics of care emerge from real life practices and can offer a new kind of urban category. We ask ourselves: what if we, as architects, recognize and use care-focused values such as sensitivity, compassion and feeling in our work?

The ethics of care focus on qualities and values such as interdependence, responsibility, empathy, respect and solidarity. In the 1980s feminist ethicist and psychologist Carol Gilligan introduced care as an attached way of human connection, requiring listening and understanding differences and needs, in contrast to what was perceived as male ethics of justice and hierarchies.[3] More recently architect Kim Trogal has elaborated on care as an ethical and relational way of acting in contemporary spatial practices.[4] As Trogal, we see a strong potential in a feminist understanding of *care*, and how it can help us to reconsider the importance of marginalized or despised urban activities.

* * *

The ethics of care can be said to be present in Mierle Laderman Ukeles art piece *Hartford Wash* from 1973, specifically in her exploration and re-evaluation of different *acts of caring* present in the process of cleaning. Ukeles' installation consists of the artist cleaning a museum during opening hours and deals with questions of the everyday and low-paid labour, the invisibility of maintenance work, the body and the personal. By using her daily work at home as a mother and wife in her art, Ukeles transforms the low-paid maintenance work into an activity that symbolically deserves an audience and, above all, recognition.[5]

Art practices can, in the words of Doina Petrescu, 'provide tools and critical methods to approach what goes beyond strict management, to reveal the political nature of space. Artists are also sometimes better positioned to deal with the 'messy, complex, lives of users'.[6] We find Jeremy Till's expression 'messy, complex, lives of users' as potentially demanding 'undefined' strategies of inquiry, as a valuable addition to conventional comprehensive planning. To deal with the complex social urban fabric, we would argue, presupposes a certain level of openness and maybe even some form of 'ad-hoc strategy'. In the film we used both analytical and imaginative accounts to do so. The first scene of our film, a staged interview, was our point of entry. By performing and re-enacting, we tested literally other positions than our own. We staged ourselves as knitting home caretakers, not as architects, to see the area in another way. The low-paid work of the care-workers and their movement from home to home, a daily presence in the houses and streets of Bagarmossen, interested us. The act of fictionalizing helped us reflect both on content and authorship, and was partly inspired by Ukeles and the way she uses herself in her work, making us go beyond our initial roles.

We argue that the ethics of care can inform us both in how we act as architects/planners and in how we relate to our objects of study. Many of the people

we have encountered, and featured in the film, can be described as urban caretakers. As Kim Trogal notes 'in other professions such as nursing, or roles like parenting, the caretaker is looking after *by*: nourishing; stimulating; healing; loving; teaching and so on. What is it that "urban caretakers" *do* when looking after public space?'[7]

The personal key to our mapping of Bagarmossen was the traditionally female gatherings around the practice of handicraft, handwork and bodily practices primarily using the hand.[8] The hand often plays an important role in actions of caring – in Swedish "ta hand om" means to take care of – the hand symbolizing a care-full approach. Practices of handicraft and various forms of 'hand work' became a key to conversation and dialogue in our urban mapping. These practices inform our method to talk through the work of the hands, which is a basis for the film.

As the social interactions of traditionally female handicraft groups – such as informal knitting, crochet and sewing gatherings – show us, occupying your hands can be a way to create an informal and trusted dialogue, as well as being an interaction between people. An important aspect in this is time, more specifically, the significance of a slow dialogue where questions and answers are not already predetermined. Giving others and ourselves time let us build relationships and trust through several visits, long conversations and engagement in different activities such as taking part in a drumming class at 'Rhythm Works'.

The focus on dialogue and hands allowed us to first discover and eventually, through moving images, convey how practices of caretaking are important as social and political forums for learning, exchange of ideas and support. All crucial for the development of sustainable social communities.

Practices of handwork have historically not been visible in the public sphere and have mostly been referred to private homes, which in many ways is symptomatic of

Figure 13.2
'I always think of the people that live here when I'm around'
'I've developed a relationship to many of the houses, to many addresses, and to the history. Many have lived in the same place for a long time, they moved in when it was newly built.' (*quote from Underground Urban Caretaking*)

Figure 13.3
'... and then she brought her ...'

'I think it was her brother, a relative, a guy. But wasn't it supposed to be for women only, was my question. But he is so kind! She said. And then men started to come along. Neighbours come, drum enthusiasts from here and there, sometimes people who don't know left from right and don't know anything, sometimes real professionals come. And then I put together a drum ensemble according to the current conditions.' (quote from *Underground Urban Caretaking*)

how women have been, and to some extent still are, overlooked in questions regarding public space. As Swedish urban and gender researcher Carina Listerborn points out, both feminist critique and post-colonial theory reveal an existing generic blindness towards certain citizens, because of ethnicity, gender, class and sexuality.[9] Through new methods for participatory mapping and knowledge making, we can transgress the boundaries of this narrow focus.

Combining feminism and art practice, we therefore suggest a method of mapping and interacting that go beyond the role of an observing ethnologist. Going further and closer, it demands personal engagement or simply care. The film *Underground Urban Caring* aims to open up all kinds of micro expressions as sources for knowledge such as bodily gestures, the speakers' voices in calm conversations, the sound of the weaving or the tattoo machines.

* * *

So how can we use the care-full, small-scale activities of the here and now to develop an architectural strategy of caring? How can we promote the need for spaces where social, non-commercial and micro-commercial activities can take care of people's collective, political and creative needs, longings and desires? What stories of a place can these practices tell?

The up close and personal look at the details of social practices, the hand, generated a broader understanding of the spatial needs for social and community building.[10] It also led us to discover the importance of Bagarmossen's many relatively cheap, but almost invisible, rental basements. If it weren't for them these activities would not flourish. There is a sense of caring in the design and layout of the 1950s

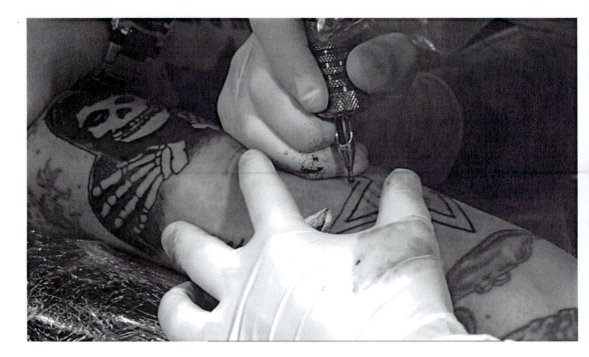

buildings in Bagarmossen. The rental houses were built with several free spaces open to all its tenants to use as social rooms. To provide a common space that is flexible, accessible and free of cost means that meeting, talking, partying etc are all activities that belong to and take care of a community. Today these spaces are legally designated as non-residential or commercial spaces, allowing the main municipal landlords in Bagarmossen to rent them out. Even though the semi-subterranean spaces are not accessible for tenants to use for free, their rent has remained relatively low due to their lack of suitability as conventional shops.

Common and social spaces like these have disappeared from contemporary housing typologies, where at best a commercial space in the ground floor serves as an alibi for social sustainability. There is therefore, in our view, a need to defend the role of *both* common and collective surfaces, *as well* as cheap-to-rent spaces for urban practices of care. The feminist ethics of care can help us to go from a generic blindness to a growing ability to interact, and a sensitivity towards the small gestures and activities creating fellowship and togetherness that don't stand out at first sight, but make a crucial difference in everyday life. We argue for an unconstrained search and a somewhat obsessive attention to detail in order to find what is not obvious or easily seen from a planner's perspective.

Figure 13.4
'We make our decisions together and we don't want to go over anyone's head'
'It wouldn't work any other way. Now everyone is equally responsible, which is both good and bad, but mostly good. And you earn so much more. We've learned so much about economy and other things. It's such an amazing feeling, that we can manage this on our own. We don't need anyone pushing us around. What the heck, we'll do it ourselves instead! And do it as we want it, and avoid the humiliation of trying to get into that environment. And instead own ourselves the place we want to go to.' (quote from *Underground Urban Caretaking*)

Notes

1   Clarence Perry introduces this concept in North America in the late 1920s, as an American version of the garden city as a self-contained neighbourhood unit. Narrow streets with apartment buildings, shops and services would surround a community centre with a school. The neighbourhood unit concept had initially a strong focus on pedestrian safety, but came to include aspects of social structures and community-building connected to physical design principles. See Clarence Perry, 'The neighboorhood unit', in *The Urban Design Reader,* edited by Michael Larice and Elisabeth MacDonald. London and New York: Routledge, 2007, pp 54–65.

2   Sandra Harding, 'Introduction. Is there a feminist method?', in *Feminism and Methodology. Social Science Issues,* edited by Sandra Harding. Bloomington, IN: Indiana University Press, 1987, p 9.

3   Carol Gilligan, 'Moral orientation and moral development', in *Women and Moral Theory*, edited by Eva Feder Kittay and Diana T. Meyers. Totowa, NJ: Rowman & Littlefield, 1987, pp 19–32.

4   See Kim Trogal, 'Caring for space. ethical agencies in contemporary spatial practice'. PhD Architecture thesis, University of Sheffield, October 2012.

5   See for example: http://sites.moca.org/wack/2007/07/25/mierle-ukeles-manifesto-for-maintenance-art-1969/ and http://www.artinamericamagazine.com/news-features/interviews/draft-mierle-interview/, (both accessed 27 January 2014)

6   Doina Petrescu, 'How to make a community as well as the space for it', in *re-public: reimagining democracy* (http://www.re-public.gr/en/), 2007, p 3.

7   Kim Trogal, 'Affective urban practices: a feminist approach to the ethics of care and creativity in contemporary urban practice'. MPhil upgrade paper. University of Sheffield, 2009, p 34.

8   In our mapping, the activities taking place in the half-hidden basement spaces that the film conveys, were predominantly performed by women.

9   Carina Listerborn, 'Who speaks? And who listens? The relationship between planners and women's participation in local planning in a multi-cultural urban environment", in *GeoJournal*, September 2007, Volume 70, Issue 1, pp 61–74.

10 In this we are inspired by the work of muf architecture/art and their focus on the detail as a key to successful, emancipatory projects. In *This is What We Do – A Muf Manual*, Katherine Schonfield describes how to move from the close-up to the bigger picture and then back to the particular, as a method for critical spatial practice. See Katherine Schonfield, 'Premature gratification and other pleasures', in muf, *This is What We Do – A Muf Manual*. London: Ellipsis, 2000, pp 14–23.

Index

Notes: page numbers followed by *n* indicate note numbers; page numbers in *italic* indicate illustrations.